biogenetic paradoxes of the nation

Experimental Futures: Technological lives,
scientific arts, anthropological voices
A series edited by Michael M. J. Fischer and Joseph Dumit

biogenetic paradoxes of the nation

FINNCATTLE, APPLES, AND OTHER GENETIC-RESOURCE PUZZLES

sakari tamminen

Duke University Press *Durham and London* 2019

Printed and bound by CPI Group (UK) Ltd, Croydon, CR0 4YY

Designed by Drew Sisk
Typeset in Whitman, Univers, and EB Base Mono by
Westchester Publishing Services

Library of Congress Cataloging-in-Publication Data
Names: Tamminen, Sakari, author.
Title: Biogenetic paradoxes of the nation : Finncattle, apples, and other genetic-resource puzzles / Sakari Tamminen.
Description: Durham : Duke University Press, 2019. | Series: Experimental futures | Includes bibliographical references and index.
Identifiers: LCCN 2019010881 (print) | LCCN 2019016271 (ebook) | ISBN 9781478003465 (ebook) | ISBN 9781478001959 (hardcover : alk. paper) | ISBN 9781478003069 (pbk. : alk. paper)
Subjects: LCSH: Biodiversity conservation—Finland. | Biodiversity conservation—Government policy—Finland. | Nature and nurture. | Life sciences—Social aspects—Finland.
Classification: LCC QH77.F5 (ebook) | LCC QH77.F5 T366 2019 (print) | DDC 333.95/16094897—dc23
LC record available at https://lccn.loc.gov/2019010881

Cover art: Eastern Finncattle calf. Photograph by Sakari Tamminen. Illustration and design by Drew Sisk.

CONTENTS

ABBREVIATIONS

ABGR	National Advisory Board on Genetic Resources
ANGR	animal genetic resources
ANT	actor network theory
CBD	Convention on Biological Diversity
EJA	Animal Breeding Research Group
FABA	organization of Finnish artificial insemination cooperatives
ISK	Eastern Finnish Cattle Breeding Society
LSK	Western Finnish Cattle Breeding Society
MAF	Ministry of Agriculture and Forestry
MENV	Ministry of the Environment
MTT	Agrifood Research Finland
PGR	Plant Genetic Resources Programme
PSK	Northern Finnish Cattle Breeding Society
PVPA	Plant Variety Protection Act
STS	science and technology studies
UPOV	Union for the Protection of New Varieties of Plants

ACKNOWLEDGMENTS

Thank you . . .

. . . to all the scientists, experts, and policy makers who allowed me into their worlds and shared their way of seeing the world, animals, plants, and life's mysteries beyond biological bodies.

. . . to my academic colleagues for the intellectual companionship, never-ending discussions, debates, and arguments that develop thoughts and ideas further.

. . . to friends, old and new, that I first encountered during my research, writing, and presenting, wherever you are, near and far.

. . . to Mike Fischer, for coaching and for detailed comments pushing the initial manuscript ideas to a much better expression, specificity, and format.

. . . to the Academy of Finland for providing the grant to finish this book.

. . . to Ines, Mai, and Taina, for their unconditional love.

INTRODUCTION

the new biopolitics of nature and the nature of (mis)stakes

It had already been a long day, but the sun was nowhere near setting. As is typical of late-summer afternoons at Nordic latitudes, it would take many hours to reach the horizon. Our day was not over yet. We had finally completed the scheduled lab session and headed back to a little office tucked away in the farthest corner of the building. When we stepped through the frosted-glass doors that separated the lab area from the domain of paperwork, the senior plant researcher sitting within passed me a document from her desk. I was looking at a black-and-white printout listing hundreds of names accompanied by variations on them and locations that had been prepared as part of the Finnish national Plant Genetic Resources Programme. Handwritten notes were jotted next to some of the entries. "That's the initial census of Finnish apples," explained Dr. Antonius. Then she described our mission: to compile the official list for the national mandate for laying claim to "native Finnish" varieties in global forums. "It's more work to do this properly for the plants than the animals because there are many more cultivar variations for a plant than there are breeds for a given animal species. But that you already know from working with the animal-program people, don't you?" she remarked. Dr. Antonius went on to clarify that it was by no means certain that all the cultivars on this initial list qualified for inclusion. The criteria were simple enough—the apple cultivars on the list needed to be alive and found living within Finnish territory. "Of course," she continued, "once we establish that, we need to prove that these apples are natively Finnish, genetically distinct from

Russian and Swedish cultivars." In 2005 "genetically distinct" would be determined through the techniques of genetic fingerprinting (to be explained in chapter 2); as time progressed, techniques for what counted as "distinct" changed, complicating matters. And so the seeds of our journey were planted.

This brief encounter was back in the summer of 2005, when I was conducting ethnographic fieldwork on Finland's national genetic-resource programs. As I reflect on these experiences from the fieldwork in 2004–2009 and my follow-up interviews between 2014 and 2017, I find that this encounter nicely conveys the key challenge facing these programs—that the identification of natural populations (plant varieties and crop cultivars, animal species and breeds, microbes, and so on) had become a national problem both scientific and political. On one hand these programs were aimed at the biological identification of living beings that were considered native to Finland. At the same time they had a goal of compiling population-level inventories and producing politically potent "mandate lists" that would be imbued with the power to represent a nation's native life forms in the global context of biodiversity protection and its legally enforced frameworks. In this wider context, the ethnographic account is not unique to one country. It is far from exceptional in how it reflects the attempts made—with a range of means—to protect natural resources in 173 United Nations member states as of August 2017.[1]

In particular, the account above lays out the first steps in the anthropological exploration of an emerging global biopolitics of nature both in global discourse and as implemented at national level. Thereby it highlights the central themes and related lines of inquiry that are followed in this book. What kind of politics of nature drives these large-scale efforts globally, or why do nations seek to define life forms as "native" in the first place? How do such identification programs deal with the seemingly fundamental contradiction rooted in the division that is so commonly drawn between "nature" and "culture" and wrestle with issues that stem from the historically contingent and constructed nature of the idea of nation in the context of natural life forms and their genetic differences? And what technological, legal, and institutional conditions enable the identification of national forms of natural life en masse?

The answer to these questions must be sought by uncovering the radical changes in how we think about, conceptualize, and govern nature and life at global level while charting a new, complex biopolitical terrain of nature conservation. A close examination of these changes points toward a clear conclusion: the stakes in global biopolitics have shifted.

Most discussions of biopolitics that are inspired by the Foucauldian tradition focus on human populations and fail to consider life forms beyond *Homo sapiens* that have long been central to the development of biopolitical ideas, techniques, and programs (see Pyyhtinen and Tamminen 2011). Others have looked at the so-called nonhuman actants in human networks (Callon 1986; Latour 1993), and some consider animals that have been created by biotechnology for medical research, as with OncoMouse, which was explored by Donna Haraway (1997), or work to understand basic biology through such bodies as *Drosophila* fruit flies (Kohler 1994) or reproduction with the aid of Dolly the sheep (S. Franklin 2007a). Others have looked at crop or animal breeds (hybrid wheat, genetically modified crops, cotton using Bt insecticidal properties, genetically modified soybeans and the like; see, for example, Stone 2010) or at breeds of working dogs or bovines (Derry 2003). An ecological perspective changes things radically, but few anthropologists or social theorists have seriously considered the larger institutional changes required. This book is an attempt to do so while examining efforts to rearrange the meanings of nationhood that tie in with these changes. While other works have offered symbolic analyses of nonhuman icons and national identity (as in Ohnuki-Tierney's [1987; 1993] examination of rice and monkeys in Japan), the interest there tends to lie less in the technoscientific elements as they are analyzed in this book.

A new scramble for resources was set off in 1992 when the Convention on Biological Diversity (CBD) entered the scene, even amid efforts to regulate and contain this predicted result. The CBD, hailed by many as the key symbol of a common global vision for saving what remains of Earth's biodiversity, was signed by 167 nations at the Earth Summit in Rio de Janeiro, Brazil. By 2017 the number of signatories stood at 192. With the goal of protecting biodiversity, the CBD began as an effort to empower and implement conservation biology via the tools of market discourse. By ushering in new articulations of natural objects, such as genetic resources, and reinventing political treaties through national sovereignty over genetic resources, the CBD led to a series of ethical dilemmas and legal aporias, however. And once let out of the box, these continue to stubbornly resist anything more than temporary rebalancing.

The dilemmas and contradictions stemming from the CBD and its implementation are also potent and generative in that they have unintended consequences radiating to adjacent fields of global nature politics such as biosecurity governance. From early on commentators warned that the CBD "has the potential to hamper disease monitoring" by making it harder to share samples quickly and smoothly across borders and seriously hampering efforts to monitor drug resistance, outbreaks of *E. coli*, and so on, thereby creating roadblocks to synthetic biologists (Cressey 2014, 14). This was highlighted when the potential pandemic of avian influenza was raging and Indonesia refused to share samples with the World Health Organization in order to spotlight the inequity represented by the likelihood that such exchanges would lead to none of the much-vaunted benefit sharing benefit-returning, affordable medications to Indonesia (see Fischer 2013). Such developments in a post-CBD world create and in turn are shaped by the constant technoscientific rearrangements that are mediated by political treaties, administrative institutions, economics, and efforts to protect the commons. The unfolding results entail changes within and between the concepts that are at the heart of the most fundamental of our ecological, economic, and political relations. These dramatic shifts come about as new challenges emerge in managing open ecological futures, the dynamics of rights and sovereignty discourses, and historically manufactured legacy identities. I suggest that if one follows these challenges to their source, one finds a hot spring that pours forth radical but fragmentary lines of a philosophy of nature and the nation. A closer analysis reveals how vexing questions about global nature conservation and on issues such as access and benefit sharing are only the most visible symptoms—like the itching rash from a tropical disease—betraying a more far-reaching and experimental political philosophy that renders these discourses possible. In the end, what is at stake is the constitution of a new form of international biopolitics aimed at healing nature's body, a body with marks seared deep into its flesh by unevenly distributed strings of power in the global context.

This book uses four case studies for a multilocale or multisited ethnography of the Finnish effort to honor the mandates of the CBD and subsequent protocols. The aim in this is to explore the ethics dilemmas (attached to ideas of equity and benefit sharing) and legal aporias (nationalizing natural resources and creating ex situ and in situ genetic archives) of biodiversity preservation along with the encroachment of the problematic replacement of the biodiversity framework with the economic and political discourse of "genetic resources." The four cases involve plants, animals (historical and contemporary), and the experimental formulation of administrative policy and institution building. These all exist in parallel with the biopolitics of human populations, and they act in combination with said politics in co-constituting new forms of national imaginaries.

More concretely, the cases I use to contextualize and ethnographically address the Finnish implementation of the CBD cover, in addition to the effort, touched upon in the opening vignette, to establish a "Finnish apple" by what is termed genetic fingerprinting (chapter 2), the transformation of a Finnish "native breed" that grew out of a nineteenth-century search for a "pure breed" in parallel with racial purity (chapter 1), all in conjunction with historical analysis. The work tells the story of how a national animal breed was literally built to mirror the key ideas of a nation. The next chapter in that story is one of writing life into a national digitally managed set of biobanks, both ex situ (as genetic information and physical samples) and in situ (with small live herds), in which parallels can be seen with a digitally managed national human health-care system (see chapter 3). With these building blocks in place, we can ascend the ladder to consider the high-level policy work and the tightrope it has walked between concerns of administrative and institutional economics (including national wealth) as articulated in the Ministry of Agriculture and Forestry and considerations of the Ministry of the Environment (which is presumably less economically driven, more ecologically driven, or at least more focused on the eco-body of the nation).

While the phenomena showcased are not unique to Finland, the country is well situated to show their patterns clearly and perhaps earlier than many others. Finland is one of the pioneering countries in biodiversity sciences; it is home to the first published studies on biological problems caused by the Green Revolution in both the animal and plant kingdoms. These date back to the 1960s. Today the research institute charged with implementing the CBD is the 1,400-scientist-strong Natural Resources Institute Finland (formed in the 2015 merger of Agrifood Research Finland [MTT], whose scientists I follow in this book; the Finnish Forest Research Institute; and the Finnish Game and Fisheries Research Institute), which features the largest biodiversity research institute in the Nordic region with offices in fifty-three locations across Finland. This network is enhanced by close cooperation with the Nordic Gene Bank and its globally branded Svalbard (Spitzbergen) Global Seed Vault in Norway, and its efforts are spurred on by the climate change that is evident in its Arctic regions. These factors combine to make the Nordic region one of the global centers for the future of global biodiversity thinking—materially, conceptually, and in terms of experimenting with institutional implementations. Echoes in larger patterns can be seen in the implications of negotiations over varieties of grain on the platform provided by the Consultative Group on International Agricultural Research (CGIAR), the International Rice Research Institute, and other such research and seed-banking institutions.

In addition, the historical perspective is rich here. Finland has well-maintained national archives pertaining to agriculture that accentuate the fact that it has always kept detailed records of national life (Finland has more than 250 years of detailed records of its human population, and other life has long been part of the story). These are kept under the auspices of an important contemporary institution of another sort—the umbrella organization of Finnish artificial insemination cooperatives (FABA) is overseeing a new transformation in the political economy of plant and animal breeding.

The paradoxes evident in the Finnish work and beyond—ethics dilemmas and legal aporias created via the CBD—stem from unresolved contradictions related to the protection of the biodiversity commons by way of economics-anchored notions of commodifiable "genetic resources" that are placed under the sovereign control of nation-states. The aims behind the CBD were coded as three goals that (perhaps to some idealists or to those who saw profit in such cover terms) seemed compatible at first: biodiversity, sustainability, and benefit sharing.[2] Soon the dilemmas and aporias that arose were creating challenges for the unfolding of successive treaty conventions internationally, such as the Nagoya Protocol, and the deployment of institutions and administrative arrangements within domestic (national) power structures.[3] Genetic resources as conceptual, corporeal, and legal objects are difficult to manage because they cut across normal institutional arrangements and their political mandates.

The resulting turbulence, with rearrangements remaining in constant flux, is generated by three main paradoxes or contradictions among those three goals of the CBD and the later protocols (or, rather, the philosophies guiding such efforts more generally). The first tension is between scientific management for high productivity and, on the other hand, concerns over gene loss (forms of benefit sharing and sustainability) or of the hopes held out for the first Green Revolution in the 1960s and 1970s with the fears of threats to long-term biogenetic robustness. Those fears are stoked as monocropping faces challenges in response to issues of pest resistance and overreliance on fertilizers and irrigation and as industrial farming comes under similar pressure related to biochemical factors: antibiotic resistance, new viral infections, and overuse of hormonal stimulation. The second paradox emerged from the uneasy relationship between ecology and economics, in tension between the ideals of conservation biology and imperatives of the "genetic resources" stance. This contradiction was actually already present in conservation biology as soon as it began struggling to make its goals practically attractive, but the balance shifted with the CBD's enshrining of national sovereign rights and the value or potential of genetic resources. Paradox three is found in the conflict between the global commons and a sense of national sovereignty wherein natural resources are increasingly seen as commercially exploitable, with powerful vested interests overriding the original intentions to save biological materials holding genetic diversity for the common good of humankind. This final tension is between wealth as conceived of by economic interests and something to be treated as a freely accessible, usable, and circulated source of biowealth.

In the remainder of this chapter I provide a brief introduction to the core idea expressed through the CBD and the Nagoya Protocol, set out the three biogenetic paradoxes proceeding from the related dynamics in more detail, explain how each of the empirical chapters elaborates on these, and discuss the methodological challenges of writing an ethnography of patterns developing around a global treaty such as the CBD and subsequent developments—from the crafting of the Nagoya Protocol to the handling of national implementation at higher levels or on the ground.

NATURE ACCORDING TO THE CBD

The idea of exploring, collecting, circulating, and banking nonhuman life—biowealth—is not new. Nonhuman life has been mobilized to the ends of empires and, more recently, nations through much of recorded history, and here the exploitation of exotic species is only half of the story. The export of familiar forms of life to new lands has been as extensive for colonial purposes as the import of exotic species for capitalization. Some claim that the whole colonial enterprise would not have been possible without mobilization of European nonhuman species for repopulation of conquered territories with familiar species. Nonhuman life served as the biological lifeline of colonial practices: "explorers" brought animals and plants along in large quantities and introduced them to the colonized territories. In his classic analysis, Alfred Crosby (1986) has called the effect of these large-scale mobilizations "ecological imperialism." Neither is the issue of the politics of nature, or power struggles over plants and animals of a certain human population, new, especially in the context of the historical accumulation of biowealth (see e.g. Grove 1996; Schiebinger and Swan 2005).

Since the waning of overt colonialism, nonhuman life—plants, animals, and even microbes—has become a focus of renewed global concern of a new sort. In the past five to six decades the practice of bringing animals and plants to new lands on one's travels, which evolved from the traditional approach to colonized territories in the early twentieth century, has given way to a worldwide network of "agricultural introduction stations" created for the ready collection and circulation of exotic materials. Among this modern colonial system's other underpinnings is the planting (introduction) of newly bred high-yield varieties of plants ostensibly to advance Third World agriculture (Kloppenburg 1988; Pistorius 1997). These practices had effects also in the rapid spread of European human and nonhuman life at the expense of local forms of life, and they also extended the reach and speed of bioprospecting—which is typically described as the exploration and extraction of valuable local natural components for agribusiness and "big pharma" dominated by the global North (see, for example, Parry 2001; Hayden 2004b). With this network the international circulation of the extracted life forms and their valuable components has been convenient and, in most cases, highly lucrative, afforded by "friendly" economic mechanisms such as patents and licensing fees.

In 1992 the Convention on Biological Diversity changed most of that. The usual way to explain the CBD is through the three key objectives cited for it: the conservation of biological diversity, the sustainable use of its components, and the fair and equitable sharing of the benefits arising from commercial and other utilization of genetic resources. Yet even while its signing was hailed in public as a landmark event in the global management of biodiversity for sustainability and for fair and equitable sharing of benefits arising from that use, it brought powerful changes to international nature politics. In biology "biodiversity" is an umbrella term denoting differences found in nonhuman life on scales as far ranging as ecosystem, species, and population level. Within the CBD, however, the term predominantly performs functions other than that embodied in the call for preservation. It is employed for common application in the context of several problems of global ownership and issues of rights over nonhuman life. Here, it no longer denotes a shared global resource. It has become a contentious category of nature within a web of powerful international geopolitical interests and politics of nature. In many ways the convention is, as Corinne Hayden (2003b, 1) put it, "a living and much-contested document," not least because it deals in foundational elements and concepts that are open to alternative political and legal interpretations. The fact that many aspects of the CBD are contested should not come as a surprise since it is in part an international response to an outcry about alleged biopiracy and the practice of bioimperialism within the territories of a biodiversity-rich South by multinational companies based in the North. While this convention is only one on the long list of global instruments aimed at securing rightful distribution of the profits derived from natural resources among nations, it stands out in one key respect. In its assignment of rights and responsibilities related to various objects of nature, it is much more far reaching in its implications than are other global contracts. It cannot be readily ignored.

Article 15 of the CBD granted sovereign power over what it calls "genetic resources" to the signatory nations. Quite interestingly, the CBD remains decidedly ambiguous as to what counts as genetic resources. These are broadly defined as "genetic material of actual or potential value." This ambiguous definition gives the signatory nations an opportunity to claim sovereignty over nonhuman life of all kinds as long as they contain genetic material. The only condition, and a crucial one for the work presented in this book, is that the genetic material be native to ("originating from") the relevant signatory nation. Therefore the CBD potentially covers all nonhuman life that has a (scientifically) proven "country of origin," the condition set within the convention's text itself. With the CBD, then, the previous relatively free global mobilization and circulation of nonhuman life across national borders was restricted. This effect stemmed from three operational (re)definitions found within the convention.

First, with article 15, the only internationally recognized hard-law part of the treaty, biodiversity was effectively transformed from a biological understanding into something quite different. It became rearticulated through a genetic understanding of life with the concept of genetic resources, or as a collection of genetic material found in nature that could be turned into valuable resources—in actuality or potentially. Second, biodiversity became tightly enmeshed within particular political geographies of nation-states through this novel figure of genetic resources. By signing the convention, the parties (with the United States notably absent) decided that all nonhuman life in all its forms could be identified with a country of origin, or a nationhood, and that these forms should become objects of sovereign national genetic governance and should be subject to national-level policies on access and benefit sharing. Under the convention, all genetic materials exchanged (irrespective of their use or the presence or absence of a compensation agreement) between nations ("parties to the convention") must have prior informed consent for the exchange and a certificate of origin for the materials.

Finally, the signatory nations became bound to a new obligation to "as far as possible and as appropriate . . . identify components of biological diversity important for its conservation and sustainable use" (under article 7): they are to provide an identified inventory of their nationally distinct biodiversity "components," including species and communities, genes and genomes, all amenable to interpretation as being the nation's genetic resources. Previously at issue had been individual cases of animals and plants, species, and other forms of life, all representing nonhuman nationhood. With the CBD, however, we see a novel imperative to calculate the totality of nations' nonhuman material across all traditional biological taxa (such as the plant and animal kingdoms). The convention compels every signatory nation to identify and produce a national inventory of "its" genetic material (or at least that of value), regardless of its place within the taxonomic system applied in the life sciences. With these new operationalizations, the differences in nonhuman life, as biodiversity, are defined through the politics of nationhood in the three senses explicated above within the politico-juridical sphere of the convention.

These are important political translations between nature and culture that have both symbolic and material effects. The CBD demarcates nature by national boundaries cast in terms of nonhuman genetics, and the scientific universality of "nature" is particularized by political divisions. Not surprisingly, the division of Earth's natural entities into collections of the nature of particular nations that is implied by the CBD—and even its sheer possibility—has been subject to heavy scientific and political criticism. The very concept has prompted moral outrage among natural science, social science, and legal scholars. This critique has come in many forms and shapes, beginning within the very bodies that prepared the first provisional drafts for the treaties (e.g., Kloppenburg 1988; Raustiala and Victor 1996; 2004). The scientific critique has focused mostly on problems derived from the twin concepts that are held as the core elements of the criteria for the nationhood of genetic resources under the CBD: the "country of origins" and the in situ element. These arguments hold that it is virtually impossible to determine the origin of a species since all species continue to evolve, mutate, migrate, and cut across political state and national boundaries. The CBD demands that besides fulfilling the "country of origin" condition, any nation claiming sovereignty over genetic resources must possess those genetic resources within in situ conditions. This concept suggests that genetic resources are found within their natural ecosystems and habitats—and, in the case of domesticated species, in the surroundings where they have developed their distinctive properties. Perhaps it need not be said that the definition of "distinctive property" is as unclear and open to interpretative flexibility as is the second criterion for nationhood mentioned in the convention.

Hence, with the convention biodiversity became tightly nested within the sovereignty of nation-states through the concept of national genetic resources. The global cartographic demarcation of nonhuman life took place as these objects of nature were grafted to the foundations of national sovereignty. Quite simply, they also became a new object of nations' politics over life, requiring a new form of nonhuman biopolitics.

This convention and its global effects still inform much of what is going on in global nature politics. The speed of signatories' adoption of the CBD; subsequent problems related to the global circulation of natural bodies that are now heavily restricted by restrictions based on access, use, benefit sharing, and ownership rights; and nations' slow movement toward adopting strict measures for conservation of nature beyond the legal protection of genetic resources have all come as a disappointment to many in the decades following the convention. In 2010, eighteen years after the Rio Earth Summit, the global call to action to save biodiversity (and genetic resources as its particular materializations) was subjected to new reflection by Achim Steiner, executive director of the United Nations Environment Programme (UNEP). In the third edition of *Global Biodiversity Outlook* (GBO-3), the official global letter from the Secretariat of the Convention on Biological Diversity (SCBD) reviewing the progress on biodiversity protection, Steiner expressed his disappointment with the governments' response to the action plans they had agreed upon via the CBD for stopping biodiversity loss at all levels by 2010. The director painted a gloomy picture of the state of biodiversity affairs: "A new and more intelligent compact between humanity and the Earth's life-support systems is urgently needed in 2010—the UN's International Year of Biodiversity. This was the year when governments had agreed to substantially reduce the rate of biodiversity loss: this has not happened" (Steiner 2010, 3).

Steiner continued by pointing out that failure in the global regulatory system had a negative impact on the way national governments reacted to the call to action: "A successful conclusion to negotiations on an international regime on access and benefit sharing of genetic resources is needed. This is the missing pillar of the CBD and perhaps its financial mechanism: a successful conclusion would indeed make 2010 a year to applaud" (Steiner 2010, 3). This "missing pillar" has been one of the most problematic aspects of the global contract since its birth, one that is still under consideration and review by the signatory states. Disagreements about the access to and benefit sharing in successful use of nature's most precious objects, genetic resources, stood in the way of what he termed an intelligent compact with nature.

The pillar missing from the CBD's original text was negotiated, drafted, and agreed on by the signatory states over the course of the first decade of the twenty-first century. The parties to the CBD first, in 2002, agreed on the Bonn Guidelines, a set of nonbinding global guidelines for the drafting of national legislation on the issues of access and benefit-sharing related to genetic resources (SCBD 2002). However, for reasons of inertia inherent in global politics and decision making, the international work advanced slowly; the work culminated in the Nagoya Protocol only at the tenth Conference of the Parties (COP) held in Japan in 2010. That protocol defined fair and equitable benefit sharing to be based on terms agreed upon mutually between the provider and the user of genetic resources and addressed the terms of access, which was to be based on prior informed consent—all more or less articulated in the terms that had already been employed in the Bonn Guidelines and other preparatory documents.

The Nagoya Protocol brought, or was thought to bring, "legal certainty" to the access and benefit-sharing system of the CBD, and all signatories were assigned a target of national implementation by 2015.[4] This extension protocol to the CBD already shows well how the translation of discrepant global visions into an international agreement codifying one formalized vision in a binding way takes years or even decades to negotiate within global bodies of policy yet still has gaps. In all its legal certainty on the principles for access and benefit sharing, the protocol leaves other conservation measures and their national implementation as they were: unregulated and uncertain.

At the very same meeting in Aichi Prefecture, the CBD targets for a ten-year period (2011–2020) were revised and explicit goals for conservation action defined. The Aichi Biodiversity Targets were born. The conservation measures now extended to twenty more specific actions to be promoted globally, ranging from establishing awareness-raising campaigns to ensuring that the benefits of biodiversity are enjoyed by all of humanity, and beyond.[5] Quite interestingly, the name for the ten-year strategy that was agreed on in Aichi is "Living in Harmony with Nature," although many of the biodiversity target actions that it envisioned have less to do with "Nature" than with issues that are properly human: the global politics of nature and the economic and legal instruments guiding people toward the newly envisioned relationship with nature and laying down the rules for the use of its resources.

The CBD and the Nagoya Protocol are the output of three interlinked processes unfolding within their own trajectories, imbued with related crisscrossing discourses that allow for a reframing of nature and life: first as a system of biodiversity and then as genetic resources to be indexed, conserved, and used in accordance with global agreements. Here, life is simultaneously vital global capital to be utilized in agricultural and pharmaceutical business, corporeal life forms that are in danger of extinction and needing conservation by conservation scientists, and valuable matter that is subject to national policies and legal frameworks only to be governed by globally agreed-on fair rules on access rights and benefit sharing. In these three processes, the figure of genetic resources has played a key role from the very beginning as a central symbol of the value of nature's diversity and the locus of global power politics. As such, it is the figure that best encapsulates today's unresolved paradoxes in the CBD and the related global protocols.

THE FIRST PARADOX: THE GREEN REVOLUTION × GENETIC EROSION

We can now begin delving into the factors at the heart of the three core paradoxes that are interwoven in the relations we explore. This necessitates a word first about how the factors fit together via the shorthand employed for referring to them. In my use of "×" in the section headings, I am indebted to Michael Fortun (2008) and his notion of the chiasmus in the graphic description of double-binding forces that bring to bear both conjunction and disjunction. The factors are signed largely for contradiction, but we also see a multiplication symbol characterizing the emergence of each paradox as a multiplicative outgrowth of its factors, loaded with many possible senses of production. The emerging relations and problems are *products* with roots in the apparent constituent elements, not *sums* of them.[6]

The first root of the CBD is an outgrowth of advances in green biotechnology and related technological advancements, the latest phase of which has been described as following "the molecular vision of life" (Kay 1993). The Green Revolution in agriculture that began in the 1960s rearranged nature through biotechnology's strivings toward genetic uniformity, toward greater control over and capitalization of the vital processes of nonhuman life. This process and its methods of producing genetic monocultures in plants and animals were so powerful that they prompted widespread scientific concern about genetic erosion and the need for genetic conservation starting very soon after that revolution began—late in the 1960s (e.g., FAO 1967)—and gaining prominence in the last decades of the twentieth century alongside the social inequalities and problems that they more directly generated (Shiva 1991).

Perhaps surprisingly, it was the agricultural scientists themselves who first raised the issue of genetic conservation of traditional animal breeds at the regular meetings of the United Nations Food and Agriculture Organization's (FAO) Animal Breeding Committee. One of the new key technologies of reproduction, the artificial-insemination techniques used for breeds' improvement, had already prompted concerns about unwanted "gene loss" and the emergence of local endangered breeds of animals at conferences in the late 1960s (Tamminen 2015).

One of the first to crystallize the concerns about the negative effects of the Green Revolution on breeding and the management of agricultural species was the young Finnish population scientist Kalle Maijala. In a paper he presented at the European Animal Breeding Committee meeting in 1967, he claimed that "before the beginning of rational animal breeding—that is, 50–100 years ago—there were numerous local native breeds of different species. . . . The problem arises mainly from the fact that effective utilization of the best animals today automatically means setting aside the poorer animals, strains, breeds, and even species." His main message was of a need to reevaluate the rationality of "rational breeding," with "the purpose [being] to consider (1) whether this elimination of genetic material will have undesirable consequences, and (2) if so, how these could be avoided" (Maijala 1971, 404). On the plant-breeding side, the FAO's Technical Advisory Committee to the CGIAR has been another key site of expressing the worry and ongoing struggles surrounding the conservation of diversity of plant genetic resources starting at about the same time in the late 1960s (Pistorius 1997).

For agricultural scientists the threat of genetic erosion meant less genetic material to choose from under the new paradigm of rational breeding, which needs raw material if it is to function. Suddenly, and after only a short while, with new breeding techniques, the diversity and genetic stock found in animal and plant populations began running low because of the introduction of more uniform, high-yield agricultural life forms, which were preferred. This genetic erosion resulting in uniform breeds and lines made them also more vulnerable to pests and plagues. The more daunting side effect of the accordant genetic uniformity and intensive farming was the simultaneous endangerment of species that were not suitable for agricultural production and the destruction of their natural habitats along with larger parts of natural ecosystems. Ecologies that were once suitable for a variety of life forms were transformed into standardized agricultural production platforms that were suitable only for advanced, highly bred forms of life.

Here the destruction of diversity in tandem with the drive toward more genetically uniform species is a symptom; it is visible testimony of the complex power relations found within agricultural policies that lead to such action. However, these actions become understandable only if one considers them in view of the relationships that are enacted in the historically intertwining development processes of agricultural science, business, and the other ideas affecting the desirability of particular forms of life in both its symbolic and material senses—such as the notion of the "purebred production animals" or "native crops" that was born as a result of the dominant breeding logic.

After the Green Revolution, the animals and plants that were not initially seen as attractive for agricultural business and had been replaced by new, "better" breeds and varieties became important and interesting again to agricultural business. This time, however, the species that had given way to life forms producing a higher yield were valued for something other than their agricultural output qualities. These breeds and varieties were now seen as the raw-material pool of genes ensuring that industrial production could continue despite its tendency to restrict or homogenize the genetic makeup of production animals. The agriculture industry needed this raw material for its own continued existence. Therefore, native or nonbred animals and plants came to be seen as the embodiment of interesting genetic features to be conserved as genetic stocks, which could potentially be used in the creation of ever more productive life forms of the future.

In chapter 1, "Finncattle: Biowealth as National Life," I will take an in-depth look at how this process unfolded in Finland over one century, from the late nineteenth to the mid-twentieth century, with the aim of demonstrating how national biopolitics aligned a particular agricultural mode of production with the breeding sciences of the day and how a national animal breed was literally built to mirror the key ideas of a nation. This all served an explicit nationalistic ideology and created a "pure" national form of life, a bovine population that was articulated simultaneously in the economic and scientific terms of the time. Accordingly, chapter 1 tells the story of Finncattle by rereading the official histories of the breed (Kaltio 1958; Myllylä 1991) against the background of original documentary material found within the archives of the largest national historical archives pertaining to agriculture. These archives are maintained by FABA in Helsinki. With the permission and kind help of that organization's staff (mostly agricultural scientists), I spent about a month in 2005 going through the genealogy of Finncattle starting with the late nineteenth century. The archives were in a vault built into the cellar of the building, filled with the original herd books, letters to the breeders, yearly reports, and yearbooks about Finncattle-breeding activities. Thanks to these time capsules, I can reconstruct a story about the intertwined nature of a bovine breed and a nation in the making through analysis of those herd books and letters along with cooperatives' reports and breeding-association journals found in the FABA vaults. The narration is based on a discourse analysis of the material, with the findings contextualized with other research-based literature on the relevant historical development of Finnish agriculture.

Why start the empirical work here, especially in a book about the CBD and genetic resources? First, the Finncattle breed is one of the first reported examples of breeds falling victim to genetic erosion on the global stage and within the circles of agricultural scientists. In fact, this was one of the local breeds that Dr. Maijala cited early on at the 1967 European Animal Production Conference to exemplify the adverse effects of "rational breeding" on life forms that were bred for other values than just maximizing agricultural profit as defined by milk or meat yield (Maijala 1971). As such, Finncattle are among the first animals to embody the criticism of modern rational breeding practices and the concern about the genetic erosion of local breeds within the global discourse of animal production.

Further, this bovine breed came to embody some of the most central relationships that went into the making of an autonomous and independent nation of Finland in the latter half of the nineteenth century and the first half of the twentieth. The 1800s, the point in chronological history that has sometimes been called the springtime of nations, witnessed not only the emergence of national movements that affected human populations and were produced around them; the creation of national human populations and their demarcation from others were complemented by the emergence of new, nonhuman ones for nationalistic ends in Finland (as in other countries). I show how Finland was centrally concerned with this animal breed by offering an analysis of its codification in language through new scientific conceptualizations of heritage and old myths of the origins of the Finnish race, its corporeal breeding practiced in the name of purification of blood, and the social institutions that were built to stabilize its meaning and to foster the new economy built around its bioprocesses. The analysis also depicts how the breed literally became a part of the national wealth—an early form of biocapital in a globalizing world. In other words, Finncattle became the embodied nexus of relationships through which major parts of Finnish life were arranged: new professions, a new economy, new institutions, and novel links between certain human and nonhuman populations and territorial areas were molded together through its figure.

This breed is a good starting point for another reason, too. The story narrates a certain way of understanding national nonhuman life, how a certain matrix of intelligibility is created and mobilized for many purposes that are collected under the transparent wings of the theme of nationhood. Through the story, I try to show how a particular constitution of the nation with modern grids of intelligibility—a constitution emphasizing the split between nature and culture and another between past and present forms of life—is made and mobilized as a legitimator of the authenticity of Finnishness in both its natural and cultural manifestations. What this empirical example shows well, I think, is how the three threads of national theory—Man, territory, and double-temporality (as conceptualized by Homi Bhabha 1996)—work in producing national forms of nonhuman life. The "double time" of the nation was constructed such that the continuity of the national genealogical past was readable in the bodies of these animals as far as the national history was rememberable. Finncattle were companion animals of Finns from time immemorial with their particular roots in Finnish territories. The carefully woven myths and the disciplined corporeality of the breed gave one form to the nation, thereby satisfying a "national longing for a form" (to appropriate Brennan's 1990 concept). Finland, once born, required also the birth of a particular nature: the idea that Finland consisted of particular national human populations was complemented with matching bovine breeds, naturalizing the whole idea of nationhood itself.

Case studies of the making of a national animal such as Finncattle are not particularly unique. Nonhuman biological entities have a long history of nativization for the purposes of nations and territorial bio-geopolitics (Ritvo 1992; Pauly 1996; Mansfield 2003; Raber and Tucker 2005; S. Franklin 2006). The story about the cocreation of the Finnish nation and Finncattle between the late nineteenth and mid-twentieth centuries serves here as a contrasting device for teasing out the differences in how nations' nonhuman lives are rearranged today. I claim that in Finland, as elsewhere, these instances of naturalization involved single species, such as varieties of trees, horses, and bovine species, until very recently. Also, it serves to point out the paradoxical relation between the drive toward the production of more efficient agricultural species by breeding genetically homogeneous populations and the need for keeping the species vital by preserving the genetic variation that the breeding practices are acting to reduce. In this biogenetic paradox, the most efficient breeding practice, aimed at reducing unwanted genetic variation, is fully dependent on its other, the genetic variation. The historical developments in the production and management of agricultural life forms, exemplified in this book through the genealogy of Finncattle, also contributed significantly to the emergence of the science of conservation biology in the mid-1980s (Meine 2010). This mission-oriented biological discipline is operating today as one of the drivers behind biodiversity conservation and its methods. I will explore these in detail in chapters 2 and 3, contextualized after the historical background below.

THE SECOND PARADOX: THE MISSION OF CONSERVATION BIOLOGY × THE MISSION OF THE CBD

Around the time when agricultural breeders recognized the problems they faced with excessively uniform populations, environmental biologists outside the agriculture business voiced their concerns about the effects of the Green Revolution on the broader ecological landscape beyond agricultural lands, and they found a way to articulate their worries effectively. They were successful in seeking political weight for the ideas of conservation by shifting from the previous discourses on practices and modes of operation of traditional biology that were interested in individual forms of life toward a system that draws heavily on the premises of ecological thinking, initially conceptualizing diversity as a function of energy flows, the "currency" within the circuits of ecology (Odum [1953] 1975). Yet, from nineteenth-century proto-conservationists to mid-twentieth-century prophets of approaching ecological peril, the arguments for conserving nature gained only a little support, largely among biologists themselves, who nonetheless saw the calls for conserving nature as ethically biased and in contrast to a more scientific, value-neutral approach (Takacs 1996).

However, the effect of the Green Revolution on all living beings, extending beyond agriculture, seemed to give justification for ethical concerns by providing real-life examples: shrinking natural habitats for wildlife and the actual loss of species. Thus, in the early 1980s a new scientific discipline and political discourse emerged. That discipline, which came to be called conservation biology, was ushered in by the First International Conference on Conservation Biology. Held at San Diego's Wild Animal Park in 1978 and organized by San Diego–based biologist Michael E. Soulé, the meeting was an interdisciplinary gathering that brought together "an odd assortment of academics, zoo-keepers, and wildlife conservationists" (Gibbons 1992, 20) and, belying the initial suspicions expressed in many quarters, proved successful. In the next few years the discipline gained ground. One of its early key figures, Stanley A. Temple, defined that the movement's mission was "to develop new guiding principles and new technologies to allow society to preserve biological diversity" (Gibbons 1992, 20), and later, in 1985, Soulé characterized the discipline he had helped found as unique in that it "differs from most other biological sciences in one important way: it is often a crisis discipline" (Soulé 1985, 727).

In 1985 David Ehrenfeld, a politically active biologist motivated by deeply rooted ecology ethics, took action, establishing the Society for Conservation Biology and its journal, *Conservation Biology*, first published in

1987. The explicit aim was the conservation of Earth's biological diversity, the pure difference found within nature and life. According to the mission statement, however, conservation biology should be seen not as wanting to turn nature into a museum of living beings but rather as advancing the idea of the sustainable management of natural resources, an idea borrowed from scientific management in business contexts. Sustainable management of the ecosystem ecology, eventually the whole planet, was the aim, which in its turn influenced related policies and governance. The conservation biologists moved out of the realm of science and into politics, and, indeed, environmental ethics and ecology quickly became a "mission-oriented" advocacy science (Takacs 1992; Escobar 1998; Meine 2010).

With the discourse of conservation biology comes the interesting issue of how science being both "pure" and an espoused aim of advocacy can be wedded or even seamlessly coexist. The very first general textbook on ecology, from 1953 (Odum [1953] 1975, 1–5), pointed out the close connections between ecology and economy on its first pages yet accorded them separate aims and methods. Conservation scientists instead, in efforts to gain more political power for the message of conservation and to demonstrate rationale beyond valuing the intrinsic value of nature and preserving its diversity (many considered "nature" too general and/or too romantic a notion), added the economic calculation of the value of biodiversity to their toolbox. An illustrative example of reasons cited for which the economic discourse should be adopted to further the causes of conservationists comes from the founder of the Worldwatch Institute, Lester R. Brown. He explained the reasons for the friendship between ecologists and economists thus: ecologists understand that all economic activity, indeed all life, depends on the Earth's ecosystem—the complex of individual species living together, interacting with each other and their physical habitats. These millions of species exist in an intricate balance, woven together by food chains, nutrient cycles, the hydrological cycle, and the climate system. Economists know how to translate goals into policy. Economists and ecologists working together can design and build an eco-economy, one that can sustain progress (L. Brown 2001, 4).

The language of conservation biology created a new discourse filled with idioms borrowed from liberal economics in the latter part of the twentieth century in order to speak of scientific ecological management and to "talk hard policy," to provide easy-to-understand cost-benefit calculations to conservation's ends, to help policy makers set conservation priorities based on the cost of the losses, and to create sustainable policies and further progress. Early articulations of this were presented by C. S. Holling and W. C. Clark (1975). For nature to become manageable, it had to become rearticulated as a resource since resources can be assigned a market value—a value that needed to be protected in a liberal economy, optimally managed by the conservation community, and finally translated into policy measures. In his provocative book about conservation of biodiversity, Joseph Vogel went so far as to claim that biodiversity can be saved only when genetic information in genetic resources is privatized because "self-interest can achieve that which inadequate noble intentions cannot" (Vogel 1994, 7).

The mission-oriented science of conservation biology was also responsible for the introduction of the concept of biodiversity, which really took off when it gained institutionally powerful support. The concept was thrust into public and biological discourse in the 1986 National Forum on BioDiversity organized by the highly esteemed National Academy of Sciences (NAS) of the United States and cosponsored by the Smithsonian Institution. More specifically, the forum was first suggested by the senior program officer for the Board of Basic Biology, Walter Rosen. He managed to sell the idea to the notoriously conservative, neutral, and objectivity-focused NAS even though the notion of biodiversity already hinted at arguments on behalf of nature's conservation. He invited influential biologists such as E. O. Wilson and Peter Raven to be conference speakers early on.

Prominent biologist Daniel Janzen recalled the event some years later and admitted how, for researchers of his ilk, it was all about "coming out of the closet" to raise awareness of the impending destruction of nature's diversity: "The Washington Conference? That was an explicit political event, explicitly designed to make Congress aware of this complexity of species that we're losing. And the word [biodiversity] . . . was punched into that system at that point deliberately. A lot of us went to that talk on a political mission. We were asked, will we come and do this thing? So we did" (Janzen, cited by Takacs 1992, 37; see also Vogel 1994, 8–14).

Environmental groups and the ecological movement at large had found a useful concept in biodiversity, which was promoted in the media and became the meat of very successful lobbying in political institutions to bring a change in prevailing conditions and practices driving the loss of diversity, a shift toward more sustainable policies. As a concept, biodiversity entered print in 1988 in an edited book composed of the presentations given at the BioDiversity meeting. The book, simply *Biodiversity*, was edited by Wilson, who credited the invention of the term to Rosen. The key element in this part of the chronology is that while the idea of and research on biological differences found in nature long predates this conference, it is here that those differences were formulated simultaneously as a "global resource, to be indexed, used, and above all, preserved" (Wilson 1988, 3).

With the CBD, and through redefinition of "global resource" in terms of nationally claimable genetic resources as described above, a point of contention has formed around whether and to what extent these efforts to conserve biodiversity are, in fact, thinly veiled forms of bioprospecting. Are genetic resources that are already collected, preserved, and commercially used in practice a resource that can be considered part of the global commons or not, and how should any access and benefit-sharing issues arising from the scientific and commercial prospecting and use of genetic resources be addressed? Quite a few works of various kinds have been written on the subjects of biodiversity, bioprospecting, and global contracts (Shiva 1993; Hayden 2003b; Agrawal 2005; Hall 2007). In addition, there are various treatises about their historical developments over the years within international institutions such as the UN and at high-profile botanical gardens (e.g., Pistorius 1997; see also Parry 2004, 201–11), none of which offer an easy solution to the questions above.

What has been left largely unexamined in previous studies is the way in which particular forms of life become nationally identified as genetic resources in the local practice of biodiversity conservation. The CBD not only rearticulated biodiversity as genetic resources but also translated the general mission of conservation biology into national missions that were enacted and supervised by the sovereign signatories to the convention. Thus, a new, complex territory of decision making emerges: How, with what technologies, and under which intersecting rationalities are the genetic resources brought to life and managed in the national implementation of the CBD? This question cannot be answered without consideration of two key challenges in the local implementation.

The first is this: How can particular species and breeds be identified as having a nationhood or belonging to a particular nation through genetic identification? Second, given our long-standing modern dichotomy of nature versus culture, how and by which technoscientific apparatus can nature become culture? How can nationhood be identified in and located within genetic difference? Once identified, how is the value of those national forms of life pragmatically managed and optimized through the selection-specific bodies representing the purest forms of national genetic resources (see Hayden 2003b, chap. 6)?

In simple terms, there can be no nationally valuable resources without the identification of distinct genetic profiles and the transformation of the life forms into practically manageable forms of life, all in order to ensure that this vital material is available for processes of economic optimization and political naturalization. This bricolage work in a space of highly productive contradictions (K. Fortun 2001) is an expression of double-bind imperatives (Bateson 2000) that leads to ethical plateaus where national values, multiple technologies, and local decision-making practices meet the global Convention on Biological Diversity to create new configurations of national forms of life.[7]

Hence, what I am interested in are the articles of the CBD (especially article 15) as far as they are the basis for biological nationalization guaranteeing the internationally recognized genetic sovereignty of each signatory. National genetic sovereignty involves a novel redefinition of the signatory nations' natural resources and their boundaries with new instruments for identifying or fingerprinting all national "genetic material of actual or potential value" (in the words of the definition in the CBD's article 2). This amounts to literally inscribing the national identity in flesh, matter, and life. What is of interest in the protection of native rights under the biodiversity treaty is the recasting of those rights in economic and genetic terms. Value, potential or actual, is defined exclusively in terms of the origin claims of nations that are mediated by globally recognized institutional instruments of calculation and audit. The naturalization and indeed nationalization of nonhuman life translates the older or more mundane forms of biological national wealth into an explicitly genetic one. What is more, the nation itself, by the same token, becomes newly defined by these emerging nonhuman genetic corporeal boundaries. The new biotechnologies—the technoscientific means—that make this translation possible have, in human contexts, been sources of major debate in recent decades, especially with regard to the definition of national populations, the markers of difference at population level, and the sparking of questions about ethnic profiling at the level of the individual. However, they have not been fully examined with regard to nonhuman nationhood. If the Finncattle in chapter 1 are one way of showing how the totality of a nation's life—human and nonhuman—is connected and produced through various nature/culture interfaces creating each other, the rest of the book asks in what ways the practices by which the collective life of a nation is collected and reproduced now operate in a different mode, especially with regard to the definition of nonhuman populations, and how, in a very concrete way, novel space-times of nations are created, requiring a novel constitution of the nation.

With chapter 2, on the Alexander apple, my account of the national genetics programs starts to reexamine the three key threads of national theory that need to come together in the identification of nationally distinct genetic features: population, territory, and the double time of the nation. These are explored thread by thread in relation to the question of nationally identified forms of life beyond human populations. First, following the crafting of nonhuman forms of life as made possible by new biotechnologies, I analyze in chapter 2 how genetic fingerprinting and the creation of national populations of plant genetic resources problematize the territorial rooting and historical explanations as principles in the identification of national forms of life. More specifically, I study how a variety of apple tree called Alexander is becoming genetically identified as part of Finnish nature. The chapter offers an account of the work of a population scientist employed at the national research institute that was assigned scientific responsibility for corporeal identification of Finnish plant genetic resources. The material for this chapter was collected between 2005 and 2007 through participant observation, with the documentation of field trips around Finland in search of apple varieties and the accompanying laboratory work aimed at their genetic profiling.

The chapter takes on the problematics of territorial and temporal dimensions of national theory within the context of twenty-first-century nonhuman nationhood. In the context of scientific fact making, Bruno Latour has argued that "most of the difficulties we have in understanding science and technology proceed from our belief that space and time exist independently as an unshakeable frame of reference inside which events and place would occur. This belief makes it impossible to understand how different spaces and different times may be produced inside the networks built to mobilise, cumulate and recombine the world" (1987, 228). Analyzing the ways in which DNA fingerprinting practices work in the identification of nonhumans, I argue that new genetic technologies and practices complicate national identification and reconfigure the creation of national nonhumans. Here, different times and spaces become relevant in comparison to the historical case of Finncattle. In short, another grid of spatio-temporal intelligibility is laid down for assessing the nationhood of nature's species inventory.

Developing this line of argument, chapter 3 ("Stilled Life") contextualizes the creation of genetic resources in the national and international political economy over nature and follows the construction of new infrastructures of life illustrated by animal gene banks. The empirical material for this analysis comes from extended participant observation over the four years I spent visiting the scientists working for the Animal Genetic Resources Programme. What took a long time for me to understand about the politics of genetic resources—the manner in which multiple rationalities and values condition the living corporeal matter that will be recognized and optimized as representatives of nations' genetic resources—was something that is exemplified in the event I describe here. The chapter tells a story about a weeklong field trip taken in 2006 to the world's largest breeder of white Finnsheep, which was aimed at banking the gametes of this animal breed for conservation purposes. I ask how and under which matrix of reasoning particular gametes are selected as the purest representatives for the Finnish sheep breed stored in the national gene bank. To paraphrase Donna Haraway (1997, 7), I am extremely curious as to what kinds of bodies, what forms of frozen as well as motile sociotechnical alliances (also called social relationships), the nonhuman nationhood in Finland consists of in the twenty-first century—here embodied by the Finnsheep gene bank.

I claim that three central interests intersect within the materiality they embody and that these condition their identification processes all the way down to their corporeality. Thus, while different spatio-temporal configurations are required for the identification of national genetic resources, they are enacted by large-scale networks and gene bank infrastructures that are needed to guarantee their local figure—a rooting as national beings of nature. Paradoxically, these networks also provide for their easy global mobilization.

To unpack this argument, the chapter empirically analyzes the creation of the first national ex situ animal gene bank (which is usually the only conceptualization of gene banks applied in the popular media). I claim that two central matters of concern, the threat associated with ecological extinction and anxiety about economic losses related to diminishing global genetic variance, have merged into a distinctive field of global reasoning. Within this scientific-economic apparatus, ecological and economic interests are not readily subsumed by each other. My account follows how the concerns are translated into material interests that radically transform the Finnsheep breed by conditioning the process and the instruments by which particular genetic resources are collected, processed, and finally stored in the gene banks, the new infrastructure for conserving national life.

THE THIRD PARADOX: GLOBAL COMMONS × NATIONAL SOVEREIGNTY

Finally, the idea of biodiversity as a global resource, as defined by Wilson in the quotation above, is related to the development of the international politics question of commercial exploitation of natural resources, especially of genetic resources. The development of international nature politics has followed the paths of larger processes of globalization, questioning the idea of national sovereignty and its powers to control the flow of capital, information, and—most importantly—corporeal forms of nonhuman life. In the latter part of the twentieth century, bioprospecting, the search for capitalizable forms of life, as perpetrated by the multinationals of the North within the territories of the biodiversity-rich South, disrupted the latter nations' old ways of protecting their national interests and led to accusations of systematic bioimperialism and biopiracy, or the unwarranted prospecting for and use of traditional knowledge and useful genetic materials (Shiva 1993; Moran et al. 2001).

Early international agreements on plant breeders' rights made in the wake of the Green Revolution, such as that in the 1961 formation of the International Union for the Protection of New Varieties of Plants (UPOV) among European nations and the 1970 Plant Variety Protection Act (PVPA) in the United States, helped identify ownership rights only for commercial varieties developed in the North while deregulating the raw material of those found in the South. This left both the nations and their plant (and other living) materials without international legal protection against one-sided bioprospecting (Kloppenburg 1988). Thus, the older agreements and acts functioned, and still function, as a fragmented global regime dictating the access to raw materials and derivate outcomes of some key forms of life that are vital to agribusiness while many other forms of life found in nature were left unregulated at the global level.

Aware of these previous developments, international nature-conservation institutions, such as the World Conservation Union (IUCN), the United Nations Environmental Programme, and in later years the FAO, too, explored a more ambitious global contract: they envisioned a political and legal possibility of setting up a global convention on biodiversity. In 1987 the UNEP Governing Council came up with an ambitious plan. It wanted to coordinate international efforts to protect biological diversity, and the ad hoc working group that was set up to identify the key elements for a globally coordinated action identified that a global treaty would be needed to bring the world together around the conservation of biodiversity. In the working sessions of the ad hoc group, the idea of conserving and protecting the rights to raw materials was extended beyond plants to animals, covering domesticated and wild species both in their natural habitats and in managed gene banks (or in in situ and ex situ conservation). It was in the preparatory meetings for the CBD that one of the working groups dealt with fundamental issues such as the scope for the convention and the legal obligations of the signatory parties. That group came up with the propositions by which "the scope for the Convention was gradually broadened to include all aspects and facets of biodiversity" (Glowka et al. 1994, 1–2).

Looking beyond the scope of the convention, another working group had been appointed, tasked with considering the conditions for the convention, especially the access and benefit-sharing rights related to biodiversity. Although the first working group came up with the proposition that biodiversity is a common concern of humankind, it was the second working group that then qualified this proposition. Thus, according to one of the negotiators who was present, the "proposition that biodiversity should be considered as the 'common heritage' of humankind was rejected at an early stage, since most components of biological diversity are situated in areas under national jurisdiction" (Glowka et al. 1994, 3). In other words, the negotiators ran into the global power politics between the North and South, between the technologically advanced but biodiversity-poor countries and the biodiversity-rich yet technologically less advanced ones.

What happened, then, was a rearticulation of sovereign rights over biological diversity, especially over valuable resources found in nature: genetic resources, in line with the earlier Stockholm Declaration, or the Declaration of the United Nations Conference on the Human Environment held in Stockholm in 1972. Principle 21 of that declaration proclaimed a global understanding that the signatory states had "the sovereign right to exploit their own resources pursuant to their own environmental policies." This right was articulated anew in the CBD's preparatory work, which again recognized the signatories' sovereign rights over their natural resources and, hence, also their sole authority to determine access to genetic resources—as long as these are recognized as "national" and embody "actual or potential value" (CBD, article 15).

Yet, and as is now obvious from the above, the "common concern" over the conservation of biodiversity was reframed in the final CBD text in language speaking of "a common responsibility to the issue based on its paramount importance to the international community as a whole" (Glowka et al. 1994, 3). This recognized that biological resources fall under the national legislation of each signatory country while simultaneously restating the moral global obligation to conserve biodiversity. The initial regimes for fair and equitable access and for benefit sharing that were envisioned in the CBD have attracted much critical commentary from legal, ethical, and social perspectives since even before the convention was opened for signature. At base, the argument goes that the CBD claimed to address key issues for the conservation and sustainable use of biodiversity but offered no valid mechanism for doing so and that the focus on ownership and genetic resources "delaminated" biodiversity, rendering other layers the focus of global politics. However, the key tension still revolved around the genetic resources. The G77 group, the largest organization of developing countries in the United Nations, promoting the voice and economic interest of the countries of the South, repeatedly called for more specific and legally defined terms for access and benefit sharing related to genetic resources.

Eighteen years after the CBD's initial adoption, the G77 group stated in 2010 that the conservation of biological diversity "cannot be achieved without the sustainable use and the fair and equitable sharing of the benefit arising from genetic resources. . . . In doing so, an effective international framework must be in place," and "the Protocol on Access and Benefit Sharing at the next meeting . . . to be held . . . in Nagoya, Japan, is of a strategic importance" (Alsaidi 2010, 1). The Yemeni ambassador to the UN, Abdullah Alsaidi, also reiterated the call for all G77 countries to work toward the adoption of a globally binding policy on genetic resources. His message was that "the G77 and China takes this opportunity to underscore the need for great mobilization and political will such that we will be able to adopt the protocol on access and benefit-sharing and to ensure that the post-2010 [biodiversity] targets are able to be met" (Alsaidi 2010, 2–3).

And so the success of conservation measures and compliance with biodiversity targets were explicitly linked to the global recognition of sovereignty and ownership over biological resources by the G77 countries in 2010 in a process that led ultimately to the adoption of the Nagoya Protocol. That protocol, which entered force in October 2014, serves as a clarification and a more legally refined supplementary protocol to the CBD, specifying some of the aspects that the initial treaty left too open for implementation (see above, and the guide to the Nagoya Protocol in Greiber et al. 2012). Thus the Nagoya Protocol reiterated the legal sovereign power over biological resources that was specified in its mandate, and its reception has followed a path uncannily familiar from the mixed reports on the adoption of the CBD that were quoted earlier.

In 2014 a piece in *Nature* reported that "a major international agreement is coming into force to combat 'biopiracy'—profiting from biological products while failing to compensate the community from which they originate. The Nagoya Protocol aims to ensure that developing nations benefit when their plants, animals or microbes are used by foreign scientists" (Cressey 2014, 14). The author concluded that "new rules will also present challenges for synthetic biologists, who combine genetic code from many different organisms to create drugs or sensors" (Cressey 2014, 14–15). As is obvious, the tensions between countries and scientists, health officials, and biotechnology industry stakeholders are not going to be resolved with the simple introduction of the Nagoya Protocol, and perhaps they will never be resolved in a satisfactory way. It is easy to see that the ethical plateau created by the intensified confrontation of power between the South and the North has continued after adoption of the Nagoya Protocol. Several excellent works have been written that explore the inherent tension of interests connected with access and benefit-sharing issues from the standpoint of various disciplines both in light of the CBD's entry into force (e.g., Brush 1998; Parry 2001; Hayden 2003b) and in the wake of the Nagoya Protocol (Kamau et al. 2011; Vogel et al. 2011).

What has been left largely unexamined in previous literature, however, is the distribution of power and renegotiation of the social contracts within the nations that are implementing the CBD. The CBD is not only a global, international political treaty but also a political challenge, an experiment in domestic implementation, for it questions the existing boundaries of national political institutions and their powers. As Philippe Le Prestre (2002, 270) has stated, the CBD "touches not only upon man's relationship with nature and international relations but on the distribution of domestic political power as well." Different interests and institutional topographies at the national level have a significant impact in shaping how genetic resources are naturalized as national objects of nature politics.

In the final, empirically oriented chapter, I follow the shaping of genetic resources within Finnish nature politics where policies on genetic resources are explicitly made: in the Ministry of Agriculture and Forestry. Although the CBD had already been signed by the European Union as a nonstate party in 1992, Finland was affected very little in its national implementation of the convention until the adoption of the Nagoya Protocol, after which an EU-wide regulation on genetic resources (Regulation [EU] no. 511/2014) was issued in 2014. In practice, this regulation still requires only that the EU member countries establish a minimal institutional framework to oversee national compliance, consisting of a national focal point for coordination with other relevant parties and a competent authority to check whether users of genetic resources comply with their obligations. Hence, regulation at the level of the EU region leaves most of the implementation in the hands of nation-states and their institutions. I wanted to look at what is forming in the space left to those actors.

Institutional observations within the national Board for Genetic Resources at the Ministry of Agriculture and Forestry provided me with access to the highest level of political decision making related to genetic resources in Finland—the drafting of policy and juridical evaluations of the appropriateness of the legal frameworks now in place. I first sat down in a cushioned chair in the ministerial meeting room in the spring of 2005, and I completed my silent observations at the end of 2007. In that time I also gained access to the Access and Benefit Sharing subgroup, which was charged with the task of providing Finland with a draft policy on access and benefit-sharing issues related to national genetic resources. To draft the policy, this group had to survey the complex interrelations of national and international regulations pertaining to various natural entities and how these are connected with the novel objects of genetic governance.

I also followed the legislation-drafting process over the years and conducted follow-up interviews in 2014–15 at the time when the draft national legislation for genetic resources was about to be passed forward in its first form for official approval by the Parliament of Finland and again shortly after the law had been brought into force in 2017. The policies and political principles specified in the draft and in the final accepted text, together with the infrastructure in which it is embedded, constitute the key site where particular conditions of possibility for the nationhood of genetic resources are constructed. It is in this process that propositions are drafted in order for science to prove valid the domains of nature that are turned into genetic resources—simultaneously setting the stage for the political, juridical, and material emergence. It is here, in short, that the sovereignty of a nation is exercised through inclusions and exclusions of natural entities. I will explain these observations in more detail in chapter 4.

What becomes clear in following the unfolding of the national policies in the making is how much they, in turn, are conditioned by something more than the humans working at the ministry—how national interests are a matter of constant negotiation between actors with different potentiality for agency above and beyond each individual member of the working group for genetic-resource policies. The political infrastructure and national principles for delegating political power among ministries, the CBD and its partial reaffirmation in the Nagoya Protocol, the weighting between actual and potential value of genetic material, and the suggestion to bifurcate national nature through an amendment to the constitution all show how complicated and relational a figure of nature Finland's genetic resources really are. Indeed, not only is the ontological base of "genetic resources" questioned; so is the Constitution of Finland, providing clear categories of nature and culture. What is at stake here is not only the definition of rights of ownership over living bodies of animals, plants, microbes, and the information these contain within their genetic makeup but also the matter of how the sovereign might claim the right to decide on those rights in view of the fact that private ownership of fleshly living beings is at present ultimately protected in the national constitution.

My analysis focuses on the institutional and domestic power relationships and their effects on the definition of criteria applied in identification of genetic resources: some forms of nonhuman life are considered national while others are not. I conclude the chapter by analyzing Michel Foucault's claim that "sovereignty and discipline, legislation, the right of sovereignty and disciplinary mechanics are in fact the two things that constitute—in an absolute sense—the general mechanisms of power in our society" (2003, 39).

I strive to show how this is still one of the most important unresolved paradoxes of the living communities in the form of a "nation" and the biopolitics it is based on: to have a sovereign right to include select life forms within the communal sphere of the nation and as part of its natural body, to discipline and manage its vital forces, while at the same time excluding certain other life forms from entering the sphere of the nation. In application of the latter right, the sovereign renounces its sovereignty with regard to itself, and the paradox flows from the fact that the sovereign nation is the sovereign itself and cannot thus dismember or divide itself. The sovereign entity also must set limits with reference to the other, nonnational and alien forms of nonhuman life, in order to discipline and take care of the native species of Finland. Quite simply, this is a new articulation of the paradox of sovereign power in relation to biopower, the right to kill and to let live. According to Giorgio Agamben (1998), this is the "hidden foundation" of all politics. I will elaborate on and evaluate this claim, too, in chapter 4.

WRITING THE BIOGENETIC PARADOXES

The arguments presented in this work have grown out of experiences gained via participant observation, whether scribbled down in unorganized field notes or encapsulated by photos taken for visual evidence as authenticating devices. Only later were these to be cross-pollinated with archival and theoretical work. This confession is a reiteration of the classic distinction between field and home in anthropological practices, which has been contested as a spatial metaphor to situate research theoretically or in practice (Appadurai 1988; Gupta and Ferguson 1997a). As in most anthropological works, the distinction does not hold as a clear-cut boundary with natives associated with one or several bounded geographical locations. Yet I want to keep to this metaphor of location for several reasons.

During my fieldwork, I spent a considerable amount of time directly involved with genetic-resource-program activities—in and around laboratories, fields, meetings, and offices of scientists. My first experience with the genetic-resource programs was in the plant program (PGR) in January 2004.

I then met my first informant at her office at MTT's headquarters some one hundred kilometers north of Helsinki. She was Mia Sahramaa, the plant scientist nominated to be coordinator of the national efforts involving plant resources. She and her work became a very fruitful entry point to the large network of the national programs. Dr. Sahramaa provided me with interviews and contact information for the people and institutions directly and indirectly involved in the calculation of national genetic resources. She also took me to meetings that extended beyond the usual boundaries of her work as a scientist and required her to act as a top-notch networker. Most importantly, she made possible my access as an observer of the national Board for Genetic Resources under the Ministry of Agriculture and Forestry. With her kind support and interest in the work, I was brought into the fold of the ministry and gained access also to the internal draft documents that were produced and circulated between the meetings. However, Dr. Sahramaa left the post in 2006, and new coordinators took over her work.

Those new coordinators were two of her colleagues who both had many years of experience in genetic-resources work, Merja Veteläinen and Kristiina Antonius. I first interviewed Dr. Veteläinen in 2004 about the national genetic programs, around the time she returned to Finland after having spent several years with the Nordic Gene Bank in Alnarp, Sweden. She provided me with very insightful interviews and background support for my work before the actual fieldwork began. But it was Dr. Antonius who brought me closest to the scientific work performed in the PGR context. I followed her apple identification work—genetic fingerprinting as it is called—for almost as long as I did the field research.

I first entered her office in the spring of 2004 not knowing that one of the chapters of the book would be about her work. I began to take interest in her apples only a year and a half later. Since then, as chapter 2 makes clear, I shadowed her in the fields in the hunt for apples and also acted as her assistant in the laboratory. The prolonged observation period, almost three years of following her work, is explained by the seasonal rhythms of nature: not much work on apple identification can be done between late fall and late spring in Finland since the trees are hidden under a thick layer of snow and thus are practically unidentifiable or even unfindable. Because of these environmental conditions, the work must be performed during the right seasons, the summer months of June to August, to gain easy access to the trees and to their fruits, the apples.

My first contact within the Animal Genetic Resources Programme was with Juha Kantanen in the spring of 2004. The first meetings consisted mostly of interviews and of Dr. Kantanen pointing me to the basic literature on animal genetics. He kindly granted me access to his research laboratory after my request to see the practical work he performs with the team. Since then, I have been a regular visitor to his laboratory and have accompanied him in his research with animals and on fieldwork travels around Finland. He also arranged a mentor for me in laboratory work, Ilma Karhu, who patiently initiated me in the secrets of genetic assays and thereby added further value to the lab access.

Most herds of animals such as of Finnsheep are kept by individual farmers who, from the viewpoint of the genetic-resources programs, provide outsourced shepherding for the national aims of conservation. The scattered herds are all easily calculated by the national programs since they are subject to nationwide controlled population management—all but a small fraction of the professional animal breeders are already enrolled in centrally managed national breeding programs run by the artificial insemination cooperative FABA. The constantly updated vital statistics of sheep populations are readily accessed via the internet, so they are at any given moment just a mouse click away. This simplifies the planning of the future direction of the breeding (with the central database and related calculation operations handled by associated software recommending mating partners within the flock), and it makes day-to-day practical breeding management very easy for the farmers (by allowing the comparison of current vital statistics of the flock with those of flocks owned by others). These benefits are also the main reason behind their enrollment in the programs. Together, these geographically separate animal populations form what is called the national herd of Finland, merged in databases and in the genetic-program calculations by the conservation scientists.

However, while the national herd is easy to compose digitally in the database and textually in planning documents aimed at maintaining genetic diversity in the genetic programs, genetic conservation of this flock—the transformation of live animals from their in situ mode of existence into genetic resources ex situ—is a tricky business. The aims of the individual farmers must be aligned with those of the animal program (for animal genetic resources), and, in more practical terms, the animals themselves must be willing to go along with the plans of the scientists. I learned this in the autumn of 2006 when I followed the construction of the first ex situ gene bank for the national sheep, Finnsheep. The week's fieldwork, which gives a real-world animal backbone to chapter 3, was done on a semiprivately owned farm in southern Finland.

Similarly, most Finncattle, also taken to be one of the native Finnish animal breeds, are in small herds around Finland. The interesting part of the story here is that many of these animals are on two prison farms (in Pelso and Sukeva), where the in situ gene bank is maintained by the prisoners. I was along for two trips to these facilities in 2004 and 2005 during which Dr. Kantanen surveyed the cattle population and planned future conservation strategies. Besides the northern geographical location of the prisons, what is interesting here is the institutional location of the cattle. During the fieldwork I began to wonder whether there might be something more than a metaphorical connection between the human and nonhuman prisoners. In Foucault's classic work on the birth of the modern prison system, the overarching aim is made clear to be no longer that of punishment. It is disciplinary action aimed at making bodies docile and productive, to contribute to the national economy. With this theoretical analogy to jailbirds, I began wondering why the Finncattle were put in prison in the first place.

I returned to FABA's Finncattle archives with that question at the front of my mind. After systematic study and analysis of all available documents and some related interviews, the reason for the Finncattle's imprisonment slowly began growing more understandable. I will return to this issue by recounting the genealogy in chapter 1, so I will note here just that their imprisonment serves both as a metaphor and as a very real power effect on their corporealities that was brought about by the larger developments in agribusiness over the past two centuries. The same developments have been instrumental in transforming them from an animal breed into genetic resources, from a matter of fact to a matter of concern that is emblematic of the entire global family of genetic resources.

Finally, the institutional observations at the government ministries have provided me with a first-person view of how the genetic resources became a political concern in Finland. The focus of my observations was on two aspects of ministerial work in preparing the official background memo on the access and benefit-sharing issues related to valuable genetic material. That is reflected in the argument presented in chapter 4. On one hand, I traced how genetic resources became an issue for official politics and how the Finnish political infrastructure first identified valuable genetic material institutionally. Tellingly, it was the Ministry of Agriculture and Forestry rather than the Ministry of the Environment that was officially tasked with preparing the first national stance, even though the official representative of the latter was joint leader of the group in her capacity as secretary. The institutional location alone betrays how, at that time, genetic resources were considered primarily economic resources of the nation, not ecological objects of environmental concern. The institutional location of the issue of genetic resources has shifted again in the 2010s, and drafting the first legislation proposition ended up being a task of the Ministry of the Environment. I wanted to find out how this institutional relocation affected the political framing of the issue, so in 2014 and 2015 I interviewed the key persons drafting the new legislation. Accordingly, my first observations were focused on the role of institutional location, the distribution of domestic power over nature, and the valuation processes related to the institutions and their political mandates. The second set of observations is about what gets written in the draft and preparatory documents and how, that is, the ways in which the issue of the ownership of genetic resources challenges the existing social contract between the citizens and the state, between private individuals and the body of the national community.

Thus, the initial site of this ethnographic study, a national program, emerges in the course of the work as a collection of multiple sites dispersed across various sets of spatial and temporal coordinates, as a heterogeneous network of various nationally relevant locations, and as novel emerging forms of life (Fischer 1999) in themselves. An early recognition in science and technology studies (STS) is that, of course, science and technology are not separate realms nested in, or situated outside, society but form part of the same social fabric and practices that coconstruct it (Latour and Woolgar 1986; Latour 1987; Woolgar 1988; Knorr Cetina 1999). The methodological mobility with regard to my field, or the makings of genetic resources as my object of study, is accounted for by the fact that, for the most part, this particular formation of culture and these novel objects of nature have been created in a constant movement back and forth between places.

This kind of ethnographic method can therefore be characterized best as what has been called a "multisited ethnography," also referred to as a "multilocale" or "multisite" ethnography (Marcus 1995; Fischer 1999; K. Fortun 2001; Sunder Rajan 2006; Callison 2014; C. Ozden-Schilling 2016; T. Ozden-Schilling 2016): it is very much a mobile ethnography aimed at following the actors through their multiple trajectories in a nation-gathering technoscientific enterprise. While observing this gathering practiced by scientists, my own narrative is a special kind of cultural gathering that itself loops back to the production of biowealth as a marker of accumulated national identity as wealth (Clifford 1988).[8] The challenge in this type of fieldwork-based research is the question of the borders of the field and the constitution of the object of study itself. Does the field travel with the scientists themselves, and what about the other key unit of analysis, the nation? The problem of the local and the global persists in the anthropological literature as a question about the field of observations (e.g., Gupta and Ferguson 1997a; 1997b; Mitchell 2002; Tsing 2005), especially when scientific activity is taken as the object of observation.

Various metaphors other than that of the field have been suggested for science-in-action (E. Martin 1997) and the traveling facts of science. While the problems related to fieldwork are deconstructed in detail in anthropological literature of recent decades (fieldwork as authenticating device, the field as too limited a research object, the field as a narrated homogeneous fiction, and so on—see, for example, Clifford and Marcus 1986; Clifford 1988; Gupta and Ferguson 1997a; Clifford 1996), I wish to use it precisely because of its naturalistic connotations and to see how the metaphor sometimes falls in relationship to very literal field topographies during the work. In this, I am concerned not so much with asking what kind of narrative fiction the metaphor allows for as with purposes of locating the interplay between the narration and the material, the very articulation of what is thought to be social/cultural and natural/biological.

The work traces the links between spatially bounded, special sites of observed practices and is an attempt also to discuss these simultaneously with previously (predominantly) disparate theoretical locations. Thus, in the following stories refined ministerial boardrooms in the nation's capital are interwoven with the provincial barns where the national herd is kept, and the well-organized and spatially bounded laboratories that are equipped to read off genetic signs of nationhood are linked to locally contingent practices and to the vast geography of the dispersed knowledge of local breeds and varieties of nonhuman. In other words, they address the idea of the universality of biological sciences versus contingent differences in scientific reasoning that could be termed national in their pursuit of identifying national genetic resources as particular nonhuman forms of national life. Lately, questions about location and movement, about locality in its relation to the global, have been cut short within some of the arguments presented in science and technology studies, most notably in actor network theory (ANT), where the question is rephrased as being about the length of translations in strivings to resolve the problematic difference of scale.[9]

Here, of course, one may question the reason for performing any translations at all and what could be made of a pure description of them. I find Kaushik Sunder Rajan's (2006) argument about the inherent tensions in creating biowealth at the junctures of local and global rather illuminating with respect to the problem of articulating what is at stake here methodologically. His claim is that "it is impossible to write about global processes of exchange simply by localizing them to their manifestations at particular field sites; but it is equally impossible to appreciate the complexities of these global processes without making them specific, since for all the hegemonic potential of globalization today, it does manifest in particular, tendential ways in particular, tendential places" (Sunder Rajan 2006, 233).

However, analytically, it would be too simple to resort to only this kind of methodological argument, specificity, which itself tends to naturalize difference in spatiality, in local differences assuming—and, perhaps even worse, justifying—a preconceived national/local existence. Writing is what all anthropologists ultimately do, and it is through this writing that "we become aware of creating more and more gaps. Hence our activities forever magnify a background of potential significance against which—whatever the scale—we try to actualize subtle re-imaginings, and build models that will take everything important into account" (Strathern 1991, 119). Therefore, rather than just assuming a specific localization and its assumed tendency for cultural difference, I am interested more in what makes a difference or how it is possible for a difference to manifest itself and how these differences are found in the nonhuman life that is made to constitute a genetic demarcation of a locality—a nation—from the rest of the world through a figure of genetic resources. As I will argue later, the existence of a nation consists of marking off boundaries in and through living bodies and the populations from which individual bodies are derived, a very Foucauldian standpoint. But to see how this empirically plays out requires a methodological orientation of seeking to understand how national genetic resources suddenly came to be in all their modalities of existence—conceptual, institutional, juridical, corporeal.

Numerous studies have shown that things called facts are constructed through meticulous practices across the boundaries between scientific fields. Although STS and the anthropology of science are more broadly considered to be approaches to rather than theories of scientific and technological practice in all its shapes and forms, they still are approaches that are tuned to understanding the emergence of the new in science and through technological means. Yet for seeing how and in what sense genetic resources are a novelty, I suggest, a dialogue with the theory of nation must be opened. Nation and nationhood as particular communities of life have been approached in the theory in terms of human identity, in the discursive sphere limited by an inherent humanism.

The discussion has for many decades been the domain of historians and historically oriented social scientists, and the gaze has seldom been directed toward the ongoing mundane practices by which nations are currently being reproduced. The early notion of nations as a "daily plebiscite" became, of course, taken for granted after Ernest Renan's lecture in 1882 (Renan [1882] 1996), but insight into how our contemporary communities are continuously reproduced by a multitude of (scientific) practices is in the quantitative minority in the academic literature (but see Billig 1995). In taking part in the associated dialogue, I situate this book at large among the texts and approaches found within the anthropology of science and, more specifically, flag the kinship with the anthropology of emerging forms of life (Fischer 1999; 2003) and multispecies ethnography (Kirksey and Helmreich 2010). *Biogenetic Paradoxes* is about the practices of identification and negotiation required for assembling the nation in a new way—a new way to perceive and write about the intersecting worlds of the human and the other forms of life, of the simple species boundaries, the social communities and the interconnectedness of life within the sovereign sphere of the nation, and the new modes of governance within the global biopolitics of nature today.

CHAPTER 1 finncattle: biowealth as national life

Is it surprising that prisons resemble factories, schools, barracks, hospitals, which all resemble prisons?

—MICHEL FOUCAULT, *DISCIPLINE AND PUNISH*

Cows are not just cows; they are (bio)technological artefacts, and their scientific study has produced considerable knowledge-power.

—SARAH WILMOT, "FROM 'PUBLIC SERVICE' TO ARTIFICIAL INSEMINATION"

About six hundred kilometers north of Helsinki and three hundred kilometers south of the Arctic Circle lie two central prisons—the Pelso and Sukeva correctional facilities. The prisons are in cold and swampy areas, some one hundred kilometers apart, making them geographically isolated and hard to reach even from each other. The nearest town, Kajaani, is about a forty-minute drive away, and the nearest city, Oulu, twice as far. My first visit to these prisons was in October 2006 when I accompanied the national coordinator of the Animal Genetic Resources Programme, Juha Kantanen, on one of his yearly visits to the important genetic conservation sites.

The Pelso and Sukeva prison facilities keep quite nontraditional inmates: a threatened bovine breed that is considered indigenous to Finland, Finncattle. This special breed comes in three distinct colors, or subtypes, each said to indicate a specific geographical point of origin. A white coat designates Lapland, for it resembles the snowy conditions of northern Finland; the uniformly brown animals come from western Finland; and the third type, sporting a playful dappling of white and brown, originates from

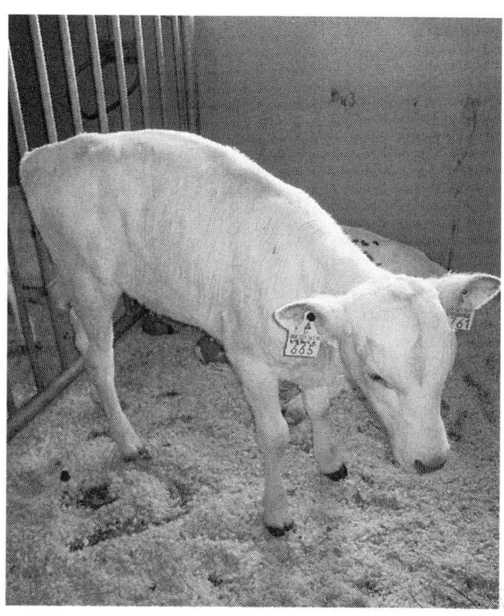

FIGURE 1.1 Figures 1.1 and 1.2 show three very young Finncattle calves born in 2006. The white calf here is a northern Finncattle. Photo by the author.

FIGURE 1.2 Figures 1.1 and 1.2 show three very young Finncattle calves born in 2006. The calves here are eastern Finncattle (*left*) and western Finncattle (*right*). Photo by the author.

eastern parts of the country. One can readily spot this morphological difference by walking around the prison cowsheds and associated grazing areas. In their distinguishably colored coats, the cattle are an interesting sight behind the prison fence as they mingle with their keepers, the prisoners.

The two prisons double as national gene banks for the national bovine species. They serve as a refuge for the last surviving live animals of the breed, amounting to three thousand individuals of the western type and about five hundred each of the two other types in 2009. Only a marginal population of live animals can be found outside the prisons, scattered around the country in small herds, and a small amount of their reproductive material, sperm and embryos, is cryopreserved in ex situ gene banks by Agrifood Research Finland (I will return to the issue of gene banks and cryopreservation in chapter 3). Without the constant care provided by the prisoners, the breed would soon wither away. In a story stretching back many years, such a threat of extinction dovetails with the claims of the breed's nativity to give it special status as nationally significant genetic resources.

There exists an easier way to meet Finncattle than to visit these remote prison farms. In attempts to promote flourishing of the breed, Finncattle have been included on the short national list of indigenous species in Finland. In this connection, the breed has gained international status, too, as a threatened one worthy of conservation-related attention, and, as was noted in the introduction, this breed was one of the first agricultural animals to be presented as being in danger of genetic erosion and extinction in the late 1960s. Although the breed has been considered native to Finland since the country first became independent, the tools of comparative genetics have only recently allowed identification of its actual genetic relationship to other breeds, though only in the present day. The research has enabled the breed's placement on a map in terms of its genetic distance from other European bovine breeds to show its "territorial belonging."

The worldwide Domestic Animal Diversity Information System (DAD-IS),[1] accessible through the World Wide Web and maintained by the Food and Agriculture Organization (FAO) of the United Nations, now holds this and other vital information on Finncattle in its global archives. Here, one can browse through various physical characteristics of the breed along with digital images of its representative members, typical uses, performance data, and the contact information for the organizations monitoring developments related to the threatened cattle. If the breed becomes extinct in its corporeal form, the archives will provide immortality for it as a digitalized memory of a form of life that once contributed to the biodiversity on planet Earth. The difference between the digital and corporeal sites and the modes of conservation they represent reveal something important about the Finncattle as well as about larger, global politics around the management of nonhuman populations. In a telling way, the two stand as mutually connected techniques for ordering life in the twenty-first century.

The first is focused on local care for individual animals at particular sites, illustrated by the two prisons. The traditional practice of animal husbandry in this case is relegated to Finnish correctional facilities, localities that are removed and geographically distanced from civil society and its knowledge-related practices such as the science and the laboratory that once assigned the animals there. Threatened forms of life need special care and high visibility for those responsible for their management, thereby requiring nonhuman animals to be incarcerated, to be individually indexed and monitored. The second technique operates at the level of national or international species indexing and the production of extensive bioinformation on the species, with the data available to all internet users through the right keywords typed into Google. The digitalization of threatened species and breeds (Whatmore 2002) in these archived collections helps them transcend local boundaries and circulate in international networks of science, bioeconomy, and politics over nature. Here, this widely accessible bioinformation is easily made a commodity (Parry 2001) while simultaneously the digitalization augments conservation scientists' vision (Roth and Bowen 1999) of taking on a global scale, and it rearticulates the political territorial boundaries through the life of indigenous species as it is translated into "genetic resources" (CBD 1992).

Alongside these two forms, corporeal and digital, and forming another thread in the complex contemporary problems they raise about nonhuman life in the fields of economy, science, and politics, the third way to encounter Finncattle is through the breed's genealogy. This is a method of teasing out the historical relations that once made the animal an embodiment of national biowealth and of tracing the trajectory that later reconfigured it as a national genetic resource. This also serves as a practical way to lay ground for later chapters, which examine more closely the differences between the production of national natures before and after the assumed "molecurization of life" (as discussed by, for example, Kay 1993; see also Rose 2007) effected through advances in biotechnology and by new political divisions of nature such as those formed in Rio de Janeiro in 1992.

This chapter analyzes the politics of nonhuman belonging created through Finncattle's service of pronouncedly nationalist purposes in Finland from the late nineteenth century until the close of the 1950s. More specifically, I ask in this chapter how Finncattle as a class were created and how they served as a corporeal nexus of the ambivalent natural and cultural identities of the nascent Finland. The central empirical argument in the chapter is that this breed, as a national bovine population, has acted as an important national intermediary in naturalizing human populations called "the Finns" and has in itself been a constitutive form of life for several of the central cultural developments in the making of the Finnish nation. Simply put, these animals have been coproduced with the life of the nation itself, a national "nature" that is symmetrical with and inherently connected to the creation of the national "culture."

In the course of the chapter I also start tracing how changing technologies of the management of nonhuman life—from ecological to institutional arrangements, from type definition to enhanced reproductive control—have historically been central to the body politics of a nation. I do not analyze these techniques merely to demonstrate a change in them and the associated development in the knowledge practices of animal industry (this has been done before in a much more detailed manner). Rather, my aim is to show how a strong national interest—indeed, an interest of creating a particular nonhuman nationhood—has become steadily embodied in and through the matter, life, and flesh of Finncattle.[2] The purpose of this analysis is to provide tools for starting to question the anthropocentricity of the theory of nations analyzed in chapter 4 by showing how nonhuman populations are important in naturalizing national human populations and, more broadly, the cultural idea of nationhood itself, not just as representations of nature but also as corporeal beings. Here, Finncattle serve as a perfect animal guide both to the historically intimate ties in the creation of Finland and to the current forms of power in use to maintain particular nonhuman populations as genetic resources.

EARLY FORMS OF NATIONAL BIOWEALTH

Among the earliest letters issued from the first institutionalized office of Finnish agriculture—the Grand Duchy of Finland's Board of Agriculture established in 1892—was a plea addressed to the Senate,[3] which was the highest political institution of the day, overseeing both economic and judicial issues of the grand duchy. The board requested an additional budget for developing a systematic breeding program for agricultural animals. The reasons proposed for the betterment of livestock were conveyed with a pronouncedly nationalist tone, setting the work put into animal breeding equal to that devoted to other economic activities that increased the prosperity of the nation. The letter boldly stated that domestic animals were, in fact, the basis of the national wealth.

It read, "A major portion of our national wealth consists of domestic animals, and, within those, horses and cattle are definitely the most important ones. All actions that aim at the betterment or breeding of domestic livestock, or that more or less improve their output or value, must in the same proportion thus add to our national wealth."[4] The Senate granted a significant amount of money, 18,000 marks, for establishing a program of betterment to be overseen by the board.

The grant made possible a state-led shift in systematic breeding work and paved the way for new, national cattle types.[5] Over the next few decades, the breeding of a national cattle type was systematized: the ecology of the countryside, cooperatives and professionalized institutions, and a national economy based on dairy products started weaving together a network that was embodied in and by one domestic animal. This animal was a national breed distinct from other countries' animals. It was to be called Finncattle.

Three interconnected developments had led the Board of Agriculture to pursue the idea of developing a national—Finnish—breed: an impetus for creating a new national culture, the development of international markets, and cattle-breeding experiments and cattle disease.

The first can be traced to ideological, or perhaps more accurately, nationalistic, aspirations. Finland had been annexed as a war cession to the victorious Russian Empire in 1809 after being a territory of the Swedish Crown for six centuries. At that point, the territory was granted autonomous political existence and became known as the Grand Duchy of Finland. The autonomous status made Finland fertile ground for the emergence of widespread nationalism as could be seen in so many other European countries in the nineteenth century. While early conceptions of the German romantic ideas of organic nations (see von Herder [1789] 1968) had gained some support earlier, the society, granted autonomous status and administratively set apart from direct Russian governance in 1809, developed a growing sense of national identity in the second half of the century.[6] The ideological aspirations in the creation of a distinct Finnish culture were given form with the question of language as "Finnish nationalists found in language the binding element of nation" (Kirby 1975, 2).[7] The promotion of the Finnish language as an official language of Finland—a status granted in 1863 with the language edict of Alexander II—was not, however, enough for the nationalists. The Fennomans, as they were called, also demanded novel forms of Finnish economy.

The Board of Agriculture was led by well-educated men who were driven to prove nationalistic ideas, such as Nils Grotenfelt. With his good knowledge of agricultural practices and even better connections with members of high society, he managed to reach the most exalted position in agricultural governance. In 1892 he was appointed as the first director general of the newly formed national Board of Agriculture. This board was in charge of every official decision made in the area of agricultural development in the Grand Duchy of Finland. The position granted him great institutional authority and economic means to decide on the direction of Finnish agriculture, and his choice was to start developing "landrace" cattle breeding (Lähdeoja 1969, 15–19, 41–50).

The second major development was the opening of international markets, especially for agricultural products. In the late nineteenth century Finnish agriculture was on the brink of major rearrangements with the other countries of Europe. International markets began to reform on account of a change in the doctrines of political economy wherein most countries were moving from mercantilist policies to self-regulating markets of a liberal economy (e.g., Polanyi [1944] 2001). Until then, Finland's primary agricultural product had been food crops: mainly barley and rye, which had been cultivated in the fields for centuries. Domesticated animals were kept only in small herds, and none of the species—cattle, pigs, horses, or poultry—had a major economic role in wider agricultural exchange networks (Rasila et al. 2003–4). Indeed, agriculture involving cattle did not even make an appearance in the Finnish Society for Economics list of the thirty most important national economic questions in 1820 (Nylander 1906).

To cope with new international trade, the Senate first gradually relaxed previous mercantilist taxes and export bans in 1852 and 1859. Later, in 1864, the Senate finally removed all agricultural duties for an indefinite period, thereby adding Finland to the long list of European countries to adopt liberal economic policies in the second half of the nineteenth century (previously, duty-free trade in grain and export for agriculture had been possible only with the Russian Empire). This liberal movement was a reaction to the continuous pleadings of farmers, who demanded more freedom in their agricultural trading and believed in overseas grain-export opportunities. However, what they did not expect was that duty-free grain trade with other countries would see Russian, German, and American food crops quickly come to saturate Finnish markets. Consequently, in just over ten years (in the 1880s), the price of crops dropped to two-thirds of its initial level, and imported grain became available year-round. The changes in tax policies in connection with international agricultural markets, alongside the developments in the availability and price of food crops, resulted in a crisis of Finnish agriculture, which was then heavily based on cereal cultivation. At the beginning of the 1880s it was starting to become obvious that the domestic cultivation of grain could never reach competitive price levels again because of the imported grains. Cereal cultivation became an economic impossibility. Instead, cattle breeding and a dairy economy started to look economically viable to the agriculturalists. By the early 1890s dairy farming, especially trading in butter, was hailed as the savior of the Finnish economy. Government actions were strongly directed toward developing this new direction for the agricultural economy, and a time of "butter fever" ensued. In 1903 cattle- and dairy-based income accounted for around 90 percent of all sales of agricultural products for the (landless) farmers (Peltonen 2004, 83), and dairy products amounted to 90 percent of total Finnish exports between 1905 and 1909 (Simonen 1949, 133; Peltonen 2004).

For the start of dairy farming and butter production, the initial agricultural configurations had to be changed so as to favor producing milk in vast quantities. Previously, a shortage of fodder had led to problems with the feeding of cattle and, consequently, low milk yields. This began to change with the introduction of liberal grain policies. Food for human populations was now secured with the cheap imported grains, and the use of tilled land could be rethought. In consequence, the fields, which initially had been used mostly for growing food crops, were put to another use. They were harnessed for grazing and growing fodder for cattle populations. The change in the use of fields was dramatically fast. As late as 1870 only about 1 percent of tilled land was used to grow fodder for feeding cattle. By 1910 more than 60 percent of the fields were used to grow fodder, and barely 20 percent for food crops. Accordingly, the whole ecology of the countryside changed (Simonen 1949, 125; Vihola 1991, 17–21; Östman 2004, 36).

Third, even if dairy production in Finland really started to be seen as a potential form of economy only in the late nineteenth century, cattle breeding had for centuries been a leisure-time hobby for the Finnish nobility. The first imports of foreign animals to Finland date back to the sixteenth century, and regular imports followed after that. The Senate itself had done some experimentation with cattle breeding in the 1840s and 1850s. Different types of animals were gathered at the manors of their wealthy owners, and various experiments were conducted for producing exemplary livestock. "Blood refreshment," a typical technique in Europe at the time (Ritvo 1995), was the most common way to experiment with cattle. This was an outbreeding technique wherein vital animals were bred with those considered to be of low value in the hope that vitality would be transmitted to the offspring through the mixture of blood. This was a general technique of experimentation for augmenting the vitality of animals, though it was not consciously used for breeding particular traits. However, it seemed that something other than vitality was spread with this technique. Deadly diseases became a common problem plaguing the experimenters. For example, in 1818–19 an anthrax epidemic raged in northern Finland, disappearing for years only to emerge again in 1831, once more killing cattle in large numbers (Forsius 1979a).

An outbreak of cattle plague in 1849 in England and in 1850 in Germany suspended imports from these countries for a number of years. However, this did not stop the infections in Finland. In a national health control, cattle tuberculosis was diagnosed to be widespread and common. This incidence was quickly attributed to the imported animals. In 1862 a local epidemic of foot-and-mouth disease in Helsinki was diagnosed in cattle imported from England, and in 1863–64 the "Siberian plague" raging in Russia was seen to threaten Finnish animals also (Simonen 1964; Forsius 1979b). The reasons behind the diseases were considered to be many—from bad climate to poor feed quality to bad spirits. But as the middle of the century neared, the mortality statistics started to point in one definite direction for the source of the diseases as almost every one of the infected imported animals died. An outbreak in the 1880s infected almost 90 percent of the national cattle population. While 90 to 95 percent of the imported animals soon died, the plagues left most local cattle alive. Imported animals were increasingly suspected of carrying contagious and deadly diseases.[8]

These violent outbreaks finally led to strict restrictions and reductions in the number of imported animals since there were no known cures for the blights. The only option upon diagnosis was to kill all infected cattle, rendering the diseases a fierce economic adversary to farmers (Forsius 1979b). Imported animals were considered to contaminate the healthy cattle in the country and were viewed as disastrous to the newly born dairy economy. To prevent future disastrous outbreaks, the Senate imposed a total ban on the import of any cattle for ten years between 1885 and 1895 (e.g., Kaltio 1958, 15; Myllylä 1991, 11). During the ban, the interest of the cattle breeders and especially the attention of the Board of Agriculture turned to the animals that had survived. They seemed to be resistant to the diseases that were threatening the rising cattle economy.

These three intertwining developments during the nineteenth century—the growing awareness of national culture, the shift toward international liberalism in agricultural trade, and problems with animal health—led the Board of Agriculture to write a successful appeal to the Senate: the Fennomans demanded the creation of something truly Finnish; the sources of a viable national economy had changed from cereals to cattle, and the foreign blood imported for breeding purposes was deemed contaminated and most mortal. The board concluded that national wealth could be augmented by creating a national breeding program, the result of which would be a healthier, productive, and purely Finnish animal, the embodiment of a new form of national biowealth.

ARTICULATING LOCALITY WITH AGRICULTURAL SCIENCES: FROM "LANDRACES" TO "BREED"

Animal types forming breeds are each a collection of a particular set of distinguishable structural (or morphological) characteristics—height, color, horn type, and so on—that are easily visually witnessed and together give an animal its representation in language, a codified and categorized identity. The first animal breeds that were thus demarcated and successfully capitalized on were developed in England in the middle of the eighteenth century by Robert Bakewell and other well-known breeders of the time (Walton 1986; 1999; Ritvo 1995). The result of their entrepreneurship was a number of valuable breeds: the Shorthorns, Herefords, and Ayrshires. In the developing cattle economy, these competed especially with breeds that were developed later in Holland, such as the Holsteins.

However, the capitalization on breed was for a long time dependent on the valuation of individual superstar animals, such as the Durham Ox or Duchess of Geneva, that became the metonyms for a particular cattle stock (Walton 1986; Ritvo 1995). People did not buy entire stocks; rather, they bought animals of good reputation, and this reputation depended on which breeder's stock they came from. As a result, the fame they gathered on both sides of the Atlantic in the international cattle economy was attributed to individual breeders and their efforts in developing better animals.[9] In most European countries the breeding of animals remained a matter of individual-level efforts for almost two centuries, or until the Second World War (Gaudillière 2007, 528). In a marked contrast to this approach, the Finnish Board of Agriculture sought an animal whose origins would be attributed not to any one breeder but instead to the nation itself.

It should be clarified that the board and its Fennoman members were not the first to promote the creation of a national cattle breed. Early debate from the 1840s onward concentrated on a comparison of the economic benefits of imported breeds with locally available, non-selectively-bred animals (also called mixed cattle) as found on most farms. The trouble within these discussions was that the latter animals could not be seen as forming any clear group among themselves, and this rendered comparisons difficult. These sentiments are best captured in some of the comments made on cattle breeding at the 1847 national agricultural conference held in Turku, then Finland's largest city. Addressing a public panel on the suitability of locally available animals for agricultural purposes, local farmers stated that they had made some comparisons of their milk yield against that produced by an Ayrshire cow, an expensive breed to import. They had found that the local animals were almost identical to the expensive breeds in productivity qualities. However, according to the same farmers, the animals compared with the imported breed did not form a natural group—they did not share structural or aesthetic characteristics with each other. The only group they formed was constructed by a broad linguistic categorization that made it possible to talk about these dissimilar bovine animals. They were called the "landrace cattle" in a folk categorization that covered all nonbred animals in contrast to the bred ones (Nylander 1906, 16; Nissinen 1923, 35).

The problem of a landrace without a natural existence highlights two quite distinct contemporary scientific ideas about cattle breeding that were popular at the time. The first was based on the theory of breed constancy. Jean Gayon argued that the theory emerged first among breeders in Northern Europe and has no clear point of origin. Its adherents subscribed to the view that "the longer the character had been transmitted without crossbreeding, the more powerful its 'hereditary force' became" (Gayon 2000, 71). The doctrine was perfected by the German August von Weckherlin in the first half of the nineteenth century. His theories on animal breeding became well known in German agriculture and were carried over to Finland from there (Myllylä 1991, 12). According to his theory, all breeds were "natural"—meaning that breeds were fundamentally different from each other and that the differences by which they were recognized would stay within a breed as long as it remained free of artificial crossbreeding. This also meant that, in essence, all individual animals belonging to a breed were identical—that, in fact, there were no true individuals in a breed. Later, Francis Galton and the English biometricians took up this idea and called it the proposition of "ancestral heredity." This doctrine was prevalent throughout Northern Europe during the nineteenth century (Gayon 2000; see also Derry 2003).[10]

The other theory was based on ideas related to individuals' potency. This competing theory, developed by the German Herman Settegast in the 1860s, enjoyed great popularity in the breeding practices of the time. It proposed that the inheritance of traits depended only on individual animals and had nothing to do with larger populations, such as breeds—that breeds did not really exist. The most important issue in cattle breeding, accordingly, was to find the desired trait in individual animals, to ensure that the animals could pass that trait to their offspring, and to mate as many animals as possible with the ones having the desired potency. This technique, the blood refreshment mentioned earlier in the chapter, assumed the results to demonstrate a new, better mixture of blood in the offspring together with the desired inherited trait. The theory led to large-scale crossbreeding of animals all over Finland. Imported animals, usually superior bulls, were introduced to an old cattle population to refresh its blood (Nissinen 1923, 17; Simonen 1950, 40; Kaltio 1958, 12; Myllylä 1991, 12).

Both of these theories belong to an ahistorical understanding of breeds. Accordingly, they have not yet carved a modern epistemic space for heredity (Müller-Wille and Rheinberger 2007). Foucault ([1970] 2001, 139–70, 235–52) has argued that this scientific epistemology still belongs to the field of natural history. Here, living beings are not considered to possess history, or, more accurately, they are not considered to be "life" at all. The main argument of the two theories was of the essential fixity of characteristics, either expressed in the surface of an individual animal or visibly present in a group of animals, a species or breed. This fixity defines a stable modality of a being—an ahistorically unified and unchanged being—based on characteristics that are visible in animal breeds and individual bodies, such as visible veins on udders signaling both vitality and the prefiguration of a good milk yield from the animal. However, this fixity of character (or hereditary force) and not the characteristics themselves could be altered by human intervention, and because of this, the nature of the relationship between the characteristics and their hereditary force alternated between the two opposing solutions (see Gayon 2000).

The two theories guided cattle breeding in an ambivalent manner in the latter half of the nineteenth century in Finland. The two principles of breeding were applied side by side, and often they were mixed.[11] The board, however, wanted to replace both for two reasons. First, the Senate had imposed the aforementioned ban on animal imports to fight animal diseases. In practice, the old means of developing better cattle were not possible because neither individual potent animals nor "the best possible cattle" could be imported from outside. Second, importing animals meant that the development of a local animal was rendered impossible, for its blood would be contaminated with the foreign—it would always remain a mixed breed. As an alternative the board found a rational and scientifically valid solution to the problem: a new theory of breeding.

The new theory at hand was developed by Victor Prosch of the Royal Veterinary and Agricultural University in Copenhagen. At the time, this was the only university in the Nordic region to teach agriculture as a university-level subject. Interestingly, some members of the Board of Agriculture, most notably its leader, Grotenfelt, had been studying agriculture under his supervision. Prosch had started to develop his theory in the late 1850s, and he was teaching his ideas to his students already in early 1860. This theory, *Stedegenhetslæren* (the local trait doctrine), was published for the first time in 1863. The central argument was very much what one could call quasi-Darwinian: local breeds do exist; they are created by their milieu of living; and because they are shaped by this milieu, they are adapted perfectly to the local conditions of their origins. The milieu and its conditions encompassed all the central environmental factors that were important in cattle breeding: climate, feeding habits, and diseases. In his *Haandbog i det almindelige Huusdyrbrug* (Handbook of general laws of animal breeding [1863] 1872), he described how different breeds develop. He contested previously held assumptions in a subtle way, criticizing, in particular, Weckherlin's constancy theory: "This view [referring to Weckherlin 1851] is not without some justification: in every clean breed, there is an unmistakable concordance among all the individual forms and manifestations of life, such that they all cooperate together toward a single objective—namely, to fit the animal essence into all of the external conditions in which it is set, whether these be natural or artificial" (Prosch [1863] 1872, 141; my translation).[12] The key aspect of the theory was that it did not deny individual potency or the idea of breed. Instead, it accommodated both and connected them with new elements. Prosch ([1863] 1872) argued that individuals do form natural herds, which after quasi-Darwinian selection will establish a pure breed that "in its smallest details" is adapted to the local environment. Accordingly, the breeds that are developed this way are more resistant to diseases and are best adapted to the effects of climate and local traditions of cattle keeping, as manifested in their efficiency in feeding/milking ratios. The theory does not, then, share the relative fixity of a species predicted by Darwinian theories; rather, it subscribes to a quite fluid conception of natural groups of animals, or breeds.

This theory also embraces quite practically both natural and human selection mechanisms in the formation of new adapted traits that characterize breed types. In a very simple way, it brings together all the contested and previously discrepant elements—breeds, individual animals, milk yield, and even resistance to diseases. Its effect was to gather these elements under the figure of the original local breed—a breed that was superior to others because it was bred by local conditions, both human and natural—and give scientific justification for treating the "animals of no breed" as a real breed type. The theory codified that previous "breed of no breed" as a truly scientifically proven animal breed. It was not just a true breed; it was also a breed that was better than the imported ones. Hence, the only reasonable action was to start breeding local animals, what had earlier been called landraces.

The ideological consequence is comparable to a new way of understanding the true origins of living beings at the beginning of the modern episteme as described by Foucault: "Historicity has now been introduced into nature—or rather into the realm of living beings; but it exists there as much more than a probable form of succession: it constitutes a sort of fundamental mode of being" (2001, 300). In scientific terms, the fundamental mode of being for landrace cattle was now superimposed with their local history, to which they testified through their particular corporeal traits developed in interaction with their cultural and natural environment. The new theory established the first condition for the possibility of thinking that a landrace might be a natural group, a breed. This also marked a starting point for the possibility of a new identity category, that of original Finnish cattle.

Even if the scientific figure for a national breed was now established in theory, it still remained a theory, made up mostly of novel relations between ideas of individual traits, heredity, and locality, and, after all, these were still just printed words on paper. To make the ideas really matter and to breathe life into this new figure of local origins, different methods were to be used. The aforementioned 18,000 marks provided by the Senate would be used to find the best representative individuals among the local cattle and to start breeding programs around them. The easiest way to do so would be to gather all local cattle in one place and organize cattle exhibitions for the landrace breed.

THE PRIMORDIAL FINNS: BREED TYPES AND NARRATIONS OF NATIONAL MYTHS OF DESCENT

The first countrywide landrace cattle exhibitions, organized by the board in cooperation with regional agricultural societies in Kuopio and Tampere, were held in 1898. In the late eighteenth century and the whole of the nineteenth such shows were important sites of trade and value creation: they functioned as sites where comparisons and ensuing categorizations of different individual animals and breeders' whole herds could be developed. The purpose of agricultural fairs is to exhibit animals, to judge their qualities, and to reward the best animals (or their owners). Bringing the animals together enables their simultaneous assessment with techniques that (still today) depend heavily on visual and other aesthetic judgments.[13] However "subjective" the valuation by the shows' judges or by the animal buyers, these events were the only occasions on which an "objective" value could be given to the animals with the possibility of evaluating them immediately alongside other individuals. Particular visual traits could easily be assessed visually, such as objects of evaluation, such as coat coloring, size, and udder structure.[14]

However, the problem of determining what exactly this original landrace breed would consist of was obvious from the start. What was to be its objective trait, which would separate it from others and give it its scientifically proven value as the original local breed? The first show in Kuopio saw in total 251 animals, which did not form a recognizable herd by visually exhibiting a certain type. The animals that were brought to the fair could not be translated into or taken as the representatives of a prototypical landrace breed by their bodily aesthetics. Simply, there was none: no breed, no one clearly distinguishable visual marker that could serve as the basis for a type category. The description of the eighty-nine bulls present conveys nicely the divergent features of these animals. According to show records, the participating bulls were described thus: six whites, eleven red "kyyttö," thirteen red, forty-eight red-whites, two black-whites, one grayish, three black, one gray, one black "kyyttö," and three "ruunis" (Nissinen 1923).[15]

Given this heterogeneity of their physical appearance, the fact that any type categorizations were made reveals the deep-rooted nationalistic aspirations related to the evaluation and valuation of the animals. Despite the aesthetic variety of the animals exhibited, the members of the board and the farmers raising landrace cattle ended up reaching a conclusion that clearly a type—in fact, three types—could be discerned, even legitimated. This conclusion, nicely captured in print on the first page of the first herd book for the eastern type (published in 1901), is the following: "In the two first exhibitions, the eastern cattle could be distinguished from the western cattle. The north Finnish cattle were present only in some tens of animals, and so were hard to compare with the other two. Despite this, the Kuopio and Tampere fairs legitimated the division of the landrace into three types and provided the breeding directions for each of the types" (Nissinen 1923, 3).

The type descriptions themselves are vague and hard to distinguish from each other. The only difference among the three types cited is in their coat coloring and a mention of their horns. Otherwise, the official definitions given to the different Finncattle types are astonishingly similar:

Eastern Finnish cattle-breeding should strive for a middle-sized, grayish-red or grayish and white, clearly milk-type and finely shaped milking animal that also fulfills moderate requirements with regard to front and back body development and their deepness, width, and regularity. (ISK [Eastern Finncattle Society] 1901)

The Western Finnish cattle should be relatively well developed, hard but finely structured, open, and milking-type. The color should be evenly light brown, not reddish brown, not whitish or "voikko," nor should the animal bear a furry coat. (LSK [Western Finncattle Society] 1904)

The Northern Finnish cattle should be red/brown or white, middle-sized, short-legged, finely built animals, most often without horns with a clear milking style, and with a relatively well developed front and back body. (PSK [Northern Finncattle Society] 1906)

How did this tripartite division come about? If Prosch's theory of the locality of the breeds was true, there was something locally specific in the three cardinal directions that had resulted in the separation of western, eastern, and northern cattle. Here, the new scientific figure of an original local breed allowed a narrative space for one of the most common ways of narrating a true identity of modern times—the myth of national origins. In the creation of the divisions among the types, the members of the Board of Agriculture and the breeders of the landrace who were present at the fair relied on a national myth of descent, one that covered both the bovine animals and the human populations found in Finland. In their stories, the origins of the cattle and the original Finnish tribes began to weave together in inseparable ways. The passage below is taken from the first printed book on the western type of Finncattle (Kiianlinna 1907). It describes how the genealogies of ancient Finns and the bovine animals intersect and finally become assimilated at the dawn of Finnish nationhood:

In the study of the origins of these cattle, we have to move backward in time and to reach the twilight of our ancient antiquity and turn our attention to the early stages of our ancestors. These origins have been illuminated with the study of linguistics, archaeology, and ethnography (folkloristics). We know for sure that the original home for Finnish tribes was the plains of southeast Russia. . . . It is estimated that at some point between the years 1000 and 500 BC our ancestors moved from the Volga to meander somewhat south and that it is during this

> period that they learned to know the cow, to milk it, and to make butter out of milk. (Kiianlinna 1907, 4)

The story, which is illustrative of many parallel ones found in contemporary documents addressing the history of Finncattle, narrates a genealogy of both primordial Finnish tribes and their first encounter with bovine animals. On the threshold at which the tribes really become a Finnish nation—during their exodus from the Volga River toward the west—they meet the cattle and learn the skills of cattle husbandry. Finncattle become the chosen companion animals (Haraway 2003) of the Finnish ancestors. The writer of the passage above, a high-ranking officer in the society concerned with the western Finnish cattle, continued the identification of the tribes by giving more indications of the interaction among them. Notable are the number of breed types found and the basis for their naming practices since they corresponded perfectly to the contemporary ethnographic idea of three original founding tribes.[16]

> The first ones to move [to the Finnish territory] were the "Hämäläinen" tribes, then the "Karelians". . . . We cannot say whether the Lappish tribes had cattle, but it is not impossible. The Lappish people are thought to have lived in the middle of Russia before they moved to the Finnish cape and to have close connections to some of the Finnish tribes. This was the point at which they learned how to speak the Finnish language. Already then, cattle husbandry was a known skill for the Finnish tribes. (Kiianlinna 1907, 5)

The idea of nations and nationality, as Anthony Smith (2000) has noted, depends centrally on myths of ethnic descent, which "bring together in a single potent vision elements of historical fact and legendary elaboration to create an overriding commitment and bond for the community" (Smith 2000, 57). At the same time, however, these myths are themselves particular invented traditions (Hobsbawm 1990), well-formed narratives about unbroken historical activity continuing until the present, made up and told at particular historical moments to serve nationalist purposes. Myths are foundational to every performance of nationhood—they are central in performing forgotten memories of descent, usually by metaphorically mixing "roots" and "territories" (Malkki 1992) and attaching these to the destiny of a nation (Smith 2000).[17] For these purposes, the new science stressing the animals' local, territorial origins was coupled with the foundational myth of Finncattle that provided the genealogical roots with a mixture of animal and human history. The two formed a perfect combination.

In the historical narratives about Finncattle, all the founding tribes are accounted for as having their own animals. As the story above illustrates, these truths were also confirmed with contemporary advances in the human sciences through which the awakening nation had started to research and classify its human population. According to the archaeology, linguistics, and physical anthropology of the time, the eastern (Karelian), western (Hämäläinen), and northern (Lappish) tribes were considered to be the first and original Finnish races from which the whole population later descended (Krohn 1887; Sirelius 1924; Grotenfelt 1926; Itkonen and Donner 1926; Kajava 1926).[18] The narrative cited above demonstrates nicely how the Finnish founding myths of ethnic descent are mixed with the nonhuman history of bovine species. Accordingly, the cattle in the Finncattle type are as old and as constitutive to Finnish nationhood as the Finnish people are, as they have come "here" together. They moved to their present territories with each of the Finnish tribes. The narrative mixes the primordial biological roots, cultural genealogy, and territorial claims to tie the human and nonhuman Finnish populations together. The Finncattle types are as old as the primordial Finns who populated the territory, and so they also are a primordial type of national life.

This powerful mythological—or should one call it scientific-mythological?—narrative only grew stronger as time went by. Sightings of the primordial cattle slowly came to be found everywhere in the national culture until the late twentieth century. Even some of the most celebrated pieces of national literature, the Finnish national epic *Kalevala* and its companion *Kanteletar* composed by national(istic) writer Elias Lönnrot from a collection of oral folk poetry and songs in 1835, were mobilized to confirm the primordial existence of this type of cattle. While the epics are normally taken to recount the mythological pasts of heroic proto-Finns in the golden age, after the aforementioned narrative moves, these works also speak of their cattle:

> When we read the profound and soulful works the *Kalevala* and *Kanteletar*, written by our ancestors, the descriptions of the cattle, at the same time as they show how irreplaceable a guarantee cattle were taken to be, seem quite familiar to us in terms of how the cattle in these songs are described. When we read the lyrics of the song for releasing the cattle to graze the fields

"Drive the cows to yonder bowers,
To the birch-trees and the aspens,"

> there is no doubt about whether the feelings evoked by these lyrics are correct and the cattle presented in these works are the ancestor of our own cattle. . . . Its roots are as deep in this land as ours are. It belongs inseparably also to Finnish nature. (Soini 1937, 3–4, my translation)

The passage above was written by one of the historians of Finncattle in 1937 under the heading "The Foundation of Animal Husbandry Has Always Been Our Homely Cattle" in an attempt to clarify how Finnish agriculture had changed in the preceding hundred years. In this text the Finncattle become animals that are inherently tied both to Finnish culture as a lyrical figure of the *Kalevala* and to the national nature as an inseparable part—a truly cultural-natural beast. With these scientific-mythological narratives found in the letters and books that circulated nationwide among breeders, the cattle became an irreplaceable element of the narrative origins of Finnishness itself, thereby becoming an obligatory passage point for truly understanding the origins of nationhood here from its agricultural perspective. The cattle and the ancient Finns were essentially written together. This myth of descent was initially a heavily used rhetorical tool in motivating what was needed from the breeders: an immense amount of breeding work. Before we look at how these myths were taken as ideal molds for working with the animal bodies in practical breeding, we need to examine how this work was institutionally organized around the mythical animal and how the myth itself was mobilized and complemented by another rhetorical move to motivate breeder populations.

INSTITUTIONALIZING THE WORK AND CREATING NATIONAL CULTURE THROUGH NATURE

While the mythologization of Finncattle led to these animals' theoretical possibility as a breed, three institutional developments complemented the movement in which word was made flesh. The first cattle show led to the establishment of the first Finncattle society at the site of the fair. Thus the Eastern Finncattle Breeding Society (ISK) was born in 1898. The stated goals of the society were simultaneously geared toward institutionally unifying the national agricultural societies and enrolling all their members for the breeding work, a vocation that was explicitly called patriotic. One of the founding members of the first landrace society described at the fair what it meant to work with these newly found national animals together: it was to be considered not normal breeding labor but work done for a greater good, for the Fatherland, and needed cooperative efforts. "This kind of society should wake up everybody for common patriotic work. We have strengths, but they are scattered. This sad state must be eliminated through co-operation" (Brander 1898, cited by Nylander 1906). This scattered nature of strengths referred to both the few Finncattle breeders, identified as doing lone patriotic work, and the contemporary institutional arrangements of breeding. Until the establishment of the Finncattle societies, local agricultural institutions around Finland decided independently on their cattle-breeding practices. The difficulty here was that most favored old principles of animal betterment—blood refreshment with imported animals (Nissinen 1923, 80–95). Accordingly, the first item in the ISK articles of association reflected the society's aim to unify the efforts undertaken in geographically dispersed local settings: "The aim of the society is the betterment of East-Finland landrace cattle and accomplish[ing] a direction for common purebred and reciprocal interaction between East-Finnish agricultural societies, individual breeding bull societies, and individual members" (Rules of the Eastern Finnish Cattle Breeding Society [1899] 1901, §1). According to the rule, the aims were to find appropriate breeding practices for creating a purebred Finnish animal. In addition, almost any type of actor (an agricultural society, a breeding society, or an individual) could be accepted as a member of the Finncattle breeding society. The rule ensured that the networks involved in the work extended downstream to these local societies and made them conform with the strict purebred breeding aims and practices. The institutional arrangements worked also upstream in order to unify the breeding work done at the national level. The Senate approved the rules of the ISK in 1899 with one exception: the group was not given independence as a society but was instead subordinated directly under the political powers of the Board of Agriculture. Two other societies for landrace cattle quickly followed. The Western Finnish Cattle Breeding Society (LSK) was established in 1904 and the Northern Finnish Cattle Breeding Society (PSK) in 1906 with similar rules and subordination. With these institutional arrangements, the breeding of Finncattle became an institutionally state-led effort.

In the recruitment of farmers to the societies for the institutional growth and control of the directions of the breeding, the patriotic ideology that was built around the development of national cattle worked as an effective motivational resource, and the systematically repeated call to breed national animals runs visibly through the whole history of Finncattle. The ideological nature of the work was rearticulated in every public event that the breeder societies arranged as much as it was visibly present in their regular publications that were circulated to the members of the society. Not only public speeches but also wide circulation of the message in print delivered this patriotism to cowsheds all over the country: an active reminder of the nationalist ideology behind the breeding was seen in the quarterly journals that all three societies published. For decades the LSK group even printed an (extended) slogan on its journal cover, reproducing the ideological underpinning in each issue: "Landrace is our commonwealth, the abatement or evanescence of which will devalue the whole practice of breeding and devour the most important source of national income." So central was the nationalistic motivation that in 1923 the whole landrace-breeding movement was described utterly in terms of patriotism: "The basis on which the Eastern Finncattle Breeding Society was established was by nature ideologically patriotic. The thoughts that animated the founders moved both for the preparation of a better landrace and for more acceptable living conditions for that animal that had endured all the bad fates of our land alongside our ancestors" (Nissinen 1923, 113, my translation). The local agricultural institutions did not resist patriotism; in fact, they embraced it, and it was not hard to persuade them to join the Finncattle breeding societies. But the individual farmers put up harder resistance. What else would they gain from joining the breeders' societies apart from official status as supporters of the official ideology of patriotism? And why should they turn from their much larger mixed-breed cattle, which were already producing better milk yields than the pitifully small landraces? It was obviously not only the ideological side of patriotism that persuaded them to join the movement.

Here, national aspirations were backed up with an economic advantage provided by the state—individual-breeder-level subscription to the ideology was rewarded with economic compensation. Very early on, the director general of the national Board of Agriculture declared that the state would start supporting cattle shows by granting money to the local agricultural societies and that the money (18,000 marks per year, originally granted by the Senate) could be used as a prize for only the Finncattle or the Ayrshire breed. He called this declaration the Magna Carta of Finnish cattle husbandry. The agricultural societies were given written instructions on the declaration in 1895, and they were to oversee the economic compensation. The cleverness of the new instructions lay in their details: the Board of Agriculture changed the national method of granting prize money to participants in the cattle exhibitions. Where previously only a few of the best animals in the shows were awarded monetary compensation, with the system thus favoring the noble cattle owners who had resources for the decent upkeep of cattle, now almost all animals that met the minimal requirements of Finncattle breed types were awarded a small amount of compensation for simply appearing at a show. These new rules were not swallowed without resistance (Liukko 1906, 108–15), but they did finally lead to economic calculations on the farmers' part: it was profitable to exchange their mixed cattle for a pure landrace breed and to join the Finncattle movement (see Simonen 1964, 106–8).

The three Finncattle societies grew steadily as the central elements of Finnish agricultural society. However, the tripartite division was questioned early on, and alternative visions of one unified cattle-breeding society and of a single national cattle breed had been presented from the start. For many, the separation into three societies with their own cattle reflected separative national politics more than unifying patriotism. Early commentators stated in 1911 that "it's a waste of time to separate East and West; one nation and one type of cattle is how it should be" (ISK 1930, 15).[19] It was also pointed out that unification would be practical for all the societies since it would result in a larger, more influential body to lobby on Finncattle breeders' issues in Finland.[20] The problem was that the Western Finncattle society had spread over large geographical areas, becoming the dominant institution in about three-quarters of all Finnish dairy farming. The smaller societies (the LSK and PSK) not only feared for their societies but also feared losing their now-unique cattle in a possible merger. Competition between the brotherly institutions ensued. A contemporary commentator saw this as an ill-motivated competition:

> After Tampere (with the national exhibition for Finncattle in 1922), a furious competition among the breeds started. Competition about what? Not surely about who is better, but who *looks* the best. . . . This was a battle between the older brothers the ISK and LSK. In its own way, the younger brother got involved too. The PSK has shown to those playing in Southern parts that there can be no better breed than the pure white one in the areas of the Arctic Circle. (ISK 1930, 3; emphasis in original)

This institutional competition turned battle was one of the central reasons that the unification of the societies was rejected for a long time. What changed their minds, then? The first battle was institutional, but there were two other wars to come. The aftermath of the Second World War and the resulting Winter War against Russian and, later, German forces taxed

Finland heavily. Not only this, but Finland had to cede large parts of the heartland (about one-eighth of its area) from the biggest cattle-breeding area of Karelia, the home of the ISK, to Russia. More than 400,000 inhabitants had to be evacuated and resettled, in most cases without their cattle (Roiko-Jokela 2004, 27–90). The last moments of the Winter War also saw the devastation of Lapland, resulting in almost total disappearance of the northern cattle.

After the Winter War, the breed wars continued, this time against a foreign form of nonhuman life. The pedigreed Ayrshire animals were readily available in Finland and displayed good production qualities. Amid postwar reconstruction, national demand for agricultural products had increased sharply, and Ayrshires became the preferred choice of breed for many since they produced more milk. By the late 1940s this breed accounted for about 40 percent of all cattle in Finland. The Finncattle societies fought on and decided to unite against these threats. They merged into one institution in 1949. The unification gave them new energy and, above all, new members. In their year of unification, they counted a total of 18,297 (human) members; in 1952 they had already gained more and stood at 25,223 members; and in 1956 the unified Finncattle society, SK, had 35,441 registered members—more than it would ever have again in its history (Kaltio 1958; Myllylä 1991, 68–70).

This institutional merger also unified the previously distinct cattle types and their herd books—the only difference seen between the animals was now a superficial variance that was not essential to the breed itself. According to new calculations, the characteristics of the individual types indicated that they had originally been the same breed and had become different in their looks only after the advent of selective breeding because of the institutional division. Thus, the postwar reconstruction of the Finnish nation unified not only the human population but also the cattle types. This unification proved successful, and around 1954 the nonhuman population of the societies was rising, too: more than 90 percent of the cattle in Finland were Finnish breeds in the northern and eastern parts of Finland, and the figure was 50 percent in the western parts of the land, with the other 50 percent consisting of Ayrshires (Kaltio 1958, 4). Thus, on the sixtieth birthday of Finncattle breeding in 1958, Finnish President Urho Kekkonen noted how Finncattle now unified all Finland: "We have gathered here to celebrate a special day in the history of Finnish cattle-breeding. The occasion being celebrated unites hundreds of thousands of Finns all over the country, the silent laborers to whose work one does not too often dedicate a thankful and respectful thought. In this celebration they surely deserve it" (LSK 1958, 6).[21]

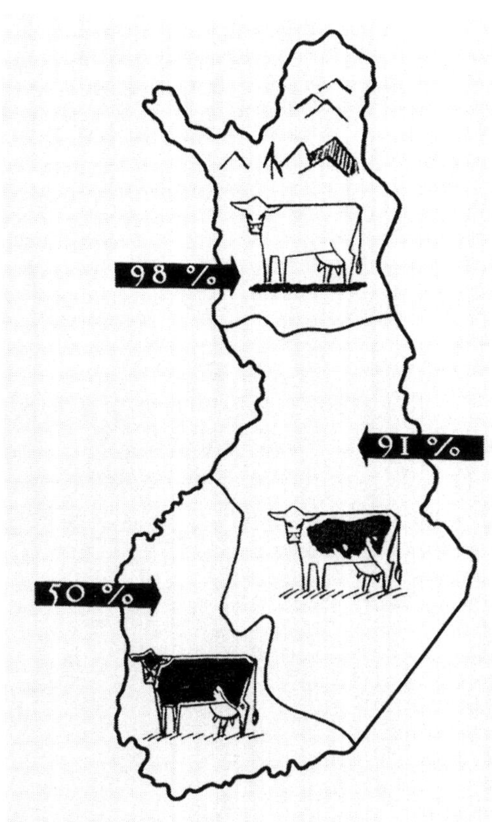

FIGURE 1.3 The Finnish territory populated by the various types of Finncattle in 1958. The percentages of northern, eastern, and western Finncattle used in agriculture in the individual regions show how national breeds had replaced other breeds almost completely in the northern and eastern regions of Finland and accounted for half of the cattle in western Finland. (Kaltio 1958, 8)

Starting with a very small membership base—only a few dozen breeders were present at the establishment of the ISK in 1898—the societies grew rapidly and steadily in membership and success. The state-led institutional coordination, the effective mobilization of nationalism, and its figure of patriotic work complemented with new ways to award prizes at the three societies' shows for individual breeders worked well as techniques of *intéressement* (Callon 1986) that brought the movement together around Finncattle. But even if patriotism and the monetary compensation for almost every participant in the cattle shows were motivating forces for all who engaged in the work, how did the animals respond to it?

FLESHING OUT THE PURE FINNCATTLE: EXTENDING THE (PHENO)TYPE

Animal breeds are necessarily, as many have noted, a social construction in that they are modeled and bred to fit existing symbols of power, wealth, or status (e.g., Quinn 1993; Ritvo 1995; Derry 2003). In other words, they are used as tokens for marking a cultural difference. But more than that, they are also corporeal forms of life that must be actively subjected to techniques of power directed to their bodies to make them conform to cultural forms of imagination—be they of economic interests, breed diversity, or (as in the case of Finncattle) embodiments of national aspirations (Holloway 2005). For every model, one also needs its corporeal equivalent. In simpler terms, for any utterance of a name, you need a living animal that responds to it if any value is to be gained in agricultural fields. In the first agricultural fairs and for a number of years after them, the ideal of Finncattle was still far from a corporeal fact.

Importantly, no a priori ideal types of Finnish cattle were presented before the exhibitions—the type definitions of Finncattle were based on a mix of the visual judgments of the animals made during the cattle exhibition in 1896 and the national myths of descent. These definitions (see above) were vague and ambiguous. Even the breeders themselves were somewhat confused about them. Tatu Nissinen, the first secretary of the ISK, commented on the first type definitions decades later by recalling that "the type instructions were not really going deep into the nitty-gritty details, but for the very same reason they also required more twigging from those who started the work with that almost blank cheque" (Nissinen 1923, 76).

Even if they were vague, the first type specifications did help inscribe the original animals as cultural objects and at the same time helped naturalize the mythical narratives preceding them. Everyone at the shows could see that the definitions and the animals matched each other perfectly: they were as real because they were irresistibly present.

Type definitions function as special kinds of inscription devices (Latour and Woolgar 1986; see also Nash 2005) mediating between the symbolic (written descriptions) and the corporeal (live animals). With these definitions, it was now possible to articulate the objectified boundaries of the breeds. The type device verbalized the essential character of the original cattle and at the same time allowed for the naturalization of the myth of origins in their flesh. After its adoption, it was impossible to say which came first, the new identity category as a linguistic device or the animals in their living flesh. Type thus opened a novel path between scientific theories, myths, and the living national animals developed in the patriotic breeding work. It stabilized these relations and made them matter.

In everyday breeding work, however, the practical problem was that only a small percentage of the animals were considered to be pure and adhering to the type. Most of the animals living within the closed borders

FIGURE 1.4 "Pisara" (a northern-type brown cow), among the first exhibition animals. Another type is shown in figure 1.5.

were not Finncattle. They were considered to be a mixture of blood between the original Finnish cattle and imported animals: between 1700 and 1850 at least fifteen breeds had been introduced to the territory (Kaltio 1958). Much breeding work (most of all, a lengthy process of blood purification) was deemed necessary to restore the real Finnish blood that had become mixed with the foreign. However, animal life that is subjected to techniques of power does not conform to the cultural imagination without resistance—bovine life is recalcitrant when faced with static models of type. Accordingly, defining the identity of the cattle into visually perceivable types was not enough for breeding purposes. Notwithstanding the mythical historical narratives and national aspirations that were embodied by the few true animals, the history of most individual animals was unknown. Before the turn of the century, few kept records of visible characteristics of individual animals, their milk yields, or their familial lineages. The type device therefore needed an extension, which would record also the history and the performance of individual animals, their inner nature (Simonen 1964, 29; Ritvo 1987; Holloway 2005).

The extension to the type device was the general herd book, which served as a public registry for the animals of a breed. General herd books emerged in Europe in the late eighteenth and early nineteenth centuries.[22]

The first one for cattle was the *Short-Horned Cattle Herd* book, published in 1822 in England. Elsewhere, general registries were published in France (1855), Germany (1864), Holland (1874), and Denmark (1881) (Walton 1986, 153; Ritvo 1995, 420; Derry 2003, 8). In Finland the first to enter use was the herd book for the eastern type, established in late 1899 and published in 1900. Of course, records of animals had been kept from very early on, but they had not been universalized and disseminated to a wider audience in printed form. Local records were easily falsified and so were suspect from the buyer's point of view. They were also confined to their local settings and could not travel far from individual farms. Centralized and printed records offered a novel permanence and dissemination power through wide circulation for the various breed types. Print media, as with other ideas, such as nationalism itself (B. Anderson [1983] 1991), acted as a key technology in the development of national animals and the forms of agriculture built around them. The Finnish pedigrees became imaginable and gained nationwide dissemination only with these books, which were published yearly by the breeder societies.

General herd books provided more permanent and powerful links between the cultural identity of an animal and the flesh itself than just type descriptions. They are tools not only to crisscross between nature and culture but also for movement between temporalities, or between the ancestral descent and the present individual. These registries provide means for creating managed breeding lines and for following the passing of the desired traits (heritability) from one individual to another through structured kinship models. They also allow for the rapid switching of a breeder's analytical focus from one animal to the whole breed. In sum, with careful use of the herd book technique, the whole breed is visually present on the pages of a book. This made it possible to use only a few well-selected animals (in Finland both bulls and cows were used as reference animals) for lineage enhancement in breeding work in anticipation of the sum of traits that they would pass to the next generation—the systematization of selective breeding. The desired traits or characteristics inscribed on paper and the records of their development in the whole population through lineage traces together make up what is called the pedigree of an individual animal. The central point here is that this management of reproduction processes is not only about producing the next generation of animals. It is about yielding better pedigrees. And better pedigrees are reached through better embodiments of desired traits: superior animals and their performance as they are inscribed in and monitored through the herd books. This is an assumption that is still largely shared by researchers working

FIGURE 1.5 Another of the first exhibition animals, "Yrjö" (an eastern Finncattle–type bull). Note that bulls with horns were accepted to the herd books for some decades, after which dehorning was to be carried out.

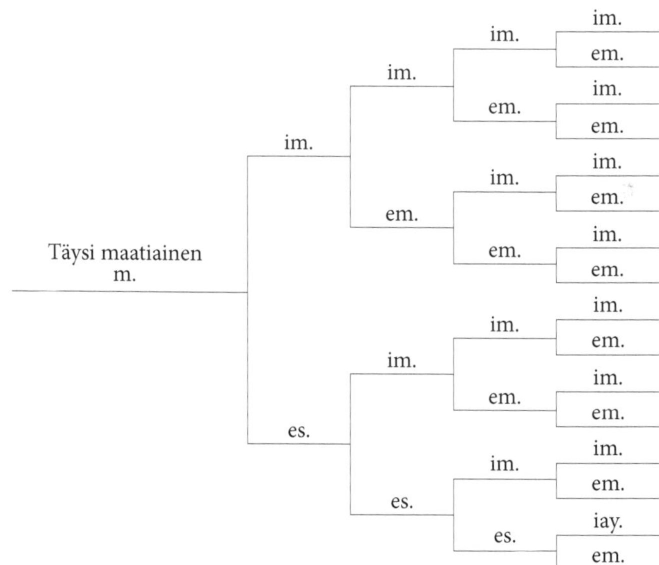

Kaavassa merkitsee: i = isä; e = emä; m = maatiainen; s = seka-rotuinen; ay = ayrshire

FIGURE 1.6 The formal pure-breeding pedigree formula for purifying from foreign blood and breeding full-breed landrace animals (*Täysi maatiainen*), where *i* = bull, *e* = cow, *m* = landrace animal, *s* = mixed-breed animal, and *ay* = Ayrshire animal. (Nissinen 1923, 59)

in the area of animal science as well as the working breeders themselves (Brackett 1981).

The first years of Finncattle breeding were "aimed at the stabilization of a general breed-type" (ISK 1922, 8). The type description provided some hints of what kind of animals the three individual types were, but how were these translated into measurable units that would guide the work in the fields and cowsheds? The first aim, therefore, was to create a set of operationalized traits based on the cattle types that would be usable in practical, everyday breeding work. The cattle societies agreed on some basic criteria for traits that would serve as a lower threshold for accepting an animal as purebred. Here, color, horns, height, and overall structure were first taken as core markers of type in the stabilization process. However, these changed quite radically over the years. For example, the type definitions of the ISK in 1915 required that the coloring be strictly "kyyttö" and that the animals be polled. In 1930, however, both of these requirements were lifted, leaving only structural and production requirements in place. Also, the PSK animals were first defined as white, red, or brown, but from 1925 onward only white animals were considered to be of the true northern variety (see table 1.1 for a brief summary of the different initial configurations and later reconfigurations of the Finnish types through the years). The only visible characteristic in the type definitions that has not changed very much over the years is the size. Authentic locally adapted animal types were (and still are) quite small, some 110–30 cm in height. This smallness was taken as a sign of the breed's adaptation to the lack of sufficient nutrition during the harsh Finnish winters. Bigger animals were suspected of carrying foreign blood, and thus of being contaminated, and were not admitted to the registries of general herd books (Kaltio 1958, 21).

Second, the traits were to be evaluated against the genealogies of the animals. The further an animal's genealogy could be traced back via herd books, the purer the animal was, attaining total purity in around the fifth to sixth generation (see fig. 1.6). The overall aim was to purify the whole breed of traces of foreign blood and to distill the pure Finnishness from the mixed cattle. For a long time—the first twenty years—it was only the level of purity that determined the value of an animal without any reference to productive qualities such as milk yield (these were recorded in some cases, however).[23]

Purer animals were favored over more productive ones, even in extreme cases wherein the milk-cream yield would have been double in animals having lower genealogical status. Concerns about the symbolic purity of the animal's nationhood overrode economic ones. Fifth-generation animals had, at maximum, one-sixteenth foreign blood circulating in their veins. This was considered to be a cutoff point for national blood purity until the 1920s. After this, the requirement was raised to one-thirty-second, or sixth-generation pedigrees. This purification and stabilization of the subbreeds reigned in all three breeding societies until 1922 (ISK 1936, 53). After that, the animals were considered pure enough en masse for efforts to start enhancing their production qualities, which have been the predominant focus of the breeding since, as is shown by the rising production requirements in the herd books' thresholds (see table 1).

For a long time the work was considered only a purification process, with breeding efforts meant to undo the previous mixing of blood. The slow filtering out of foreign traces would reveal the underlying natural Finnishness of these animals. In essence, this was not yet considered artificial selection—the breeders were just undoing what had been done wrongly in the past, thereby helping the natural nationhood to be restored in these animals. Later, when the animals were purified and selected for production purposes, these new aims of breeding were embraced as another way to demonstrate something important about the Finnish nation. In a creative manner, the difference between the two aims of breeding—and the resulting ambivalence between the natural and the artificial essence of the animals—became a positive resource. Here, nationhood was articulated through the cultural work that materialized in the corporeality of the cattle.

For example, in a key speech at the twentieth-anniversary event of the Eastern Finncattle Breeding Society in 1918 (a year after Finland gained independence from Russia), the breeding work was not said to reveal something about the animals but, in contrast, was stated to show the true nature of Finnish people. Mobilizing the theory of Herderian national creativity, Finns were actually proclaimed to be people worthy of national independence for having worked to create something really unique among the nations: "It is a well-known fact within the ISK society that the promotion of Finnish cattle and their enhancement for gaining better qualities and a breed with its own characteristics, which the world has not yet seen, is in its fullest sense patriotic work. It is said that only those nations having the ability to create something new and unique, hence contributing to the development of general human progress, have a legitimate claim to independence" (ISK 1918, 8). In this speech, which is illustrative of the register of talking about Finncattle as an object of nationalist breeding aspirations, the creation of a symbolic value for Finnish culture was enacted through the creative force of breeding behind the three types of cattle. Finncattle were no longer merely mythological, primordial nonhuman Finns. They

TABLE 1.1 Formal type definitions of Finncattle, 1898–1939 (table compiled from several archival sources and includes only major definitions)

Year	Eastern Finncattle		Western Finncattle		Northern Finncattle	
	Bulls	Cows	Bulls	Cows	Bulls	Cows
Before 1898	Only unidentified individual animals; Finncattle do not exist: "No stability of characteristics"					
1898	"Middle-sized, greyish red or greyish and white, clearly milk-type and finely shaped milking animal, which also fulfils mediocre requirements with regard to front and back of body development and as to its depth, breadth, and regularity"		"Relatively developed, hard but finely structured, open and milking type. The colour should be evenly light brown, not reddish brown, not whitish, 'voikko' nor its bear-furred coating"		"Red or white, middle-sized, short-legged, finely built, most often without horns and with clear milking style, and relatively developed front and back of body"	
1904		Milk yield must be known				
1910		Milk fat at least 3.6%				
1912				At least 3,000 kg milk or 110 kg milk fat		80 kg milk fat
1913		Height at withers < 117.5 cm				
1915	Color must be red, "kyyttö," no horns accepted, "appropriate" height	Milk fat at least 3.8%				
1916	Bull mother produces at least 100 kg milk fat, milk fat at least 4.0%					

1921			Bull mother must be in the herd book (category I: 120 kg milk fat, II: 110 kg, III: 100 kg)		Decision to concentrate only on fully white cattle, 80 kg milk fat or 2,200 kg milk (both for cows and for bull mothers)	
1922		If yearly milk yield under 3,000 kg, milk fat 3.8%; cows producing under 2,000 kg/year not accepted; if no previous genealogy/atypical, milk yields must have 110/120 kg milk fat		Milk fat requirements increasing in relation to pedigree generation: 90 kg for 1st gen. and 140 kg for 6th gen.		
1923			Bull mother must have at least 120 kg milk fat yield			
1925		Color must be red "kyyttö," no horns accepted, milk yield in relation to genealogy: 1st gen. 100 kg milk fat and 6th gen. 150 kg milk fat			Only fully white cattle accepted to herd book (black/red points allowed)	
1927			Both bull mother and father must be in the herdbook (category I: 150 kg milk fat, II: 135 kg, III: 120 kg)			

(Continued)

TABLE 1.1 *(Continued)*

Year	Eastern Finncattle		Western Finncattle		Northern Finncattle	
	Bulls	Cows	Bulls	Cows	Bulls	Cows
1928				Milk fat requirements increased: 110 kg for 1st gen., 150 kg for 6th gen.		
1929					Bull mother milk at least 4% cream in milk	90 kg milk fat
1930	Horns accepted, color can be reddish or white also (color freedom not accepted in practice), milk yield counted as the mean of two subsequent years					
1933			Bull mother must have at least 135 kg milk fat yield; no strict color requirements; list of recommended breed animals is printed (both cows and bulls)			
1939	Bulls accepted to highest class only via descendent posterity evaluations	Milk fat 4%, 4.2%, or 4.4%, depending on the class	Herd book divided into three categories with associated milk fat yield requirements: herd (125 kg), prize (150 kg), and elite (175 kg)			

were also nationally created pieces of nature that testified to the vitality of the Finnish culture, a culture capable of producing its own nature (S. Franklin 2007b, 83).[24]

Nation, and breeders as the nation's rightful representatives, stood now at the juncture of and regulated the traffic between different forms of the natural and the cultural, an early form of what Paul Rabinow (1992) has called "biosociality"—the process of creating new forms of nature modeled after cultural values that naturalize the very culture that produced them.

This circularity also nicely captures the following ambivalence between the two forms of national temporality (Bhabha 1990a): the hardly commensurable temporalities of eternal past and the immanently present national society. However, it is precisely this ambivalence that demonstrates the limits of nationness or nationhood and also brings forth how both types of temporality are involved in nationalist movements. In the institutionalized registers, and after initial interest prompted by the foundational myth, a narrative switch from past to present practices was needed for very practical reasons: the animals were now actively institutionally recognized and bred for particular purposes, no longer ancient forms of national life that had been found from the abysses of time. Here, the nation was also understood to create its culture through the bodies of the animals, and this took place through the work that breeders had put into these corporeal achievements.

The type device and the herd book functioned together as perfect devices for mediating between the cultural and the natural spheres of their time, connecting words and things by literal inscription. The cattle became the embodiments of Finnish nationhood, a bovine form of nationhood. They embodied their mythological past with shared Finnish people, and their true type communicated the signs of local biological adaptation. Within the national economy, they led the march to the future of the Finnish dairy economy. From coats to bones to hooves, they were inscribed in types and numbers in the herd books for symbolic-economic national purposes. Their small figures embodied the huge contemporary national aspirations of Finnish society. A truly Finnish breed, then.

FROM FINNCATTLE TO GENETIC RESOURCES

I started the chapter with the question of how the cattle ended up in prison and why they were put there. There are several possible answers to this question (they serve as therapeutic elements for the human inmates, they produce milk and meat for the prison facilities, they make possible the workings that serve the modern prison system's aims in teaching the prisoners new

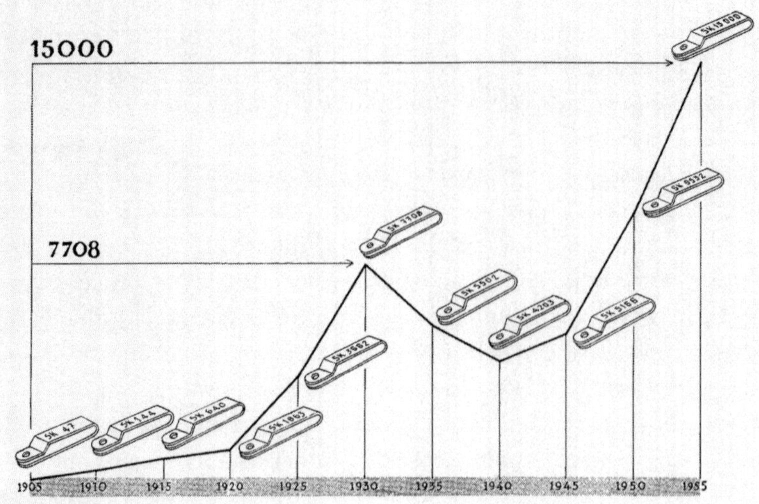

FIGURE 1.7 Nonhuman nationhood transformed into a fact. The number of cows (on the *y*-axis) in the herd books on a timeline (the *x*-axis) for all Finncattle types. (Kaltio 1958, 55)

productive skills and aid in their reintroduction to society as productive members of it, etc.), but the genealogical analysis above shows that these are only outcomes and effects of a more interesting answer to the question. Why would the national bovine species be put in prison, especially since Finncattle have long served as an embodiment of the mythological roots of the nation itself? One more piece of the genealogical puzzle has to fall into place before the answer becomes quite obvious.

For more than half a century, Finncattle were a central form of biowealth for the nation (see fig. 1.7). However, a number of interlinked events similar to the ones that had assisted in the breed's birth changed and reorganized the whole agricultural network, including its central forms of life. By the 1970s Finncattle were only one breed alongside others, and by 1980 they were in danger of extinction. The central role of agricultural animals as forms of national economy had been replaced with other forms of industry. In addition, the science that had made Finncattle the only rational choice for national purposes did not speak in their exclusive favor anymore, and the successful institutional arrangements that had once made the breed-based societies strong lobbyists for that particular animal had been reordered. As the three central relations that had made Finncattle matter started to unravel, so too did the very existence of the breed begin to "unmatter"—its membership trajectory as a natural member of society fell into question.

First, beginning with the postwar reconstruction of the late 1940s, Finland started to move from an agricultural to an industrial economy. The nation's rapidly developing industry could offer higher pay than agriculture, and people in search of work flocked to the cities. Farming was soon a fully capitalized profession for just a minority of the population, and in only forty years, between 1950 and 1990, the number of people living in the countryside fell from 1.67 million to a mere 300,000, one-fifth of the initial number. At the same time, cattle began to be more tightly connected to the new production system, aiming at self-sufficient markets. The Finncattle resisted this societal change until the 1970s—they had even conformed to new production requirements and doubled their milk yield between 1945 and 1970. But they could not resist the new government-guided milk politics, which in the 1970s shifted to favor the quantity of milk over a high milk fat percentage. This disadvantaged Finncattle as an economic animal. They had been producing less milk than Ayrshires, but until this political change they had been saved by their high milk fat percentage, which made the milk easy to turn into butter and other processed dairy products. Also, the prices for meat from cattle doubled in the 1960s and tripled by the late 1970s, a development favoring animals that were much bigger than Finncattle, the Ayrshires. Thus, Finncattle lost their central role in the political economy of Finnish agriculture (Hjerppe 1988; Myllylä 1991; Markkola 2004).

Second, the scientific principles of cattle breeding and the related reproduction technologies evolved rapidly during the century of the Green Revolution, which saw radical changes in agricultural practices and in animal and plant biotechnology in the years after the Second World War (Kloppenburg 1988; Shiva 1991). Prosch's theories of the local breeds no longer dominated breeding science, and science stopped speaking, as such, for Finncattle as the rational breeding choice. Agricultural science and loosely related advances in the technologies of breeding decoupled the national interest from the animals. A simplistic idea of a purebred animal as a simple visual type authenticated by a simple pedigree was no longer tenable. The changes in the conception of natural kinds and the relationship of that nation to the quality of purebreds as agricultural animals grew increasingly complex and contested in the latter part of the twentieth century. Emerging genetics-related knowledge practices coupled with advances in the reproductive sciences slowly became entrenched in practical breeding. While these were not reducible to any one shift, and many changes were (as they still are) questioned by the breeders themselves, they still fed into the practices of everyday work (see Walton 1986; Clarke 1998; Derry 2003; Wilmot 2007).[25]

Slowly, the corporeality of cattle was extended from types and descent to their expression in a standardized numerical fashion, making them calculable in various ways. When purebred breeding gave way to population breeding, new important characteristics emerged: statistical indices and their calculated composites, such as estimated breeding value (EBV), an index calculated on the basis of an individual animal's breeding attributes—ranging from values attached to its output yield and physical structure to indicators of reproductive capacity and health—denoting the mean effect and additive worth of an individual's genes to the population (Myllylä 1991).

This change in the scientific basis of breeding was complemented with changes in reproduction techniques.[26] Artificial insemination (AI) was first piloted in Finland in 1936, and Finland's first national AI society was established in 1946, only five years after its UK equivalent (Clarke 2007; Wilmot 2007). At first considered a controversial and unnatural technique, it quickly entered large-scale use—in 1968 more than 80 percent of the cows in Finland were artificially inseminated, and a mere eight years later all animals under population management reproduced via this technique (Foote 2002). Within a decade, the widespread use of frozen sperm for artificial insemination in cattle breeding led to a sharp increase in milk yields in tandem with a steep decline in the number of breeding lines worldwide. With AI cattle breeding truly became a form of international population management embedded in the rationalities of industrialized agriculture. Here, the new tools of the trade were genetic knowledge and statistical calculations with the global circulation of frozen sperm. I will return to discussing this particular technique of reproduction and related issues of agricultural rationalities behind its use in more detail in chapter 3.

Third, with the development of AI, the cattle lost their representative voice in human societies and politics. The nationalism that the Board of Agriculture had institutionalized with the Finncattle breeding societies now disappeared. Despite the unification of the three societies as one institution, this was slowly losing members to other societies. Worse still, artificial insemination brought different breeds' societies together in 1969 to form a single institution in charge of the reproductive technique. The Finnish Cattle Breeding Society, the Finnish Ayrshire Society, and the Finnish Pig Breeding Society were merged for practical reasons in 1969. In one of the last letters of the Finnish Cattle Breeding Society to its members, the institutional change was described in the following terms: "The aims of the society are . . . to better guide and oversee the breeding of both dairy cattle and pigs. Its work must not be overshadowed by previous restricted conceptions of breed battles. The new society will have to provide better and more equal service to all its members 'despite the members' choice of color or breed'" (SK 1969, 3). Breeds were not represented anymore by any official body; they were lumped together in an artificial-insemination society (SKJY—the association of artificial-insemination cooperatives in Finland) across species boundaries. The new society explicitly stated that it represented not any restricted conceptions of a particular breed but a technique—artificial insemination—and that it sought the highest possible levels of production qualities in cattle (SK 1969; Maijala 1971; Myllylä 1991). Choice of breed was no longer a question of societal identity for a farmer. Whichever breed was chosen, the representation was now concentrated in a single society aimed at the rationalization and cost-effective organization of AI services and the production of better milk yields. The symbolic identity of Finncattle and their representative body in national policy making were now history.

The economic, technoscientific, and institutional representation of the particularity of Finncattle were now all lost. The national animal quickly fell out of the newly emerging industrial society and its revised network of agricultural practices. The extinction of Finnish cattle began picking up pace. While in 1955 the Finncattle still were preferred by farmers, toward the mid-1970s their status as national animals, symbolic as well as corporeal, was waning, fading into history. Within two decades their proportion among all cattle in Finland dropped from 52.5 percent to a mere 9 percent (21,000 cows). Ayrshires were rapidly coming to outnumber the Finnish breed. In 1970 these imports were the country's majority breed, accounting for more than 77 percent of all cows in Finland, or 200,000 cows (Myllylä 1991, 120–25). In 1980 the national herd of Finncattle had dwindled to only some eight thousand individuals, bringing it dangerously close to extinction.

Finncattle, however, were not the only form of nonhuman life that was disappearing directly in consequence of industrialized agriculture. In the second half of the twentieth century, several European agricultural bodies, among them the European Association for Animal Production (EAAP), operating under the auspices of the United Nations Food and Agriculture Organization, were beginning to worry about new technologies of reproduction such as AI. As a result, the FAO started to organize a series of investigations of domestic animals, beginning with a symposium held in Chicago in 1959 (Hodges 1999). The initial concern resulting from these was that new and effective technologies were not just increasing production quantities;

they were also decreasing the diversity of plant and animal varieties (see the histories of plants' genetic conservation in the FAO provided by Pistorius 1997).

At the EAAP's 1969 conference, Kalle Maijala,[27] a Finnish population scientist and a member of the EAAP Commission on Genetics, took up the worrying issue of loss of diversity among animals in his plenary talk. That presentation, "Need and Methods of Gene Conservation in Animal Breeding," started with the clear assignment of blame for the problems and identification of their causes, and it pointed to the consequences in terms of genetic loss:

> The present era of frozen semen in cattle AI has re-actualized the problem of gene losses, which was amply discussed a few decades ago when AI breeding was at the stage of a final breakthrough. . . . Before the beginning of rational animal breeding (i.e., 50–100 years ago), there were numerous local native breeds of different species, obviously well adapted to the primitive conditions of that time. Many of these breeds have been replaced by other breeds, which were considered superior to them. . . . It would be interesting to prepare a list of breeds that have disappeared in the last 100 years, but, since this would go far beyond the time and energy available to me, I shall confine myself to mentioning some examples from my nearest vicinity. In Finland, the North-Finnish type of native cattle (Finncattle) has almost entirely disappeared, the frequency of the East-Finnish type has considerably decreased, and even the West-Finnish type is losing ground to the larger Ayrshire and Friesian breeds. . . . Total loss of the Finncattle genes would obviously mean a *serious decay of genetic variability* in Finland. (Maijala 1971, 403–6; emphasis in original)

As one of the first animal breeds to be named throughout Europe as genetically threatened, Finncattle became an animal example of diminishing genetic variability for the association comprising concerned scientists who were overseeing European animal production from the EAAP's Commission of Genetics. However, even if they were starting to be acknowledged as a breed worthy of conservation, they still lacked institutional representation. In the long chain of events that finally led to national institutional acknowledgment and conservation-related action, numerous national, regional, and international summits recommending conservation of biological and genetic resources were held, and international readiness for a genetic conservation movement built slowly.

In 1982 the Finnish Ministry of Agriculture set up a committee on genetic material of domestic animals chaired by Maijala. The committee's task was to "study the needs and methods for the conservation of the genetic diversity of domestic animals" (see MAF 1983, 2). In the report, the committee presented three arguments as to why any genetic material should be conserved. First were the "economic-breeding reasons." The report clarified that "the conservation of breeds that have clear adaptive qualities is extremely important, as the loss of gene complexes—a.k.a. supergenes—is otherwise permanent. In addition, the conservation of numerous breeds and stocks is a prerequisite for future crossbreeding, in order to have successful heterosis" (MAF 1983, 7). Interestingly, here, threatened breeds such as Finncattle are not objects of direct agricultural exchange but a genetic reserve making the continuation of current breeding practices possible: the viability of the future of the agricultural economy and the successful sexual reproduction of current agricultural animals depends on Finncattle. In addition, several scientific reasons were cited, such as calculations of hereditary change, in line with which animals in conservation are the perfect test animals for scientific research. The third argument set forth "reasons of cultural history." The commission's report stated that "original domestic breeds form a living cultural history, and their conservation is at least as justified as is the conservation of old buildings and cultural environments. The reasons are, among others, sentimental value, the values of cultural history, museum work, and entertainment" (MAF 1983, 8).

The commission, which started its work with an animal that had been rendered obsolete by the high-production-driven agricultural network, had now reconnected the cattle to the future fate of the whole animal industry and to scientific research and had made Finncattle into living corporeal national cultural history with a novel tripartite division. Within these animals' bodies the figures of genetic resources and past national culture now occupied the same space—they became a form of genetic nonhuman nationhood, or an articulation of cultural inheritance and national roots through genetic discourses (Haraway 1997). Interestingly, these genetic discourses were not conceived of in terms of an informational paradigm (e.g., Kay 2000), or the "code of life" binding life and information sciences together to reveal life's "secrets" (Fox Keller 1992). Rather, Finncattle as the carrier of unique genes were expressed as tokens for the viability of commercial (re)production, elements for research on heredity, and living proof of a particular material living culture. Thus, the genetic discourses were embedded within registers drawing heavily on the idioms of markets, science, and cultural difference. The set of three distinct reasons for the conservation of genetic diversity reveals well what is at stake here and in larger discourses of genetic conservation: pure difference and the possibilities it opens for end-product differentiation in markets, research, and culture.

But when the commission announced that genetic resources should be conserved—at the time, only twenty individual northern Finncattle remained—and that institutional arrangements should be made rapidly to assure the protection of the tiny populations, no ministry, not even the Ministry of Agriculture, responded with action. Only a small fund was granted for conservation purposes, and this was allocated for Maijala's use as he would see fit. He then faced a problem. He had been granted funds for establishing a national working group on animal genetic conservation to continue the work he had been so eagerly carrying on. But still no one seemed to care about Finncattle. Not until he spoke about the problem with his neighbor, who had been working for years as an inspector of agriculture for the Ministry of Justice and was in charge of the agricultural direction of its Prison Department. A number of prisons had established farms on their premises over the course of the twentieth century, and prisoner volunteers were working there in return for a small amount of monetary compensation. The neighbor asked Maijala to join the working group that was deciding on the future of farms within the Prison Department. He agreed to do so and suggested that the aims of the prison farms could encompass genetic conservation since these were not farms that were competing in agricultural markets. Rather, their aim was to provide prisoners with work and possibly training in agricultural skills, so why not use them as gene banks for living animals? The chief director of the Department of Prisons, K. J. Lång, agreed, and two prisons in different parts of Finland received Finncattle in 1986, and they still live there (Maijala 2005).[28]

THE PATHS TO OUR BIOPOLITICAL PRESENT: NATION, NATURE, AND GENETIC CONSERVATION

The story of Finncattle provides interesting insights into how nonhuman nationhood was born and made a part of the nationalistic movements of the nineteenth and early twentieth centuries. This particular bovine nationhood was anchored in corporeality in three ways that are important for this book and to the academic theory on nations at large. First, it mobilized two central discursive spaces of nationalist theory: time and territoriality. Temporal narratives—provided mainly by the national myths about the founding human tribes and territorial claims that were made possible by an emergent agricultural science—were forged together to show how the national animal was a truly natural breed. Later, the creative work of breeding was taken as a legitimating sign of a culture that was capable of producing its own nature in the form of a unique animal breed. Both forms of temporality—together forming the double time of nations—along with territorial claims operate in typical performative spaces through which nationalism works in the context of human populations (Bhabha 1990a; Chatterjee 1998). The parallel way of creating a nonhuman population, analyzed in detail above, illustrates nicely how the creation of national belonging involves the creation of a particular nature too.

Second, the state-led institutional arrangements and the economic benefits that the state provided to individuals for breeding national animals, complemented by systematic calls to perform patriotic work, proved successful in the large-scale enrollment of breeders. Interestingly enough, the scale of the breeding work entailed targeting only a few purebred types, and its organization through a state-led system all the way down is unique in agricultural history. The path to the Finnish biopolitical present, through these institutional arrangements, has followed a very nationalistic route (and, I would suggest, this occurred all over the Nordic region). That path differs from the ones taken by the United Kingdom, France, and the United States, where state-centered, nationwide breeding strategies and programs have emerged only since the Second World War era (Gaudillière 2007, 528; Wilmot 2007). The reasons for the difference are related to many elements: the political culture, the national economy and competition in international markets, the speed and trajectory of the circulation of technological means and scientific ideas (along with contingent events) and of agential nonhumans such as anthrax and tuberculosis, and the local topography of the agricultural networks.

However, the overarching idea of a distinct nation and its striving to achieve unification—the powerful ideology of nationalism in its many forms of rhetorical and institutional instruments—has still been the keystone in making the Finncattle (and other nonhumans') population over the past 150 years in Finland. One might think this a classical example straddling the forms of nationalism found in old and young nations, but I am still not confident that such binary categorizations can be made, as the complexity of the Finnish case demonstrates. Old and new elements intertwine in every local adaptation of nationalism and the technologies used to perform it (Serres and Latour 1998), and the outcome is in itself an event that redraws the boundaries between human and nonhuman, between cultural and natural, in the creation of a nation.

Finally, particularly labor-intensive breeding techniques were used to purify the national animals of foreign blood and to produce purebred

Finnish animals in order to prove the theoretical ideas of a natural Finnishness, a nonhuman nationhood. Interestingly, the nativity gained through the purity of blood and the fixity of particular types of corporeal animals created with hard labor over the course of decades were not enough to keep the breed a viable form of national life within the changed agricultural networks, where economics, science, and national interests mingle in unpredictable ways. Finncattle's nativity was successfully rearticulated as a living form of nationhood worthy of conservation only within the new context of genetic networks, where the nativity of the breed was taken as a sign of genetic variability that was vital to agriculture, science, and the nation at large—relations of nativity that are enacted through salvation stories stressing the maximization of difference found in genetic matter and cultural tradition. These insights into the creation of nonhuman nationhood may lead to answers as to why the Finncattle ended up in prison. They also reveal something important about the ongoing projects of biodiversity conservation through genetic resourcing both locally and globally.

Foucault's famous thesis in *Discipline and Punish* (1975) was that the penitentiary system of Western societies underwent a radical change in the late eighteenth century. Punishment, as a public display of sovereign power, was gradually transformed into another form of power, the power of disciplinary and normative strategies of ordering life. While the aim of the punishment was the eradication of unsuitable bodies under sovereign rule, the manifold techniques of disciplinary power were to correct the wrongdoers and to introduce them back into society as docile bodies. As Foucault put it, the prison "mechanisms are applied not to transgressions against a 'central' law but to the apparatus of production—commerce and industry" (Foucault 1975, 308). Prisons and today's gene banks are identical forms of arranging disciplinary power in its relation to life—population and individual, human and nonhuman—as special architectures within the larger systems of biopower. They hold populations that have no place in the society but that the society is unable to let die since they might prove useful later and in other contexts than those from which they emerged. They are an outpost for the nation's political life and its techniques of power from which the bodies, having entered, can only return altered if they are to be reintroduced to the social fabric of the nation.

The complete superimposition of the prison and the gene bank in the case of Finncattle is, in its physical and spatial forms, totally genealogically contingent (see above), but the application of national disciplinary power that is exercised through that arrangement is not. Finncattle crossed an economic threshold in the national agricultural production system, beyond which the breed was then left to die out. It did not fit the new institutional-symbolic, scientific, and economic formations that were operating under a biocapitalism that was extended to nature through agricultural advancements. The crossing of the threshold reveals the close ties between the economic investments in the biopolitical formation called the nation and its symbolic forms in the management of nonhuman life. It also captures the interaction between agricultural sciences and the political economy behind the creation of viable forms of national biowealth. Nonetheless, the commonalities between forms of biopower that were first created to describe the management of human life and the techniques of power that are used in the contexts of nonhumans should not be stretched too far in our discussion, however tempting such parallels may be—there are, after all, certain limits to the similarities between humans and animals.

Perhaps most importantly, by their very definition, agricultural animals have always been objects of agricultural production and, as such, a corporeal source of biowealth in different historical forms of economy. Many pages back in history, the Bible made its statements on animals as exchangeable wealth (for recent analysis of this, see Franklin 2007b). Such attention to animals far predates the forms of biopower exercised over human populations, for management techniques for animals have a long history as analysis of pastoral power (Foucault 1975; 2003) shows. But there are other limits to straightforward application of the analytical frameworks provided by the concepts of biopower and related politics that take life as their object. Recently, the animals have been articulated with new reproductive techniques as well as the pervasive genetic discourses, altering them to form new and problematic objects of economy, knowledge practices, and national power circulating globally through societies. They have become a new national and also international matter of concern (Latour 2004b) that, together with other nonhuman forms of life, is perceived as a vital ingredient in global biodiversity and an object of genetic conservation.

Genetic resources are a new set of matters of concern, ones that flirt with the former knowledge regimes but reconfigure their operational field: subjects and objects, nature and nation look very different after they enter conservation practices. This claim sums up Haraway's (1997, 245) analysis of our biopolitical condition as technoscientific present—this is "a world where the artifactual and nature have imploded; nature itself, both ideologically and materially, has been patently reconstructed. Structural adjustments demand no less of bacteria and trees, as well as of people, business, and nations." The new rationalities behind saving biodiversity are embedded in the conservation of variability and genetic difference, which generate new structural adjustments crafted through a national belonging and are dictated by novel genetic geopolitics of the twenty-first century. These are fields of conservation science and practice that are simultaneously economic, ecological, and most importantly embedded in the renaturalization of the biopolitical communities called nations by technoscientific means.

Here, all nonhuman life is profoundly displaced from the old taxonomies and is known through the new figure of genetic resources. As Stefan Helmreich (2003, 232–33) has pointed out, the efforts to save biodiversity—whether in the form of, for example, agricultural animals, plants, or life in the seas—are not easily accounted for by a simple application of frameworks such as biopolitics or biosociality because of the new *generative relations of belonging* that go into and emerge from conservation practices. Genetic resources are not readily reduced to marketable goods such as dairy cattle. In other words, they are not directly capitalizable as ready pieces of nature, so they must gain a national identity before they can enter the markets as recognized natural-cultural objects. I will detail this argument later in chapter 3. Also they are not readily rendered as objects of biopower, new figures of the informatic regime that the "molecularization of life" has brought into existence—new forms of social life enacted by means of a genetic condition or by new yet recognizable corporeal bodies such as the Finncattle were in the late nineteenth century. Rather, genetic resources are a new form of life enmeshed within ecological and economic rationalities. I will analyze these intersecting relations through their materialization in ex situ conservation practices in chapter 3 and show how new techniques of life (cryopreservation practices) and new kinds of infrastructure (biobanks) are needed for the creation and conservation of economically, ecologically, and culturally valuable populations in the post-CBD world.

However, before moving on to the analysis of the new techniques of cryopreservation wherein novel frozen populations and their ecological niches in biobanks emerge in contrast to the old practices of husbandry, we need to consider the ways in which national identification is acted out today in the era of advanced biotechnologies. The story about Finncattle serves as a historical backdrop showing how forms of a nation's life, human and nonhuman, have been connected through various nature/culture interfaces that coconstituted each other through laborious and time-consuming breeding practices in the absence of access to advanced tools enabling biological malleability. The rest of the chapters are an attempt to ask in which ways the practices by which the nation's life is collected and reproduced within genetic-conservation discourses now operate in a different mode and knowledge regime.

Not only animals but also plants are subject to the CBD, and we will see how the identification today, in contrast to the techniques analyzed in this chapter, hinges on new types of identification practices enabled by the genetic fingerprinting technique. As an illustrative example of how the new identification operates within a different modality of reasoning and how a powerful genetic identification practice offers potential to realign historical texts, bodies, and spaces across species and taxa, we are going to take a look at how apple trees were identified as national genetic resources within Finland's Plant Genetic Resource Programme. The next chapter therefore addresses how genetic individuals and national identification are cocreated and grafted together through a careful differentiation of scientific spaces of representation and the adoption of new temporal frameworks needed for performing genetic nationhood after the CBD—a new ethical plateau of national life.

CHAPTER 2

alexander and the (re)birth of nation: apple trees' genetic fingerprinting and the making of a molecular nationhood

In 1809, against the backdrop of the looming Napoleonic Wars elsewhere in Europe, a historic event took place in Northern Europe. This event marked the beginnings from which the political existence of the Finnish state and later the birth of a Finnish nationhood would gradually emerge. In the Tilsit Treaty of 1807, Napoleon and Tsar Alexander I of Russia had agreed on a number of issues related to the strategic importance of certain territories. The territory of Finland, then under the Swedish Crown, had been judged an important buffer zone for the defense of Saint Petersburg and to seal off the Baltic Sea, thereby protecting both Napoleon and Alexander against British naval attacks. Alexander promised Napoleon that he would conquer the territory and started its acquisition by force the following year. During the successfully advancing Finnish War (1808–9) between Sweden and Russia, Alexander I summoned the four estates of occupied Finland to the city of Porvoo to establish the Grand Duchy of Finland. In a historic speech delivered in response to the oath of allegiance of the estates he granted politically autonomous status to Finland, employing the exalted imperial French words, "*Cette réunion fera époque dans votre existence politique*" (Prestestånds Protocoll vid Laudtagen 1809, 456).

What this autonomy really stood for was the subject of considerable debate throughout the latter part of the nineteenth century in Finland—its political, economic, and cultural implications (mostly translated as governmental, financial, and religious) reverberated through society in various shapes and forms for a long time (Jussila 2004). What was clear, however, was that Finland was consequently separated from its long historical past as a territory under the rule of the Swedish Crown and was annexed to Russia as an autonomous state with its own *diet* and administration. Alexander's declaration—in addition to transforming Finland from a mere geographical territory into a political entity in its own right—made the idea of a discrete nationhood a historic possibility. In the national narratives, this important event in Porvoo marks the origins of a central chronotope (Bakhtin 1981): the birth of a nation, where a new national time and territorial space comes into being. Later, over the course of decades, these events prompted the awareness of a distinct nationhood for the population. Finnishness became reified as a cultural fact by various technologies of national imagination, leading to the claims of an independent people finally gaining sovereignty in 1917. The centrality of Alexander in this narrative of national birth is underscored by strange elements surrounding his death: he died on one of his many voyages in 1825, and his body disappeared mysteriously (Kirby 1975; Thaden 1984; Alapuro 1988; Klinge 1990; Jussila 2004).

Analogously to the treaty between Alexander and Napoleon, which determined the incidental and historical birth of the Finnish state (Thaden 1984), Finnish genetic sovereignty is a by-product of the larger national programs of biological diversity derived from the international juridical obligation to calculate national genes according to the Convention on Biological Diversity. Within the convention, article 15, section 1 placed genetic resources under the sovereign dominion of the signatory countries. It states that "recognizing the sovereign rights of States over their natural resources, the authority to determine access to genetic resources rests with the national governments and is subject to national legislation."

With this declaration, nation-states gained sovereign rule over their genetic resources, and with the same move, the genetic resources as objects of governance became discrete and autonomous objects of knowledge that were endowed with a national identity. Where, within the politics of state, the realm of "genetic" within "nature" had earlier been mostly the problem domain of a particular discipline of evolutionary and molecular sciences, and in some cases a problem of agricultural economics as I argued in the introduction, it had now become an international problem of governance attributed to the political authority of nation-states: genetic resources are subject to national legislation. These novel subjects of governance are not only a political trope but subjects that are deeply embedded in the paradigmatic assumptions of the science that was mandated to perform the identification and conservation of national genetic resources. Here, genetic resources are unproblematically assumed to be simultaneously natural and cultural, and as such they occupy a highly unstable ontology of being as natural resources.

The science performing the knowing of this innovated nature is situated on the borders of molecular genetics and evolutionary ecology: conservation genetics, which emerged as a discipline in the early 1980s and expanded quickly in the new millennium (Frankel 1974; Frankel and Soulé 1981; Frankham 1995; 2005; Hedrick 2001; Pertoldi et al. 2007). Ever since the very first article marking its emergence, this science has been concerned with the preservation of nature as it is understood as culture, or, more precisely, with saving the cultural heritage as national genetic property. For example, the article "Genetic Conservation: Our Evolutionary Responsibility," written by Otto Frankel in 1974—narrated a posteriori as one of the foundational articles of conservation genetics—starts by defining both the novel time scale of operations and the object of this science: "The time scale of concern: The widespread concern with the fate of the natural and cultural heritage now exposed to a hurricane of change is finding expression in the concept of the *national estate*. This concept denotes landscapes, sites or objects of social, cultural, historical, aesthetic, scientific or economic significance which are or should be preserved. By analogy, one can recognize a genetic estate which comprises the biological heritage, the genetic endowment of organisms now living" (Frankel 1974, 53; emphasis in original).[1]

First, by introducing the concept of a genetic estate and likening it to the national one, the article superimposed the meanings of culture and nature onto each other—the genetic endowment of organisms as a particular form of biological cultural heritage, labored nonhuman life as a form of cultural embodiment (Rabinow 1997). It marked the shift of focus in its topicality from biological to genetic concerns. Second, it clearly distinguished this genetic understanding of cultural heritage from the national estate not only in terms of its corporeal referent but also in its orientation to temporality:

> The genetic estate is a more sophisticated concept than the national estate. The latter is conservative and static, whereas the genetic estate is forward-looking and dynamic: its essence is its evolutionary potential. Accordingly it has more meaningful time scale. Since it deals with processes it has at least a national time dimension. This may be

relatively brief, as for the breeding of crops or livestock, or it may be infinite, as for the evolution of species in natural communities. Thus genetic conservation has a time scale of concern, which extends from a day or a year when there is a need (or plan) for conservation, to infinity. (Frankel 1974)

The genetic diversity (as part of biodiversity) of plants and animals has from the very start been understood as belonging to a particular culture, hence the close relation of the genetic estate to heritage and future potentiality. While genetic conservation practices themselves operate in the present tense, it is the time scale of concern that gives conservation genetics its peculiar temporality: the national-natural facts of biological pasts have been replaced with the dynamic potentialities of genetics oriented to the future to secure national interests. The temporal gaze of this science is directed toward a particular enactment of the future (from a recognized need to infinity). In this new temporal orientation, the historical today's matters of fact have become future matters of concern (Latour 2004b)—matters of national concern—for conservation genetics.

Against these developments, it is more than fitting that it is the discovery and identification of Alexander's body that demonstrate how a new political temporality and techniques of scientific representation operate together in the (post-)CBD world and give birth to a new kind of claim to nationhood, genetic sovereignty over a nation's nonhuman genetic affairs. In contrast to the tsar of the original narrative of national birth, the Alexander of my story is not human. It is a representative of the species *Malus domesticus*, commonly known as the apple tree. The case of the Alexander apple illustrates more generally how genetic resources are identified and put together as a new national population consisting of collections of plants and animals and derived materialities that are considered to be genetically Finnish. The collection and identification of individual plants and animals as a new national community is performed by multiple techniques of evaluation and judgment, as we will soon see. This work ultimately depends on the practices involved in genetic fingerprinting—a versatile tool for constructing genetic identities for all living beings that was invented in the mid-1980s (Jeffreys et al. 1985a; 1985b; Nybom 1991; Jeffreys and Pena 1993).[2]

The previous chapter depicted how the nationhood of Finncattle was reified through the mobilization of the double time of nation—the genealogical lines of descent and the immanence of national population—and territorial claims were legitimated by corporeal, morphological traits of the local breed. Within genetic fingerprinting practices, however, both national temporalities and the locus of the territorial rooting of nonhuman life are reconfigured radically for purposes of claiming certain genetic material to be national, to produce a technoscientific genetic belonging to a nation. Accordingly, in this chapter I will analyze how the scientists deciphering a national genetic makeup perform a novel kind of political work—the declaration of a genetic nationhood for the apple tree—and how, by the same token, nationhood itself becomes articulated through the genetic matter of the Alexander. This is an event that marks the rebirth of genetic nonhuman nationhood through the mandates of contemporary global politics over nature, armed with new, powerful techniques of national representation in and through genetic knowledge practices.

PROBLEMS OF CALCULATION

On a summer day in 2005 I find Kristiina Antonius sitting in her small office at MTT (Agrifood Research Finland) arranging papers. Kristiina is one of the two coordinators for the Plant Genetic Resources Programme in Finland and has been working with plant genetic resources throughout her professional career. Her background training is in agricultural sciences, and she has chosen to specialize in plant DNA fingerprinting. By training, then, she is an expert in developing and testing several kinds of genetic markers that allow for the molecular-level identification of plants. Her interest in apple tree fingerprinting followed on from her earlier work (Antonius-Klemola 1999) developing DNA markers for *Rubus L.*, commonly known as brambles (and including fruits such as raspberries). She is a senior researcher at MTT and the leading scientist in DNA marker development for the genetic identification and profiling program in Finland. Most importantly, Kristiina was also one of my key informants and allowed me to follow her work with the apple trees for several years between 2005 and 2008.

This visit to her office is not my first, but it is the first time she shows me some of the problematic aspects of her work. Kristiina takes one of the papers she has arranged in piles on the desk and shows me a long printout with a set of names dotted around what she calls a phylogenetic tree. About three hundred names are connected by lines representing degrees of genetic similarity. She starts to explain: "This is the list of the genetic profiles of the apples I have analyzed recently. There are many types that I need to check again for who they really are. You can see that a number of names here fall into the same line, which means they are genetically identical. Or, well, identical according to my microsatellite analysis."

The problem that Kristiina faces is that some of them are found on the same genealogical tree branch. One of the names is Alexander, and it stands on the same line as Linnan Omena. The two share a similar profile, pointing to identical genetic constitution. Since, according to the analysis, there is no genetic difference between them, the problem is that there is no way of knowing which of the names is true to the sample. Does the genetic profile point to the Alexander or to the Linnan Omena? And if the genetic identity is identical, are the trees really the same, or has there been a mix-up in the collecting of samples?

The problematic situation in the DNA profiling of apples that Kristiina describes is normal. Normal in the sense that this is not the first time I have observed problems in the work of scientists during my fieldwork. Normal also in the sense that, according to the laboratory studies literature, problems abound (Knorr Cetina 1979; 1999; Latour and Woolgar 1986; Latour 1987; Kohler 1994; Rheinberger 1997). Problems in lab work seem to be more of a rule than an exception. It is common for the nonhumans that scientists are interested in working with to stubbornly refuse to cooperate and to require persuasion to do so by other means than those initially selected. Additionally, problems in lab work point to an event in which new alliances must be forged: something—in the initial arrangement of bodies, machines, chemicals, spaces, work sequences, and those thought capable of exhibiting action—is not working in the way previously she thought it would. Problems are normal because they are what science is all about.

Kristiina quickly infers several reasons for the ambiguous identity of the Alexander and a possible solution:

> This is typical. I have to collect these samples again from our main nursery to make sure that I have the samples taken from the right trees and run the analysis again with those to make sure that we don't have mix-ups between them. The most likely reason is that our nursery has a wrong sample tree—I mean that they call the tree by a name similar to what another nursery calls another variety—or that they have picked the sample leaves from the wrong tree. Of course, there is also the possibility that a point mutation has occurred in the tree that we either can't see or don't see in the sample, in which case, the technologies can't reveal the true identity of the tree.
>
> To solve the problem of identity, another instance of collection of apple tree samples is required, and so is another round of analysis by means of what are called microsatellite markers.

We can see already that successful DNA profiling depends on something other than the technique itself. The reasons Kristiina is attributing to the identical readings are related to practices found outside her laboratory: to an erroneous sampling method in the nursery that provided the samples or to a mix-up in their naming. To her, these two reasons are the most probable ones, but a third, what she calls a point mutation, is possible also. The accuracy and reliability of Kristiina's fingerprinting method relying on DNA markers is preconditioned by the aforementioned issues. If these are resolved, the molecular method should in most cases be capable of differentiating between different apple cultivars. If not, the identification of a national apple cultivar becomes impossible, and she will never know whether the Alexander and the Linnan Omena are the same or whether their molecular makeup is indeed different after all. More importantly, as long as she cannot ascertain the true name of the genetic profile, the tree cannot be endowed with a national identity and particular genetics belonging to Finland.

I take Kristiina's work with the apples and the problem of differentiating between the Alexander and the Linnan Omena as an entry point to narrate the story about the genetic sovereignty in the making in Finland. I do this for a good reason.

Genetic resources, as objects of sovereign power, must be actively known and ordered by new techniques of national identification. The problems of identification in this work render visible how novel relations between nature and culture are made (and previous ones unmade) in the mundane practices of genetic fingerprinting required for the assembly of these new national objects. Whereas the identification of national nonhumans once worked primarily through distinctions and value evaluations performed through the observation of morphological differences and genealogy, they now work through the calculation of genetic difference. The locus of national difference is relocated from the surface of living beings to their molecular components—the visually witnessed (pheno)type of an organism has been replaced by genotype in the practices of national identification to get a truer representation of their essence. However, the narrational nature of nationality, as well as the particular phenotypical identifications, plays a big role in making the genotyping possible, and these elements are themselves reconfigured to complement the new practices. Old practices are not simply replaced by new ones. Rather, they become entwined in the new relations of practice that change their previous functions. In other words, the genetic resources, as the case of the Alexander illustrates, are a very interesting intersection of relations embodied in their molecular figure.

This reconfiguration of relations in science immediately prompts the question of what happens to the biological entities themselves within the process. Marilyn Strathern has argued that these novel conceptual relations are generative and capable of making new entities appear. She argues that "whether entities pre-exist relations or are brought into existence by them is another way of referring to the contrast between applying the creative work of the relation (invention) or uncovering its prior status (discovery). But this does not exhaust the interest of conceptual relations; above all they can be invested with creative or generative power" (Strathern 2005, 12). Reconfigured relations are generative: they transform the living apples and apple trees into national genetic resources. For making such an identification, it does not matter whether the apples as biological organisms predate Kristiina's work. What matters is that they do not exist as Finnish genetic resources before they are brought into particular generative relationships—ones that are transformative and that creatively make them autonomous objects of knowledge that are capable of being endowed with and showing forth a genetic nationhood. Biological organisms are translated to genetic knowledge and the novel forms of representation that genetic markers afford.

The Alexander's problematic situation, then, is one that will allow us to follow the formation of these generative relations and their new objects: the circulation of various forms of knowledge and material modalities surrounding the apple varieties through the whole network of identification. These finally converge as a special graph—a phylogenetic tree—printed on paper and attesting a new national kinship structure. The graphical representation marks the individual topological position of apple varieties within an overall national population. Accordingly, nonhuman genetic nationhood has a peculiar relational ontology associated with the creation of a native population together with its individual representatives—and here population is as crucial to making individuals qua individuals as it is to making populations (e.g., M'Charek 2005, 21–55). But the creation of such a population and its individuals depends on a number of other technologies of ordering and representing national belonging than just DNA fingerprinting. First, a central modality of the Alexander as a narrative character must be taken into account as this sheds light on its history and its place among Finnish apple varieties. Because this is the first reason that Kristiina doubts the outcome of her molecular identification, we start by uprooting the Alexander's historical narratives.

TEXTUAL INSCRIPTIONS: THE NATIONAL MANDATE LIST

How did the Alexander become of interest to Kristiina at all? From the inception of the national Plant Genetic Resources Programme (PGR) in 2004, the subgroups dealing with various plant species have been working to produce what are called the national mandate lists. These lists provide an inventory of Finnish plant varieties in textual form. The lists are official documents cataloguing national genetic resources within individual politicoscientific institutions such as the Finnish genetic-resource programs and the various arms of national government, the regional Nordic Gene Bank (NGB) and the European Cooperative Programme for Plant Genetic Resources (ECPGR) databases, and finally also the global CBD working groups.[3] Materially, these lists are no more spectacular than sheets of paper bearing lists of names (see fig. 2.1). Even if their appearance is quite mundane, they are key documents in the construction of genetic sovereignty in the post-CBD world. The special power these lists have can be traced to the prefix "mandate" in their name. The precise meaning of the "mandate," according to the *Oxford English Dictionary*, is "an authorization to act given to a representative," which points both to the political nature involved in the lists' creation and to the political work attributed to them with this form of representation.

Through this mandate, listed varieties are made to represent their nativity, a natural belonging to the Finnish nation. The lists are among the most visible artifacts on which nation and nature are textually superimposed for political purposes—the list is as much a representation of the new nature of nationhood as it is a minute-level description of the national anatomy of genetic nature (Bowker 2000). Here, previously discrete varieties of the species are gathered under the name of the nation, creating a novel relation—a potential genetic relation through nationhood. Thus, with its inclusion in the apple tree list, the Alexander is one of 304 apple varieties constituting a potential genetic nationality. Their biological relation (belonging to the *Malus* taxon) is transformed into the genetic (and, in the end, the molecular) through the inclusion in the national mandate list, itself a thoroughly political artifact. Both a novel form of kinship (as national genetic resources) and a novel relation of belonging (as objects of national genetic sovereignty) emerge (Strathern 2005).

What the compilation of these lists amounts to, then, is that "creative political action is required to transform a segmented and disunited population into a coherent nationality, and though potential communities of this kind may clearly precede such interventions (so that they are rarely interventions into a vacuum), the interventions remain responsible for combining the materials into a larger collectivity" (Eley and Suny 1996, 7). In short, it is through the lists that the technical declaration concerning and the political naturalization of the genetic sphere of nature happen (Waterton 2002). It is an identical form of the techniques that Benedict Anderson

SUOMEN MANDAATTILISTA

Omenalajike	Äpplesort	Ursprung	Bevaras/Förökas/Litteratu
Aholan aikainen, vaha	Aholas tidiga, vax	okänd, fröplanta, Fin	Piikkiö M & C
Alanen N:1	Alanen N:1	okänd, fröplanta, Fin	Piikkiö
Alanen N:3	Alanen N:3	okänd, fröplanta, Fin	Piikkiö
Alasen punainen	Alanen, röd	okänd, fröplanta, Fin	Piikkiö
Aleksanteri	Alexander	okänd, från Ryssland	Piikkiö
Ananasomena	Ananasäpple	okänd, fröplanta, Fin	Piikkiö
Andelin	Andelin	okänd, fröplanta, Fin	Piikkiö M & C
Anisovka	Anisovka	okänd, från Ryssland	Piikkiö M & C
Antonovka	Antonovka	okänd, från Ryssland	Piikkiö M & C
Antonovka, kameniza	Antonovka, kameniza	okänd, från Ryssland	Hirvensalmi, Eesti Pomol
Antonovka, safranoje	Antonovka, safranoje	okänd, från Ryssland	Hirvensalmi
Anttilan punainen	Anttilas röda	okänd, fröplanta, Fin	Hirvensalmi
Apilisto	Apilisto	okänd, fröplanta, Fin	Piikkiö
Arvid	Arvidsäpple	okänd, fröplanta, Sverige	Hirvensalmi, M & C
Astrakaani, Gyllenkrok	Astrakan, Gyllenkrok		Hirvensalmi, M & C
Astrakaani, iso kuulas	Astrakan, stor klar		Hirvensalmi, M & C
Astrakaani, punainen	Astrakan, röd		Hirvensalmi, M & C
Astrakaani, valkoinen	Astrakan, vit	okänd, från Ryssland	Piikkiö M & C
Atlas	Atlas	Kanada	Piikkiö
Atlas, punainen	Atlas, röd	Kanada	Piikkiö
Battleford	Battleford	Kanada	Piikkiö
Bellefleur kitaika	Bellefleur kitaika	Ryssland	Hirvensalmi
Bergius	Bergius	från Sverige	Piikkiö M & C
Björn Lindberg	Björn Lindberg	okänd, Fin	Piikkiö
Borgovskoje	Borgovskoje	okänd, från Ryssland	Piikkiö
Brödtorpin syys	Brödtorps höstäpple	okänd, Fin	Hirvensalmi
Charlottenthal	Charlottenthal	mutant av Harlamovski	Hirvensalmi, M & C
Close	Close	okänd. USA	Piikkiö
Cox's pomona	Cox's pomona		
Diana	Diana	okänd	Piikkiö
Early McIntosh	Early McIntosh		Piikkiö
Edelman	Edelman	okänd, fröplanta, Fin	Hirvensalmi
Eliakselan nauris	Eliakselas roväpple	okänd, fröplanta, Fin	Hirvensalmi
Eppulainen	Eppulainen	okänd, fröplanta, Fin	Hirvensalmi
Eqvi	Eqvi	okänd, fröplanta, Fin	Piikkiö
Långsjön päärynäomena	Långsjös päronäpple	okänd, fröplanta, Fin	Hirvensalmi
Finne	Finne	okänd, fröplanta, Fin	Piikkiö
Gallen	Gallen	okänd, fröplanta, Fin	Piikkiö
Goodland	Goodland	Kanada	Piikkiö
Grenman	Grenman	okänd, fröplanta, Fin	Piikkiö M & C
Guldborg	Guldborg		Piikkiö
Hampus	Hampus		
Hannulan talvi	Hannulas vinteräpple	okänd, fröplanta, Fin	M & C
Haralson	Haralson		Piikkiö
Harlamovski	Harlamovski	från Ryssland	Hirvensalmi M & C
Harmaa Gylling	Grågylling		Hirvensalmi M & C
Hava	Hava	Ryssland	Hirvensalmi
Hedman	Hedman		Piikkiö
Helenan kulta	Helenas guld		Piikkiö
Heta	Heta		Piikkiö
Hibernal	Hibernal	okänd, från Ryssland	Piikkiö
Huvitus	Huvitus	okänd, fröplanta, Fin	Piikkiö M & C

FIGURE 2.1 The first page of the tentative national mandate list of Finnish apple varieties with various annotations.

([1983] 1991) argued were central for the project of turning a disunited mass of people into a coherent whole in the early stages of nation building: the population census. The only difference here is that the census is performed for nonhuman populations that, by the same token, produces them. But how does one perform such a census?

The tentative apple mandate list was initially compiled by another researcher at MTT, Meeri Saario, in 1998, several years before Kristiina started her work on the molecular identification. The list was Finland's contribution to the Nordic Gene Bank program in the late 1990s for identifying local Nordic apple varieties and has remained in the archives since its initial compilation.[4] The tentative list was based on archival documents on the past and on the present that have been maintained by apple experts, known as pomologists, over the centuries. Meeri described to me later, in 2007, how she identified the apple varieties for the national list and what the practical problems of such work were. Her main source for the compilation was an early study on Finnish fruit trees and cultivated berries (Meurman and Collan 1943). In two volumes this handbook, written for horticulturists in the 1940s, provides a general pomology alongside the enumeration and description of the local varieties. Large parts of the first volume are devoted to the apple: different systematics and classification strategies are presented along with standard descriptions of varieties and comparisons of their yields. However, the work does not affiliate the apples with a particular nationhood but only vaguely points out the ubiquitous dispersion of the origins of the apple within Western cultures. The descriptions include hundreds of apple varieties, and from them Meeri selected those that she judged most likely to be Finnish. In an interview, she specified her criteria for inclusion:

> There were a couple of criteria that I followed in the compilation of the list. I thought that we needed an extensive list, so I decided not to be too picky in the selection. I thought it's better to be inclusive than exclusive, so I selected around three hundred cultivars in the list, all those that were possibly of Finnish origins or had been here for a long time already. The second criterion was a bit trickier—Should I include the cultivars that are mentioned in the old archives but nobody knows whether they exist anymore as living organisms somewhere? Well, I decided that I should, just in case we find those somewhere one day; you never know if someone has those in their backyard or something. And there was a third criterion, too. I took some of the same cultivars that my Swedish colleagues did if they were cultivated in Finland at

> the time—I mean if they had a known history here. The reason for this was that even if the names were the same, the trees themselves could be different because of mutation, and you never can be totally sure that it is the same tree even if it carries the same name. And if they later turn out to be the same cultivars, they are easily removed from the list afterward.

In the interview excerpt above, Meeri describes the very same problem that Homi Bhabha (1990a) identified as central in the study of any narrative of nationality: the literal expression and the act of writing of a national culture is always partial, relies on creating difference, and has to deal with the problem of closure. The first criterion in the selection of the Alexander and the Linnan Omena for the mandate list is their appearance as textual figures in the historical accounts of Finnish apple cultivation. Historical accounts of national happenings (as traditions) have enormous power of representing the nation as part of an unalterable historical development, as forms of teleological events in the becoming of the national time-space, even if the invention of such traditions would be easily discernible when placed alongside other narratives (Hobsbawm and Ranger 1983; see also Friedman 1992). Here, the textual traces of the apples' cultivation in the past are what make them traditional objects of Finnish nature, with nation understood literally as cultivated nature (in a process similar to the identification of Finncattle, as analyzed in the previous chapter), and connect them to the present by their inclusion in the mandate list. Past cultivation practices become contemporary culture by the mediation of textual accounts found in the pomological archives: they are partially reinscribed as national mandate lists. Objects of historical nature imply present culture; the present culture reinscribes the past nature with a nationhood.

The past, however, is not indefinitely susceptible to invention, open to any kind of narrative construction. Rather, it is limited by constraints that render the account plausible (Foucault and Gordon 1980; Appadurai 1981; Hastrup 1992). In the case of apple trees, the reconstruction of the national nature's genealogy relies on textual archives. Meeri has created her own local criteria of plausibility for the reconstruction of the past—translated into particular selection rules for apples—from textual archives. All her criteria for inclusion in the mandate list make visible the practical solutions and the rationalities behind them. As the interview extract above demonstrates, she is reflexive in her evaluation and justification of the selection: first the size (inclusive but not so much as to create logistical problems), then the problematic relationship between the archive and contemporary life (is the tree biologically alive somewhere?), and finally the question of cultural naming practices and genetic differences between national identities (the same name can be given to genetically different cultivars, or the genetic makeup of the tree itself might have mutated). The criteria are devised in the face of the problems of the initial writing of the apple varieties' nationhood. There is no recourse to other criteria, not to mention universally agreed-on criteria, for national inclusion. They are a local invention guiding the practical compilation practice based on historical archives.

ALEXANDER AS A WELL-TRAVELED NATIVE

Among hundreds of other varieties, the Alexander was identified in Olavi Meurman and Olavi Collan's (1943) book as one traditionally cultivated in Finland. In a little more than four pages (384–88), the Alexander's historical genealogy is recounted in detail. For this apple, first called "Aport," or "AportAlexander" (the book does not attribute any priority to either of the two alternative names in relation to its historical origins), the earliest recorded history extends back to early eighteenth-century Russia. However, it has spread throughout the apple-cultivating world. Its introduction to Scandinavia is dated to around 1830, and to the United Kingdom even earlier, around 1817. It has also been cultivated widely in the United States. According to the narrative, its cultivation in eastern Finland, however, started much earlier. The Alexander has been known to be part of the cultivated gardens of the Finnish Orthodox monastery of Valamo, which was established in the twelfth century. The book also claims that the name for the apple comes from that of the Russian tsar Alexander I. The long history of the Alexander's cultivated presence in (what in the whiggish narrative is called the Finnish) local territory was enough to persuade Meeri to include it on the list (see fig. 2.2).

The other apple, which is genetically identical to the Alexander, is absent from this central archival source only to be found in another text almost thirty years later. The Linnan Omena was first mentioned in a pomological book in 1977, and there its history is traced back to a small town in Finland, Lohja. According to that text (Leskinen 1977, 50–51), the apple originates from the gardens of a local horticulturist called "Linna" (hence the name) and became nationally famous in the 1950s for its rare resistance to diseases. This is the only archival record on the apple found among all the Finnish pomological texts, and its textual traces end as abruptly as they appear. However, this single appearance is enough for Meeri to include the

N:o 15.

Aport-Aleksander. Апортъ.

Kirjallisuus ja synonyymit: Regelin Pom. I, 204. — Aportovoje, (Krasnoglasoff, s. 87). — Ispanskij aport, Tulskij aport ja Aport obykı gårdsjournal II, s. 93). — Aport krasnij, (Näyttelyluettelot). — Aport — Aport bolschoj (Wohin). — Aport krasnij (Sagoskin. — Tiesenhau: Journal II, s. 77). — Krasnotokoje rebristoje (Wohin). — Funtovoje ja — Titowka (Gekel). — Korscha (Jegoroff). — Aportovoje ogromnoje (' loogi). — Aport belij ja Podaportovoje (Walamo).

Kaiser Alexander (Illustr. Handb. der Obstk. I, N:o 39). — Ka (Lauchen Pom., s. 250). — Kaiser Alexander von Russland (Rubenin Obstb Alexander (Enerothin Pom. II. 28). — Aport (Bihang till Svensk p Kejser Alexander (Bredsted Dansk Pom. II, s. 82). — Aporta (van M descriptif de la partie des arbres fruitiers, qui de 1798 à 1823 ont form s. 56, N:o 165) — Kaiser Alexander von Russland, Aporta Nalivia (] sorten II, 1823, o: 65). — Emperor Alexander (Lindley, A guide to tl kitchen garden, 1831 s. 14). — Grand-Alexandre (André Leroy, Dicti mologie, N:o 185). — Empereur Alexandre (M. Mas, Le verger, V, N:o : Alexandre (Catalogue descriptif des fruits adoptés par le congrès p

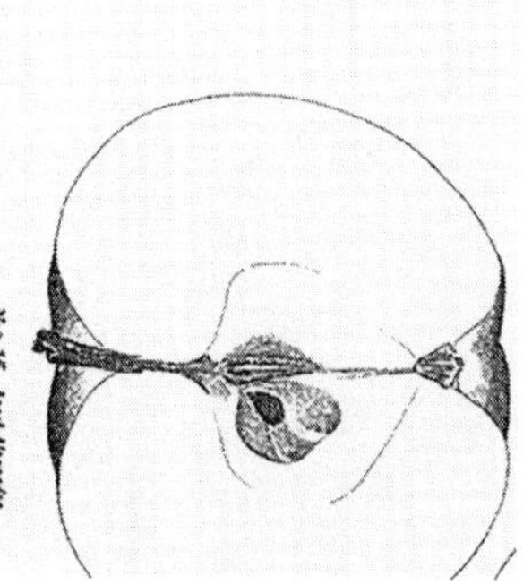

FIGURE 2.2 The Alexander's genealogy described in the first pomological book of Finland. (Smirnoff 1894)

Linnan Omena in the tentative mandate list by her criteria favoring inclusiveness in its creation.

To see why the Alexander is included in the national mandate list, a more detailed analysis of its origins is needed. At a closer look, the modern "Bible of Finnish pomology" (Meurman and Collan 1943) cited above is itself composed of other texts. Of these, it explicitly refers to one as its main source, a work published much earlier and in another political arrangement of the society in the era of the Grand Duchy of Finland. It was the Russian horticulturist Alexandra Smirnoff who wrote this first scientific exposition on apples to lay ground for Finnish pomology in 1894 (Smirnoff 1894). Again, for every apple variety that Smirnoff introduced in her book, numerous references to other texts were given (see fig. 2.2 for the list of the Alexander's references). She explicitly referred to the handbook for Swedish pomology that had been published only a few years earlier in 1884 (Eneroth 1884) along with other Swedish, German, and Russian horticultural experts of the time (Smirnoff 1894, ii). From these sources, in turn, the traces of the Alexander lead to almost every pomological directory of the second half of the nineteenth century, including Nordic, Russian, and German literature and even Anglo-American texts depicting "British Apples" (see fig. 2.3 for an example). The narration that comes together in her book is composed of a complex intertextual web weaving together different sources of knowledge originating from various times and places.

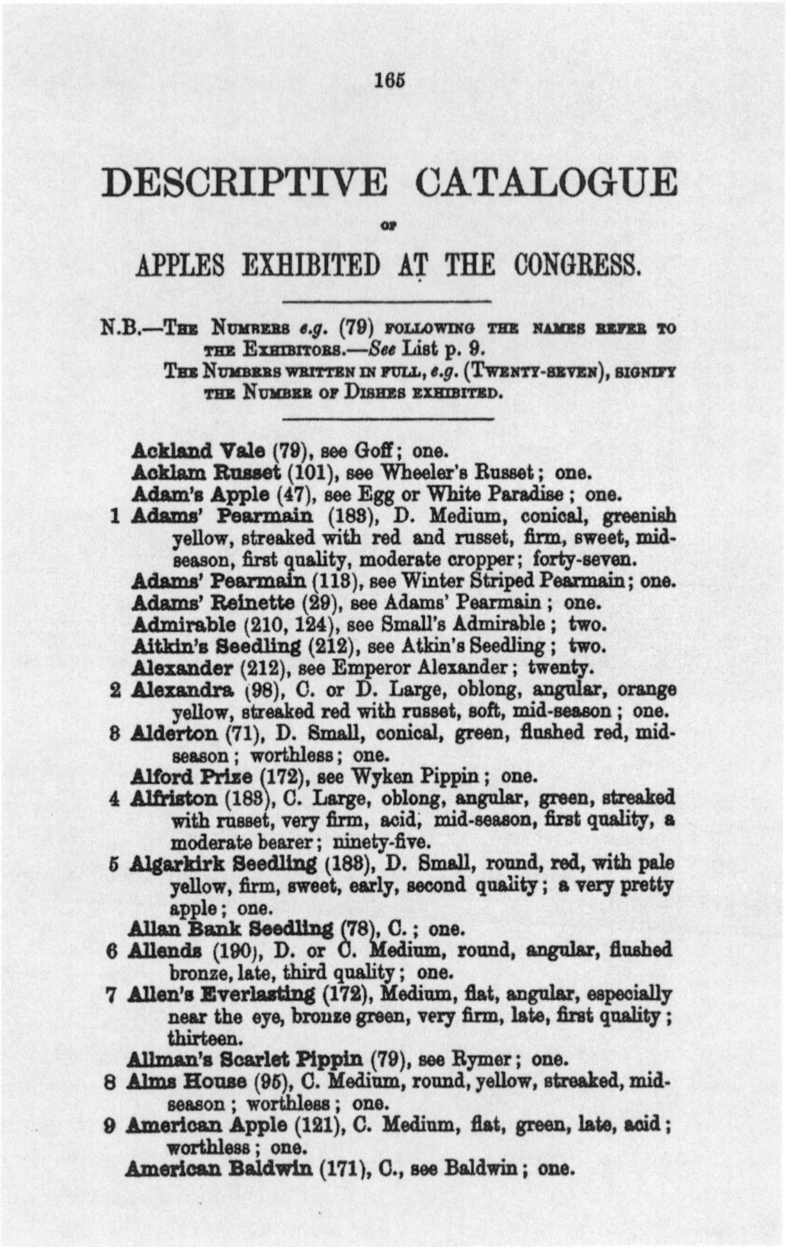

165

DESCRIPTIVE CATALOGUE

OF

APPLES EXHIBITED AT THE CONGRESS.

N.B.—THE NUMBERS *e.g.* (79) FOLLOWING THE NAMES REFER TO THE EXHIBITORS.—*See* List p. 9.
THE NUMBERS WRITTEN IN FULL, *e.g.* (TWENTY-SEVEN), SIGNIFY THE NUMBER OF DISHES EXHIBITED.

Ackland Vale (79), see Goff; one.
Acklam Russet (101), see Wheeler's Russet; one.
Adam's Apple (47), see Egg or White Paradise; one.
1 **Adams' Pearmain** (183), D. Medium, conical, greenish yellow, streaked with red and russet, firm, sweet, mid-season, first quality, moderate cropper; forty-seven.
Adams' Pearmain (113), see Winter Striped Pearmain; one.
Adams' Reinette (29), see Adams' Pearmain; one.
Admirable (210, 124), see Small's Admirable; two.
Aitkin's Seedling (212), see Atkin's Seedling; two.
Alexander (212), see Emperor Alexander; twenty.
2 **Alexandra** (98), C. or D. Large, oblong, angular, orange yellow, streaked red with russet, soft, mid-season; one.
3 **Alderton** (71), D. Small, conical, green, flushed red, mid-season; worthless; one.
Alford Prize (172), see Wyken Pippin; one.
4 **Alfriston** (183), C. Large, oblong, angular, green, streaked with russet, very firm, acid, mid-season, first quality, a moderate bearer; ninety-five.
5 **Algarkirk Seedling** (183), D. Small, round, red, with pale yellow, firm, sweet, early, second quality; a very pretty apple; one.
Allan Bank Seedling (78), C.; one.
6 **Allends** (190), D. or C. Medium, round, angular, flushed bronze, late, third quality; one.
7 **Allen's Everlasting** (172), Medium, flat, angular, especially near the eye, bronze green, very firm, late, first quality; thirteen.
Allman's Scarlet Pippin (79), see Rymer; one.
8 **Alms House** (95), C. Medium, round, yellow, streaked, mid-season; worthless; one.
9 **American Apple** (121), C. Medium, flat, green, late, acid; worthless; one.
American Baldwin (171), C., see Baldwin; one.

FIGURE 2.3 Copy of catalogue pages. The Alexander in the exhibition catalogue of the British National Apple Congress in 1883. (Barron 1884)

As the convoluted historical archive demonstrates, the origin of the national narration always precedes itself only to be found outside the particular text at hand and ultimately recedes into the mists of history. According to the archives, the same apple tree appears in multiple nations as a cultivated species. Not only does the Alexander's textual trail lead around the Western world (to Russia, Scandinavia, the United Kingdom, and the United States), but its temporal origins in the archives are located in various times, sometimes with a precise dating, sometimes in broadly defined eras.[5] Thus, the Alexander's genealogy has the same problem as narrations about the origins of nations: they both lose their origins through the myths accrued over time (Smith 2000). The more knowledge one gains about the history of the Alexander, the more its spatial origins seem to fluctuate and become blurred: the Alexander's genealogy cannot be used to judge its nationhood because it only makes the question of the Alexander's origins more obscure. But in tracing the creation of the national list, an important question now emerges. What, if anything, warrants the Alexander's inclusion in the Finnish mandate list since, according to the historical narratives, it is to be found almost anywhere in the Western world?

The problem of the varieties' origins and the closure of the list are what make it so interesting as a document of national identity. The move of simultaneously including the Alexander in a particular national community and excluding it from others seems problematic, especially because the textual traces lead everywhere. Even more so since the traces do not lead to any one place exclusively.

Because the textual figure of the Alexander occupies a multitude of spaces and times, its figure is one of multiplicities. Or, more precisely, after its selection for the mandate list, its textual figure is that of a "well-travelled native" (Clifford 1996), moving quite effortlessly through long temporal and spatial distances, and one whose roots in any one nationality or even in a specific geographical region are erased by a narrative excavation of its past. It quickly becomes nationless.

The mandate list, however, represents only one national identity. Here, we return to the rationality behind the Alexander's inclusion in it. The ambivalence in writing a nationhood through historical archives remains problematic until the enactment of a particular relation: the articulation between the archival textual material and Meeri's practical criteria out of which the initial list of national genetic matter emerges. There is nothing strange about the practical reasoning that Meeri uses in inscribing possible nationhood. Since the Alexander has been cultivated in Finland, it might be Finnish after all. The initial list is just a tentative one to be confirmed later with other identification techniques. It is a list of genetic nationhood in the making and, as such, its first condition of possibility. It is also a very special kind of writing, a form of national writing that, as Bhabha (1990a, 3) argues, is "a figure of prodigious doubling that investigates the nation-space in the process of the articulation of elements: where meanings may be partial because they are *in medias res*; and history may be half-made because [it] is in the process of being made; and the image of cultural authority may be ambivalent because it is caught, uncertainly, in the act of 'composing' its powerful image."

The Alexander, as a textual figure within the tentative list, is located in between, in medias res, not only by its national identity but also by its ontological location as an object of knowledge. It is between history and contemporaneity, between past and present, between its rooting in national territories and its spatial displacements, between textual and corporeal presence. In short, by its inclusion in the list, the Alexander is a proposition—a proposition of a national nonhuman form of life.[6] It is a textually relational effect all the way down, one that has its particular effects for its novel corporeal coming-into-beingness. The pomological archives point to the problem between the textual figure of the Alexander and its material presence as a live tree within the national territory in a given moment of time.

Meeri's last criterion for the Alexander's inclusion in the tentative mandate list is that the organism itself can be found alive within the national territory. Quite simply, without the tree, the Alexander's corporeality as a national genetic resource is lacking, and the reality of its figuration within genetic sovereignty would be reduced to a textual effect within the mandate list among other names (see Bowker 2000). It would exist only as a proposition. Therefore, the next step in the Alexander's national identification consists of something other than writing the nationhood: tracking down the living tree itself.

NATIONAL UPROOTINGS

The textual figures of the Alexander and the Linnan Omena are very different. Whereas the Alexander has an almost universally dispersed historical genealogy, the Linnan Omena only has a local and very limited one. Kristiina has inferred from this that their molecular identities cannot be identical, either, and to prove this, she wants to perform a new DNA fingerprint analysis of both of them. For this rerun, however, a new collection of samples is required since the ones used in the first assay cannot be trusted. Early in the morning on one of the last days of August 2006, I meet Kristiina in front of

FIGURE 2.4 The in situ gene bank in Piikkiö. Photo by the author.

her laboratory as she gets ready for the collection trip. The samples will be collected from MTT's central nursery, which acts as an in situ gene bank for the horticultural varieties. It holds both of the relevant tree varieties alive in its fields. After a quick chat, we get into her car and start heading for the nursery, situated in the town of Piikkiö, about an hour's drive from the laboratory.

Upon approach, the nursery is easy to recognize. As one drives along the little road branching from a highway, a large area occupied by hundreds of trees in neat rows, bushes, and fields suddenly appears. "This is it," Kristiina begins. "Our live gene bank. This is where we're supposed to find our apple trees." She drives the car near the long rows of trees and gets out. Kristiina finds the local horticultural scientist in a nearby field, speaks briefly with her, and walks back to me. "All good. There is a map in front to make sure we have the right tree. What we want to do is take the samples in the right order and try not to mix their names up this time," she says.

Kristiina hands me the map and the list of the trees that had identical DNA profiles in her analysis—including the Alexander and the Linnan Omena—and from which she wants to have a new sample. While walking between the rows of trees, I read the tree names out loud from the map to guide Kristiina's sampling. The spatial ordering of the trees and the various names on the maps and lists must match perfectly. The Piikkiö nursery is a perfect example of how the laboratory extends to the farm (Latour 1988) in order for science to do its work. The meticulous spatial arrangement and its textual inscription in maps and lists guarantee a particular order of nonhuman life and its configuration in relation to human action. What this spatial arrangement, along with maps and other lists, makes possible, then, is the quick rediscovery of what is marked on them—a clear order makes the reliable circulation of the reference (Latour 1999) easy and accessible to the scientists. Kristiina takes a few leaves from each of the trees and captures some photos of their apples. She explains her sampling:

> Sometimes we need the photo for a visual confirmation, just to make sure that the tree is what it is supposed to be. I'll compare those to the photos I have of the cultivars in the books. In rare cases, it might be possible that the tree here is not really the one that we assume it is. A mix-up might have occurred when this nursery was created, since all the various cultivars here have been created by grafting. Oh, I mean you see there's a good explanation as to why all these trees here are so small, or what we call "dwarf trees." It's easy to make them by selecting the right basic rootstock, which does not grow too big, onto which the scion from the desired tree is then grafted. Then the grafted cultivars don't grow too big, and they're so much easier to handle. Not too much space is needed for them as you can see. Much more efficient to store the trees this way.

It is here that the identification of the Alexander takes another turn (rather unexpected for the ethnographer following the fingerprinting practices). As Kristiina explains in the quotation above, the field laboratory is constructed in a reliable way only if the grafting process has been carried out successfully. This means that no unexpected combinations either between the scion and the rootstock trees or in their genetic makeup arose when the nursery was being created. Grafting, one of the earliest forms of biotechnology, is said to have been innovated some 3,800 years ago in Babylonia. With this technique, the kinds of dwarf apple trees found in the fields of Piikkiö were already being cultivated 2,300 years ago in Persia. All you need is a special kind of rootstock that will inhibit the growth of the apple scion that was grafted onto it. Various rootstocks will operate in this manner and make even transspecies grafting possible (Juniper and Mabberley 2006).

This form of reproduction is called vegetative propagation, in contrast to sexual reproduction from seeds. The target of apple cultivation is a consistent quality of fruit yield of a desired character, and sexual reproduction of highly polymorphic apple trees rarely results in offspring similar to the parents, rendering cultivation uncontrollable. However, with grafting, the reproduction of a particular tree remains possible indefinitely as long as the scion—the twig of the tree with desired qualities—will viably merge with the selected rootstock it is grafted onto. Hence, grafting is the oldest technique of cloning for the ends of horticultural production (Juniper and Mabberley 2006, 91–114). Not surprisingly, then, it is from grafting practice that contemporary cloning (of cells or animals) has inherited its name: the word is derived from the Greek *klon*, literally mean "a twig" (for its contemporary uses, see S. Franklin 2007b, 19–45).

In most archival books considering apples (e.g., the texts cited above), cultivars are just taken to exist as themselves rather than as products of intentional production, reproduction, and upkeep. Virtually all commercially available trees are, however, a fusion between the scion, or the aforementioned twig of the desired fruit tree, and the rootstock, thereby very literally making the vast majority of cultivated fruit trees on the planet hybrid organisms (for details on the principles of reproduction and various grafting techniques applied to apple trees, see Westwood 1993; Acquaah 2002; Webster 2003). It is also this form of reproduction that has made the Alexander corporeally so mobile: only small and readily transportable parts of it are needed for successful replication in other soils into which its first roots (in horticulture these first roots are called "true" or "seminal" roots) are sunk.

Kristiina continues her description of grafting:

> It is very easy to mix up the scions in the grafting process: they are these little twigs that all look similar then, and all it requires is to take the wrong one and attach it to the rootstock meant for another. That's it. Then you have one cultivar growing under the name of another. It's almost impossible to tell afterward that it's happened since the trees and the apples can look very similar. And I think, well, our DNA profiles show that this is a pretty common thing to happen. These kinds of mix-ups become visible only with the profiling method.

So a pure cultivar is a hybrid tree, a successfully created clone of a tree that was originally raised from seeds. The purity (Douglas [1966] 2002) of one of these as a representative of a certain cultivar depends on the grafting process: selecting scions and compatible stocks, making a successful union between them, and rooting it in a soil to make a new tree. The purity of the tree is a result of the purity of the grafting process. Quite interestingly, purity refers here to the process of cloning, not to the trees themselves.

The reproductive technique has made the circulation of the Alexander's body parts easy and explains why its textual traces are readily found everywhere in the archives. However, this is also why, inversely, its mobile material presence is so hard to track down: the purity of the grafting process must have been preserved over the centuries. At the nursery, locating the trees is easy with the map even if every location must be double-checked. Every sample leaf taken is placed in a small plastic bag with a code indicating the name of the tree and the sampling site. The list includes about two dozen trees, and the resampling is done in an hour or so. After the collection Kristiina packs the samples in a cooler box to keep cellular damage of the leaves to a minimum before she uses them in her lab. We drive back to the MTT headquarters, where Kristiina starts to work with the new samples, hoping that she has now secured the right samples of the Alexander and the Linnan Omena. Later that fall, I learn that the newly collected samples that were taken to Kristiina's lab fail again to identify the Alexander as molecularly different from the Linnan Omena. She says, "There's something wrong here now. I can figure out only two reasonable options for these results. Either the apple tree in Piikkiö is not Alexander and has been at some point mixed up with something else, or Alexander indeed has had a mutation that looks similar to Linnan Omena with my microsatellites."

Liisa Malkki's observation on the circulation of the key concepts in discourses of nationhood and their early translations from literal to metaphorical, from natural to cultural, is illuminating in the story of the Alexander. She wrote that one set of

> connections between nation and culture is more overtly metaphysical. It has to do with the fact that, like the nation, culture has for long been conceived as something existing in "soil." Terms like "native," "indigenous," and "autochthonous" have all served to root cultures in soils; and it is, of course, a well-worn observation that the term culture derives from the Latin for cultivation. . . . Here culture and nation are kindred concepts: . . . they both depend on a cultural essentialism that readily takes on arborescent forms. (Malkki 1992, 29)

Malkki's argument is that both in common parlance and in major theories on nationalism (e.g., Gellner 1983; Smith 1986; B. Anderson [1983] 1991) the idea of a particular nationhood has always been connected to land, territory, and soil, which serve as its common metaphoric synonyms. If the concepts of a "family of nations" and nationhood have gained so much of their vitality in borrowing the naturalness of these from the idea of literal branching of trees (e.g., the form of visual genealogical representations of descent lineages is modeled after trees) and their rooting in a particular soil, it is also true, inversely, that much of what is called nature has borrowed from culture and continues to do so. However, what becomes apparent here is that a biological rooting in territorial soil does not, as such, guarantee the purity of the native nor its automatic political naturalization. Mere biological rooting does not connect the life form with a particular form of life, the tree to its nationality, or the Alexander to its Finnishness. It might be misplaced, wrongly grafted and rooted, and in consequence another tree might be falsely presenting itself as the Alexander. All these uncertainties obscure the links that are taken for granted between a natural rooting and a national territory.

It may be that the earlier ideas, metaphorical and literal, about plant roots and their singularity, their effects as tokens of territorial truths linking natural to national, have been understood in overly simplistic terms. There are no singular territorial roots in the Alexander: direct access to a cultural tradition linking the tree to the nation is unavailable within historical archives. But if the tree has no individual national roots, it should come as no surprise that it (like other apple trees) does not have any single set of natural roots either—its biological roots are not singular, nor are they easy to track down to a particular soil. In Gilles Deleuze and Félix Guattari's words, nature "doesn't work that way: in nature, roots are taproots with a more multiple, lateral and circular system of ramification, rather than a dichotomous one" (1987, 5). Similarly to its textual figure, the rooting of the Alexander in national soil is hard to locate. It is culturally and corporeally uprooted.

IN THE FIELD, IN SITU

It is through the figure of uprooted natives—most often dubbed immigrants—that the strong metaphysical link between the idea of the nation and its soil is most often encountered. This metaphysical principle renders any "territorial displacement as pathological," and "it is in confronting displacement that the sedentarist metaphysic embedded in the national order of things is at its most visible" (Malkki 1992, 31). This national imperative becomes visible in how the uprooting of both cultural and natural belonging must be undone by rooting them in national soil. Perhaps not surprisingly, in the post-CBD world, trees (and other nonhuman genetic resources) and human immigrants share the same problematic relation to the nation: according to the international contract, any native genetic resource must fulfill the condition of being in situ, or being found rooted in the soil of the country of its origins.[7] Otherwise, these cannot be considered native or politically naturalized. Trees, like human beings, need a physical and symbolic rooting in a territory where they are identified as national forms of life.

Back in the field, our problem of locating the Alexander alive in situ in Finnish territory remains unsolved for another ten months until June 2007. It is then that Kristiina makes her final attempt to find the missing tree and to close the gap between the textual and the biological. Similar to the biodiversity sampling and plant collection elsewhere (Brush 1999; Hayden 2003b), the search for valuable organisms such as national apple trees does not happen in the wild, in the uninhabited forests and fields of Finland. Rather, it occurs within the communities that have the best knowledge of the tradition—traditional knowledge (TK), as it is called by the CBD and other international agreements and by organizations behind them.

Here, TK is considered a marketable good, as is made clear by declarations found within the CBD and numerous statements made by the World Intellectual Property Organization (WIPO) and World Trade Organization (WTO) that are aimed at reasonable benefit sharing arising from that knowledge. However, the community that holds the TK of Finnish apple trees is not non-Western native populations whose culture is being "copyrighted" (M. Brown et al. 1998) by multinational corporations. Instead, it consists of individuals making up the nation, citizens in whose name the whole claim to sovereignty is made and who are benevolently willing to share their knowledge with Kristiina.

The community that holds the TK relevant to locating and identifying apple trees such as the Alexander lives in the town of Lohjansaari in southern Finland. The town has a special soil containing large amounts of chalk and is in a temperate hemiboreal zone. These two ecological characteristics make it one of the best places to grow apples in Finland, and until the mid-twentieth century this was the national center for apple cultivation. Because of its rich history in cultivation, several amateur and professional horticulturists still live there with their own special plants. Much of the traditional knowledge of apple trees and their cultivation, along with many of the rare varieties, can be found in the exclusive possession of these local horticulturists. And, importantly, this is where Meeri Saario, the composer of the first national mandate list and herself an avid horticulturist, lives. She has promised to assist Kristiina in her search for the missing apple trees by acting as a local guide to the horticulturist community of Lohjansaari.

After a drive from MTT headquarters, involving a couple of hours and some last-minute U-turns, we arrive at Meeri's house in the middle of the slightly built-up countryside area of the town. She is waiting for us on her doorstep and calls us in for coffee. As we are sipping our coffee, a powerful cultural ritual in Finland for fostering social interaction, Meeri starts to describe to Kristiina the background work she has done to find the desired trees before our arrival. "I managed to get in touch with all the owners of the trees on the list you sent to me," she tells us. "They're all old amateur pomologists who know well the histories of their trees. They have some of the original trees that have been cultivated here from the seeds—these are the original seedlings from which all the other trees have been grafted and cultivated years ago."

After the coffee and the usual chat about apple cultivation, we head up to the first local apple expert, who should have information about the mysteriously missing Alexander. She lives in a little wooden house up on a hill not far from Meeri's house, and as soon as we arrive in her front yard, the front door opens. An elderly woman with a walking stick in each hand walks out. She introduces herself as a retirement-age amateur horticulturist and tells us that Meeri called her to help us find the missing trees. The woman explains that she herself has kept trees and berry bushes in a large cultivated area next to her house but is now getting too old to take care of them. She says, "I just have some of the trees and bushes left. Like this apple tree here." She points to a tree growing right in her front yard: "This is called Linnan Puu [castle tree]. The name comes from someone named Ilmari Linna, who is said to have discovered the cultivar. I went to school with his son and took the same classes for many years. This tree has been here as long as I remember." All three of my companions stand around the tree and marvel at its trunk. It has a big hole in the middle, "big enough for a cat to jump through" as Meeri says in wonder. "Yes, it might look a bit tired, but it is very vital," responds the old woman. The name of the tree sounds familiar—it is almost identical to Linnan Omena (castle apple). Kristiina takes some leaf samples to check its genetic profile.

This tree was not the one our guide was supposed to show us. The intent was for her to point our way to an apple tree called Alexander in the possession of an acquaintance of hers a few kilometers farther along. Accordingly, we get into the car again and pass for several minutes along the small serpentine roads winding past fields of crops. As we near the intended location, the guide starts to ponder where to find the tree: "Let me think a bit; I can't remember exactly." Suddenly, after a bend, a wooden summer house typical of the Finnish countryside emerges. The woman recognizes it: "Yes! The old main house was here, but it is gone. There's a new

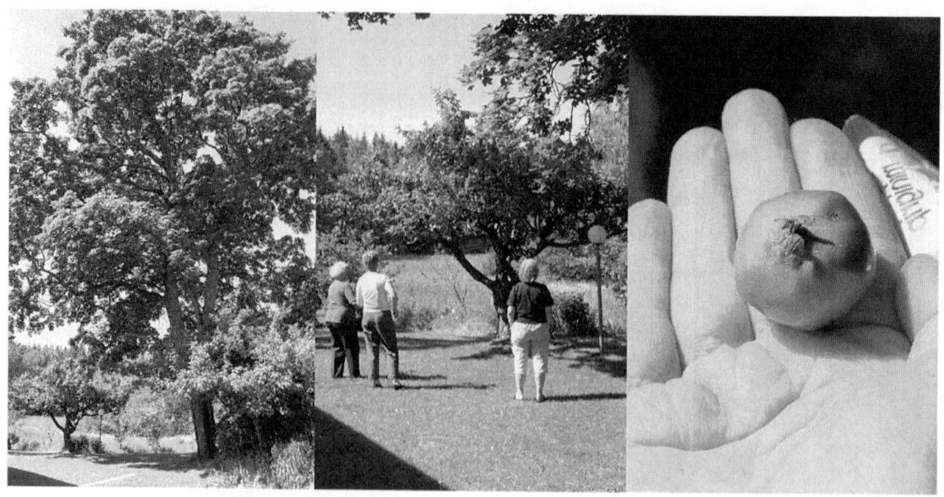

FIGURE 2.5 *Left to right:* The potential Alexander shadowed by a maple tree; the researchers and the local guide wondering at its vitality; and the samples collected. Photos by the author.

house on the premises." On driving by, we see that a small apple tree stands shadowed by an enormous maple in the backyard. Kristiina parks the car in the front garden of the house. Nobody is home, but our guide tells us that she has asked permission to go and take samples from the tree.

Meeri, Kristiina, and the local guide gather around the tree to evaluate it. The first thing they note is that this tree must be very vital to survive right beside an enormous maple—its yearly growth, according to the tips of the branches, is at least twenty centimeters. In addition, the roots and the trunk of the tree are in very good condition even if, according to our local expert, some of the branches have been pruned incorrectly. Kristiina collects some sample leaves and picks an apple. She seems surprised. She shows me what she thinks is the most important and interesting characteristic: the shape of the apple. It is pentagonal, as are all the apples. This is how the Alexander's apples should be—clearly different from the ones produced by the Linnan Omena, which are perfectly round. Kristiina thinks that she might have finally found a true Alexander.

When I ask the local horticulturist how she knows the tree and where it came from, she replies that her memory extends back to at least three generations of people who have lived in this farm estate area. She claims that it is the oldest farm in the community and that the tree has been there as far back as she remembers.

> It sounds as if this Alexander probably came here from Russia. There was an old tradition that every house built had its own apple tree. Even in the yards of the navvy houses there was, and had to be, an apple tree. The workers had it in their contract that they are allowed to use the apples together with the gentry. This is why the navvy men carried their own seedlings with them when they moved around for jobs.

After the sampling is finished, we take our elderly guide back to her house and thank her for her help. The field work in Lohjansaari continues for a few more hours yet, during which Kristiina and Meeri find other trees that have given Kristiina problematic readings in the laboratory. By the end of the day, we are back at the laboratories of MTT with fresh apple tree samples waiting for fingerprinting.

Finding a live rooting and a corporeal presence in the backyard of a summer house in Finnish territory generates the potential for national/international naturalization of the Alexander as a native genetic resource: the tree is now found in situ, fulfilling one of the conditions set for genetic resources in the CBD. However, the Alexander still needs to be biotechnologically recognized as a Finnish apple variety. This is because a political treaty such as the CBD does not simply override the potent technique of genetic fingerprinting and that process's truth claims about objects of nature. Rather, the CBD as a political instrument and fingerprinting as a technoscientific practice coproduce national genetic resources in a concerted manner. The Alexander is still only a proposition, for the binding connections between its molecular profile and its genetic belonging—together producing a true genetic resource—are crafted somewhere other than in the backyard of the summer house.

CHANGING SPACES AND CREATING MATTERING LOCATIONS

The identification technique known as genetic fingerprinting requires both a well-set-up laboratory and the right research samples if it is to work out correctly. Initially developed for identifying differences in the human genome (Jeffreys et al. 1985a; 1985b), it quickly became a tool for identifying the diversity of nonhuman life. For some years, this laboratory technique has been considered legitimate as a de facto method of producing true genetic identities (DNA profiles) for native species within the global genetic-resource programs (Ruane and Sonnino 2006). With fingerprinting the identification of the natives has shifted from morphological characteristics of living beings (e.g., the shape of the apple) to their molecular composition

(DNA profiles), which is considered a more accurate way to define their true identity. Similarly, with this technique the actual work of identifying living entities has been relocated from the field to the laboratory.

The laboratory where the Alexander's genetic identification takes place is one floor down from Kristiina's office in the MTT headquarters building. To demonstrate how she identifies the molecular identity of the apples, Kristiina has agreed to take me along as her helping hand in the DNA profiling of the samples collected three months earlier in Lohjansaari. As we enter the laboratory, an audible background hum from the large refrigerators fills the otherwise silent space. After taking a quick look at her laboratory notebook, Kristiina opens one of the refrigerators, and she takes out small plastic bags containing the collected leaves and some special liquids. She writes down an abbreviation for the samples in her notebook. These begin with the name of the collection site (*LS* for Lohjansaari), and the next two letters are taken from the name of the tree (*AL* for Alexander). Thus, the Alexander found on the last collection trip becomes *LSAL*. These IDs are copied onto test tubes with a marker. After this, Kristiina takes a leaf from the corresponding plastic bag and puts it into the tube. She explains, "The first step is to extract DNA from the leaves. The extraction process with plants is a bit trickier than with animals since you have to break the structure of the cell walls, which animal cells don't have. So I add small metal balls and special sand together with a buffer liquid to the tube to help us in that task." After filling the tube with this mixture, Kristiina puts it in an automatic shaking machine. After a minute's heavy shaking, the previously green, frozen leaves have disintegrated into a gray mass. The cell walls have now been disrupted, making the extraction of DNA possible.

The lengthy protocol for DNA preparation from frozen plant leaves starts like this with many more transformations of the mixed substance lying ahead. Most of the laboratory techniques are hard to standardize (Cambrosio and Keating 1988; Lynch 2002), but still some of them are capitalizable as general guidelines and laboratory products (Rabinow 1992; Jordan and Lynch 1998). Genetic fingerprinting is one of the many heavily capitalized techniques that are well packaged into laboratory products and set protocols. Kristiina uses these packages, and the extraction process runs in accordance with a standardized and commercialized protocol (Qiagen's DNeasy kit).[8] Before the day is out she will transform the gray liquid masses in the tubes, step by step, into clear, transparent liquids. A number of preparations, including introducing new liquids in each step (buffers and precipitation mixtures), mixing using various techniques, changing temperatures several times (or incubating), centrifuging, washing, and filtering the liquids in the tubes during the process, are constantly transforming the substance. The result of more than four hours' intensive work is ten tubes of transparent liquid—the pure DNA in surrounding buffer liquid—alongside thirty numbers written on a notepad and a large pile of plastic waste (pipette tips, used tubes, and empty bottles from the various liquids).

The extraction procedure ends so late in the afternoon that Kristiina decides to postpone the actual profiling work until early the next day. Additional transformations of the extracted and purified DNA are needed for the correct generation of the genomic locations that are used for the fingerprint. Genetic profiling depends on the segmentation of the genome, or on the identification of DNA markers. This identification involves a technique for selecting, copying, and measuring segments of a genome for various analytical purposes. The importance of DNA markers as indicators of identity (or difference) lies in their length: markers can vary from one base pair up to long repeats of a certain combination of base-pair letters. In genetic conservation practices, the markers used are usually located in the noncoding regions of the genome, referring to locations that are not known to be coding any protein. This is done to counter the possible effects of natural (or artificial) selection favoring a particular genetic makeup and to obtain more objective readings of molecular similarity between individual organisms. Because they are not considered a gene segment of the genome in everyday lab talk, the markers are called "junk DNA" (see Y. Li et al. 2002). The markers that Kristiina is using in her analysis of apples are single-sequence repeats (SSRs), also called microsatellites. These are groups of instances (containing one to six nucleotides) of certain base-pair combinations—for example, the A-T combination—that appear repeatedly in tandem in some parts of the genome (e.g., ATATATATAT). Markers are good if they have resolution power—that is, if they yield enough information about the genome for drawing inferences about its molecular composition. There are several reasons that SSRs are good at this.

First, they are considered polymorphic, meaning that the number of repeated nucleotide motifs varies greatly between individuals. This means they are good locations in the genome in which to search for differences between apple trees. Second, microsatellites are also capable of displaying allelic differences in polyploid organisms: two sets of microsatellites make up a diploid organism's genotype at a particular locus since it has two copies of the chromosomes in each cell. For each microsatellite locus in the genome, two units of information are gathered by one microsatellite assay in a diploid organism; two alleles yield two marker copies that might be similar (homozygous) or dissimilar (heterozygous). Third, SSRs are convenient to use since they are PCR based. The PCR (polymerase chain reaction) approach is a well-established technique that did nothing less than revolutionize the molecular sciences in providing means of amplifying segments of DNA quickly and easily. The amplification of segments has, in turn, provided tools for easier identification of molecular composition (Rabinow 1992). Finally, microsatellites are also readily located in a genome. Every SSR has a unique primer-sequence pair—the repeated location itself is surrounded on both sides by identifiable repeats of base pairs. In short, for most conservation geneticists, microsatellites are the marker of choice for studying the genetic profiles of nonhuman living beings and identifying individuals among them (Gianfranceschi et al. 1998).

Kristiina has given me the task of dividing the DNA into ten sample wells on a PCR plate, one for each microsatellite marker assay, and adding other liquids to them. The monotonous DNA pipetting of a full plate—one hundred wells multiplied by the number of other ingredients going into the assay (water, dNTP, buffer liquid, the reverse and forward primers, and microsatellite dyes)—is tiring, and with the rubber gloves my hands start to grow uncomfortable quite soon. After an hour I am finally ready. Kristiina takes the plate and seals the wells with a plastic coating to prevent the evaporation of small quantities of liquids and puts the whole plate into the PCR machine. Two hours later, the machine stops. Kristiina opens the machine, takes out the plate, peels the plastic seal off, dilutes some of the assays (wells) with water to match the calculated concentration with others, seals the plate again, and covers it with aluminum foil. She says, "OK, now the plate is ready. We've hopefully multiplied to the desired DNA fragments—our markers, that is—and now we are going to take this to the MegaBACE to read out the results of our assays." We drive across the research campus and give the plate to the operator of the sequencing machine. The next morning the results appear on the network drive of Kristiina's computer, to which the MegaBACE analyzer operator has copied them.

The MegaBACE is a capillary sequence analyzer, a machine that now does the real work of genetic sequencing, or genotyping, that provides for visual representations of genetic profiles. In the machine, the liquid mixture containing DNA, primers for microsatellite markers, and dyes for optical recognition is sucked into small-diameter capillaries in which the molecules within the liquid move at different rates, depending on their molecular mass—bigger molecules move more slowly than small ones. The dye included in the mixture attaches itself to a certain part of the amplified DNA (microsatellite), and the hybrid molecule is optically read by a laser beam once it passes a certain location in the capillary. This produces various readings that are translated into particular graphical representations on Kristiina's computer screen. She clicks on the visual analysis program for the sequencing, and the program displays some scales and lines with peaks plotted on them. The graphical representations are called electropherograms. "Here, you can see the markers. They produce the peaks we see now on my screen. All we have to do is assess where they occur for each of our apple trees," she explains. The visual traces on the screen are taken to indicate the length of the sliced, amplified, and dyed location of the genome in numbers of base pairs. Kristiina goes on to explicate that the visual peaks must, however, be interpreted correctly. Not only are the extraction and multiplication of DNA required but so are its visual representation and correct interpretation in order to make sense of the data within the new space of the Alexander's representation.

Incessant articulation work is required in the creation of mattering locations—the laboratory as a relational space and genetic markers as amplified locations of the genome—as has been argued by many in STS. What is more important for my argument, however, is that at this point in the process of identification, the ontological base for a nonhuman nationhood shifts as the modalities of its representation change: new locations come to matter as locations capable of representing national identity. It is here that we see how "it is 'inside' the laboratory that those master signifiers are generated and regenerated that ultimately gain the power of determining what it means to be scientific—or a broader—culture" (Rheinberger 1997, 37). The DNA markers as master signifiers of genetic identity themselves become observable only in a laboratory, and it is here that larger disputes about cultural heritage are decided in a technological manner: is the tree that we found in Lohjansaari a true Alexander or not?

In the process, the spaces themselves also transform into something else from what Kristiina started out with. Within the process, the noncoding neutral junk DNA, as a particular location along the genome, becomes politically charged. It is the junk DNA as a novel mattering location along the genome that starts to code for a nationhood, thereby reversing the well-known claim that Hans-Jörg Rheinberger has presented about current molecular technologies. For him, the "momentum of gene technology is based on the prospects of an intracellular representation of extracellular projects—the potential of rewriting 'life'" (Rheinberger 2000, 19). In other words, what happens within the process of generating these master signifiers is a dual process: the attribution of markers with the political capacity to represent nationhood and the renaturalization of nationhood through them. As much as the genetic fingerprinting and the creation of genetic resources are processes of rewriting life, with the extracellular project of global politics reinforcing the ideology of nationalism, it is also a technoscientific project of rewriting nationhood through the identification of national nonhuman life in its intracellular, molecular forms. What is at stake here is a reconfiguration of the relationship between the problematic concepts of "life" and "nationhood" understood as "nature" and "culture" (I will consider this relationship in more detail in chapter 3). This is a symmetrical event affecting the categories of both nature and nation flowing from the global politics of natural resources that have been put into practice by contemporary technoscientific practices. How exactly this process is completed is a question of other generative relations—the rerooting of the Alexander in a novel area of technoscience that is capable of creating new national populations and differentiating them from foreign ones.

THE TREE OF TREES AND THE INVERSION OF TEMPORALITY

A dual shift in the spaces of representation is the first requirement for the national rerooting of the uprooted tree. It is this that makes possible the generation of the new markers of identity. However, DNA's extraction, the amplification of its particular locations, its sequencing, and the correct interpretation of the graphical peaks is not enough to identify the trees with their novel genetic profiles. The correct spike readings must be taken down as numbers indicating their length, and the difference between the microsatellite readings must be calculated. After Kristiina's interpretation work dealing with the graphical peaks and their corresponding numbers, the differences between the Alexander and the Linnan Omena are witnessed by three markers: numbers one, four, and seven all exhibit a difference.

These readings are entered in another computer program to calculate their molecular difference. The program is called MEGA 3.1, from "molecular evolutionary genetics analysis." Using statistical methods, it calculates how different the sets of microsatellite readings are from each other. Several forms of output are possible from this calculation, most of them variations of models showing the molecular relations of discrete samples in the continuous form of a tree. The possibility of choosing from among various tree forms involves not just selection from among particular visualization techniques. More than that, the visualization itself is a calculation that provides different ways of representing the similarity between the samples and, as such, is central to how the kinship is grounded in biodiversity statistics and categories behind them (Bowker 2000). Kristiina wants to

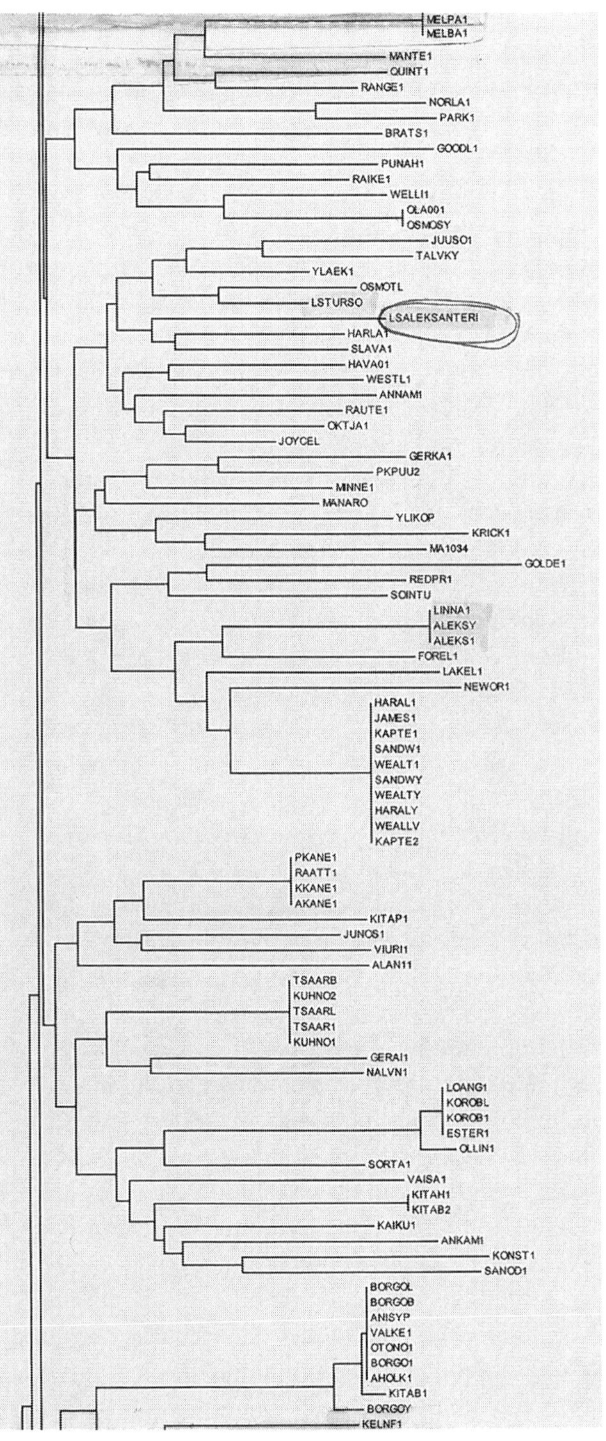

FIGURE 2.6 The Alexander's position in the national apple tree population calculated with microsatellite markers.

represent the result of the calculation as a neighbor-joining phylogenetic tree in order to see the branching of apple varieties in visual form (as shown in fig. 2.6). This tree figure represents their genetic distance as indicated by the molecular markers. The closer the cultivars are on the branches of the tree, the closer they are genetically, and vice versa. If they lie on the same branch, they are considered identical in molecular terms. This was the page on which our story about the Alexander's original nationality began.[9]

The selected tree topography, used to sort out duplicate apples going by different names, represents true genetic individuals as differing branches. What it also does is perform their unification as a new national population as genetic resources, confirming or denying their political mandate as natural beings within the initial national mandate list. It is this tree of trees that finally identifies them as a population of national genetic resources consisting of genetic individuals. These calculations therefore form novel genetic relations between previously discrete apple trees (Strathern 2005) and reroot them in the nation through the generation of genetic belonging. While this is a straightforward argument at a general level, the more important question to consider is what kinds of rerooting mechanisms this new figure offers and what constitutes the basis for the nationhood of the individual genetic beings in these molecular practices.

First, within the identification process, the temporality of national identification is reoriented from historical narratives to the time of the laboratory. Even if the name of the computer program includes the word "evolutionary," the calculation that produces the novel relations between the samples does not have anything to do with evolution as a process or with evolutionary time scales. The calculations performed in Kristiina's office for the microsatellite sets are based on apple tree samples that have been tentatively identified as Finnish from between 2004 and 2007. The temporal difference between the first and the last samples is three years, reducing the time scale to the span over which the samples belonging to the newly created population were gathered, processed, and genetically identified. Second, the computer-based calculation itself takes several seconds, and the molecular relations of the trees are formed almost instantaneously. Therefore, there is nothing evolutionary in the calculation: the relational difference—the molecular relationship of the trees—is based on novel techniques and statistical methods that have nothing to do with evolution as an explanatory theory nor with evolution as a process. Instead, the relation is enacted through the political mandate given to population scientists such as Kristiina to gather a novel population of apple genetic resources within the national programs.

As a result of this calculation, the phylogenetic tree produced here is different from the one represented by Charles Darwin in his *On the Origin of Species* ([1859] 1996) and is more akin to earlier temporal planes based on the fixity of character represented by classical natural history (Foucault 1966). Interestingly, recent theorization on kinship has claimed that genes and genetic markers function also as new units of genealogy (S. Franklin et al. 2000; S. Franklin and McKinnon 2001) and thus as signs of historical, genealogical lineages. While this is certainly correct, it is definitely not the genes or the markers based on laboratory-processed genetic material that are the cause of that linkage. There is nothing in them that per se causes the genealogical temporal orientation to be the explanatory principle behind similarity and difference, kinship, or national belonging. Otherwise, it would be impossible that genetic markers are here made to perform precisely the opposite function: they reorient the temporal explanation about national origins to the fact of the national present that is created in the laboratory. The genetic connectivity, a national kinship between the trees, is a new, instantaneously lateral one (Helmreich 2003) that is identical to the immanent, organismic, and transversal community performed in the second temporality of the theory of nation in the context of human populations (Benjamin 1968; B. Anderson [1983] 1991; Chatterjee 1998). This new temporality of gathering nonhuman populations under the name of the nation is made possible by the global politics of nature inscribed in the CBD instead of a kinship based on their genealogical lineage and its downward orientation to temporality (Kay 1993). Within this temporal reorientation, the historical narrative as a source and medium for representing the true nationhood of the apples is replaced with the laboratory-produced markers.

Second, the individual identity of the Alexander—and with it, its national belonging—is constructed through two relational differences. The markers differentiating the Alexander from other national trees confirm its individual trueness as a genetic being, a subnational difference created through genetic fingerprinting techniques. The tree now stands on its own branch of the phylogenetic figure and is considered distinct by its molecular makeup from the Linnan Omena and others listed in the national population. However, its national belonging, similar to that of other trees on the initial mandate lists, is created by another relation of difference: the standardized (Timmermans 1997; Berg and Timmermans 2000) genetic difference from foreign apples that is made possible by supranational reference trees.

Several working markers for apples have been developed in recent years, and Kristiina has decided to use those that are readily available. For her national identification program, she selected ten markers that had been publicly tested and reportedly found by other scientists who work with apple trees to have good resolution capabilities and reproducibility (Gianfranceschi et al. 1998). The reason for the selection of these particular markers was at the same time related to issues of comparability and standardization between laboratories. The same ones are in use in the Swedish genetic-resource identification programs, and in 2006 six of these markers were also selected for use in the Europe-wide European Cooperative Programme for Crop Genetic Resources for its total set of sixteen standard markers. Employing a set of markers that is identical to that used in Sweden makes it possible to compare the Swedish apple profiles (the twenty units of information yielded by the ten markers for each apple tree) with Kristiina's Finnish ones. Because Sweden is in many ways connected to Finland, most importantly historically and biogeographically, the shared set of markers is crucial for genetically distinguishing between samples with similar names that are found in both countries. The six identical markers within the European program—a number considered quite reliable for proving the possibility of identifying the unique genetic profiles of each country's apples—makes it possible to compare the samples with all other Europeans'.

There are problems with direct comparisons, however, even with standardized protocols and marker sets. Using these, each laboratory has consistently different results. Local adjustments, which are necessary for producing global comparability, are made with the aid of reference trees. Reference trees are acquired by taking leaf samples from the same tree and distributing them to laboratories with the aim of direct comparison with their results. The fingerprinting results from the reference tree are compared between laboratories, and any difference in base-pair length is then adjusted for accordingly in the analysis and evaluation of microsatellite readings.

Kristiina clarifies the collaboration between laboratories:

> According to our markers, the Alexander we found in the backyard and Linnan Omena are different apple trees. Good! We found the true Alexander then. Now we have to check that it really is a truly Finnish Alexander. I have here the marker readings from an Alexander found in Sweden, and I want to compare those with the ones from the Alexander we found. We have used the Åkerö tree as our reference material with the Swedes to find out just how much our microsatellite readings differ from each other. Our readings are off by plus-one to plus-three base pairs with these markers, so we have to adjust our

> readings accordingly. Ah . . . after these adjustments, our Alexander is different from the Swedish one. This really is a true Finnish Alexander, I would say! We'll keep it in the national mandate list after all.

Through these fingerprint analyses, the Alexander, as found in the backyard of the summer house in Lohja, becomes a proven (true) genetic resource, and Kristiina accepts it for the final mandate list of national apple trees. What becomes apparent in this process of difference creation is that it is a technoscientific reenactment of what Akhil Gupta and James Ferguson have argued is the central problem in modern national identification. In discussing possible ways in which nationhood today is made to matter, they claimed that "national identity needs to be understood against subnational ones and against supranational identities—and perhaps even against forms of imagining community that are not territorially based" (Gupta and Ferguson 1997b, 17). Alexander is a distinct genetic resource according to both subnational and supranational assessments of molecular difference. It is differentiated enough to be on the national mandate list; the existence of the two molecular differences equals national identity and affirms its new form of belonging through genetics. However complex the identification process might have been, it is not left ambivalently in the limbo of incomplete or uncompleted national identification. Instead, the Alexander, as with other genetic resources, becomes national through a multiplicity of relations of difference that mark their newly found nativity, a mode of existence belonging under a particular nation's sovereign dominion.

GENETIC RESOURCES AS EMERGING FORM OF NATIONAL LIFE

Genetic resources that are defined within genetic fingerprinting practices, as I have been attempting to illustrate with the case of the Alexander, assume different explanatory principles for their nonhuman nationality from the ones analyzed in the previous chapter on Finncattle. Most importantly, within these new practices, history as a narrative form of past temporality becomes gradually inverted and is finally erased as a principle of identification. The temporal *origo* of operations on which the identification of genetic material as national form of nonhuman life depends is reset and reoriented to the political time of the CBD and the time of laboratory practices. Previously used explanatory principles drawing on cultural histories and ecological evolution as causal explanations for national identity are replaced with others. The new principles erase the causal link between history (past temporalities) and molecular identity because of their temporal orientation. This new form of time is inherently interwoven with the new locations of identity creation, together forming a particular time-space or chronotope. Thus, extending genetic sovereignty over novel nonhuman forms of life involves a particular enactment of scientific time, one that is best captured by what Lily Kay has called the "molecular vision of life." This new vision of life, in her argument, operates thus:

> By cleaving life processes from their host organisms, the molecular biology program aimed to discover general physicochemical laws governing vital phenomena. In so doing, it distanced its concerns from emergent properties, from interactive processes occurring within higher organisms, between organisms (e.g., symbiosis) and between organisms and their environments, thus bracketing out of biological discourse a broad range of phenomena generally subsumed under the term "life." Concomitantly, this physicochemical approach bypassed historical explanations in biology and developmental and evolutionary accounts of life processes—the arrow of time. The new biology generally acknowledged only mechanisms of upward causation, ignoring the role of downward causation. (Kay 1993, 5)

Whatever "life" is in the science of molecular biology, its new principles of explanation have no connection to other organisms or environments within which they may be found or to what is generally called the in situ maintenance of an organism. The general history of organisms is erased, and the arrow of time finds its origo within the multitudes of practices of molecular science: time is always subject to local and specific sites and objects of research, and it loses its status as the key explanation (or hope) for unraveling the secrets of life. Time is arranged anew in relation to the organisms under study, and with it the accepted arrow of causation in explanation is also redefined. This is a very particular enactment of time as the empty time of nationhood and the molecular vision of nonhuman life become bound to each other inseparably. The sheer possibility of identifying genetic nationhood within the realms of nonhuman life is a matter of temporalities and causalities that flow with particular understandings of time.

If it is the case that the initial mandate list operates on the condition of success of the narrative and the biological, then it follows that the true national mandate list of genetic resources must make a detour through the laboratory on the route to its contents becoming technoscientifically recognized as genetically differentiated forms of the nonhuman life of a nation. This recognition then transforms the temporal order of the narrative, the biological, and the molecular by recalculating their mutual relationship and enabling new forms of collective life: the genetic resources. Here, the laboratory and the molecular become obligatory passage points (Callon 1986) in their formation. This is why the true mandate list including the Alexander, as confirmed by the laboratory, is endowed not only with political and cultural power but with powers of reordering temporalities. The practices of genetic fingerprinting assume and unfold in a particular time—the time of nonhuman genetic resources—through which other temporalities are now made to pass.

In addition, while the well-known theories of nation and nationalism (B. Anderson [1983] 1991; Gellner 1983; Smith 1986) hold that the very idea of nationhood depends on a unified (at least imagined), coherent culture linked to a territorial soil, the locations and the nature of the linkage to a national identification are what become radically redefined with fingerprinting practices. Clifford (1988; 1996), writing about the problematic relationship between locality and culture, between nativity and displacement as forms of identity in a world where mobility is more rule than exception, stated that the old idea of roots cannot account any longer for more complicated, much more heterogeneous and well-traveled figures of a native—such as the Alexander. The problem of the location of culture (Bhabha 1994) linking locality and culture, thereby rooting nationality in territorial soil, has been a matter of central debate in cultural studies and anthropology for the past two decades. The volumes of research on the topic have shown how these problematic links are best understood as strategic relations that are performed for the making of nationhood in boundary- or identity-making processes (e.g., Rosaldo 1986; Abu-Lughod 1991; Strathern 1991; Friedman 1994; Clifford 1996). This problem becomes once again mutated here.

In the making of genetic resources through fingerprinting practices, the national identification of Alexander is dislocated from textual accounts and from the morphological character of the apple. It is relocated to the junk DNA that codes its national identity and the relational difference produced by the national and international networks of fingerprinting laboratories. Thus, the topos of national identification shifts from a rooting in national soil to the curious relational space of molecular markers and the networks of technoscience. This topological shift of ontology marks the uprooting of nationhood from the biological and its rerooting in the globally molecular. Here nonhuman nationhood is not so much indeterminate as multiply relational—genetically grounded relational nationhood need not be any more ambiguous than any other identity. Rather, it is these novel relations of difference that create a new identity in contrast to the discovery of a primordial nationhood that is embodied by the apples.

The claims of national genetic sovereignty lead us to consider the problem of scientific legitimation against the background of larger changes in the production of scientific authority between differently located biological sciences themselves. Robert Kohler's (2002) study of the invention of the border between the field and laboratory sciences of biology in the late nineteenth to early twentieth centuries suggests that this era saw the place of reliable knowledge production shift slowly from the field (ecological sciences) to the laboratory (e.g., molecular sciences). The invention of the lab-field border produced not two separate, discrete fields but rather intertwined border regions, where a mixture of distinct but recognizable different practices prevailed. In the story of the Alexander we see how the old ways of forming relations between territory, soil, and national forms of life are played out in these intertwined borders as well. I have shown the constant back-and-forth movement between the laboratory and the field and between various literary inscriptions and types of corporeal evidence. It is neither the narrative traces nor the actual biological rooting that can link the Alexander to the soil it is rooted in; instead, the rooting must be done by another tree, the national tree of trees from which it finds its novel arborescent form as one of the national branches. This tree can only be produced by molecular techniques, whereas (as in the case of Finncattle) previously it could be formed literally in the fields (as, analogously, in the cattle exhibitions) and through the forming of genealogical trees with the principle of filial (temporal) descent.

In contrast, then, to the phylogenetic tree's normal use as a figure of genealogy, it becomes a representation of the arrested development of life—not one of genealogical lineage but one of contemporary molecular difference providing the grounds for the identification of true genetic beings. The national population gathered through the tree is based on a new and agenealogical kinship (Helmreich 2003) created through instances of junk DNA that start to code nationhood, establishing a new mediator between the domains of nature and culture. Therefore, the rerooting of the uprooted and well-traveled tree cultivars in their new national identity can only happen in the laboratory within the space of difference that national and international laboratories afford with their standardized set of markers. Accordingly, the position for speaking the truth (Foucault 1966) about the apples as national genetic resources moved from the field to the laboratory. Importantly, with the case of the Alexander we see not only how all history is the history of the present but how a particular version of the history of national apples is rewritten through the laboratory. The result—the mandate list—is a novel version of the natural history of Finland. Thus, the time of genetic resources is a particular articulation of the political time of the CBD, with the time assumed by the practices of molecular biology within the novel spaces of representation that it entails: the laboratory, the molecular markers, and the calculation represented as phylogenetic tree. Here, the phylogenetic tree cuts the individual trees away from their genealogy and identifies them as part of the self-vindicating (Hacking 1992) technoscientific network of conservation genetics that is working with the political authority to represent national nonhuman forms of life.

These two changes—in the temporal causation and the modes of authorized rooting in territory—have made possible the emergence of national genetic resources as scientific objects of knowledge: they are identifiable while older principles of explanation stemming from the sciences of evolution or ecological biology are not seen as legitimated. Their temporal orientation to the past, or a downward causation, can be ignored. History as a form of scientific conjecture cannot legitimate molecular identities, so the claims about the historical origins and dispersion of forms of life beyond national territorial boundaries can be ignored. Still, conservation genetics needs an orientation in terms of its spaces and times of operation in order to define the source for its will to knowledge. Interestingly, the legitimation of nativity as a category of identification leading to the emergence of national genetic resources is to be found outside science, in the process that politically authorized conservation genetics as the science for performing their corporeal definition and identification—with the CBD itself. A redefinition of time and causality that is identical to that in molecular biology occurred within the international politics of nature with the introduction of the CBD.

The CBD deals with genetic resources belonging under the sovereign dominion of a country of origin after 1992, thereby politically excluding both ex situ collections and genetic resources transported from their assumed country of origin before ratification. The Conference of the Parties, the political instrument by which the implementation of the CBD is steered at the international level, noted already in its second meeting in 1995 with its provisional agenda's article 59 that "Article 15.3 of the Convention defines 'genetic resources being provided by a Contracting Party' to mean 'only those that are provided by Contracting Parties that are countries of origin of such resources or by the Parties that have acquired the genetic resources in accordance with this Convention.'"[10] Since the contracting parties (signatory nation-states) cannot, as such, preexist the contract itself, their status as countries of origin and/or parties that have acquired the genetic resources is acknowledged only after ratification. In short, the global category of nations as countries of origin in the CBD is the performative outcome of the ratification of the contract itself and does not have a relation to, say, the countries of origin as understood by ecologists or system biologists.

It is true that the CBD urges the ratifying states to carry out "the protection of ecosystems, natural habitats and the maintenance of viable populations of species in natural surroundings," but it does not juridically bind them to doing so. Thus, the CBD promotes the ecosystem- and species-level planning of practical conservation practices. But—and this is the key point—it only politico-juridically orders national genetic resources, and it orders them into discrete national categories by their post-1992 territorial location. In a manner identical to molecular science's orientation to time, the CBD disregards the other types of time (for example, a historical or evolutionary time scale) and so erases any political ownership claims to genetic resources made prior to 1992. The political time of the global contract flows in only one direction, from the temporal origo of the ratification act toward the future, and (scientific) explanations about their historical linkages through evolution, deliberate (dis)placements by humans, and other causes pointing to time before the contract are not acknowledged as valid (politico-juridical) arguments as to the nationhood (or not) of a genetic resource.

Writing to counter Benedict Anderson's ([1983] 1991) and Homi Bhabha's (1994) arguments about the power of indecisiveness in the formation of modern Western nationhoods, Sarah Franklin, Celia Lury, and Jackie Stacey (2000, 75) have claimed, "in contrast, that emergent global networks offer the chosen—or, rather, choice itself—as the origin of the imagined community of global citizenship; indeed they render choice itself a necessity." While they spoke about the global consumer and the naturalization of the compulsory choice within the global network, the very same argument about locating the national origins can be advanced in the case of the Alexander in particular and of global genetic resources in general. Identifying genetic resources as objects of governance is a national and international political choice: all the signatory countries have internationally agreed to the task of identifying their national genetic resources, and in order to become global citizens in the family of nations of the UN, they are also obliged by the contract to do so. This political choice, along with all the other selections that go with it, is naturalized by the act of ratifying the contract.

In the years after its ratification, the CBD is not only the political naturalization of the autonomous status of genetic resources, locating them under the sovereign rule of nation-states and pertaining to their territorial genetic natures; it is also a choice of science—politically identifying and delegating the molecular sciences that are capable of identifying genetic resources and thus naturalizing them as scientifically valid objects of knowledge. In the end, then, the political transforms into a scientific choice,[11] scientifically choosing the genetic resources by inherently nationalizing them and motivating the action narrated in the story of the Alexander. This is not just a political choice, then. It is a choice that ultimately depends on the possibility of imagining the political as corporeal, of imagining national genetic resources that are part of national natural resources as identifiable, discrete, and self-sufficient entities—in other words, they are genetically sovereign nation-natures, or an entangled semiotic-material effect of international politics and conservation genetics. The very possibility of genetic sovereignty both as imagined political ordering and as corporeally identifiable genetic material depends on good articulation between the two truth-speaking regimes in terms of the required rearrangements of space and time: the very possibility of the choice and selection and, finally, the good articulation of national origins between molecular science and global politics over nature. It is, then, to paraphrase Kay, the molecular vision of nationhood, a vision that emerges out of the CBD itself, that gives the time of genetic autonomy its particular character.

Accordingly, one can summarize the argument presented in this chapter as follows: national genetic resources become possible through the interstices of novel relations—as objects of knowledge, they are not what ecologists and system biologists understand by the concept of genetic resources, nor are they equivalent or reducible to a biological-material understanding of genes or genomes. They cannot be reduced to either simply because the event they bring into being consists of a particular configuration between science and politics. The politico-scientific autonomy of national genetic resources pertains as much to the scientific means of conservation genetics as to the international agreement warranting this science that corporeally defines and creates them.

As new temporalities of the global politics of nature and conservation genetics operate on the principle of an upward causation, historical explanations are deterritorialized, and biological root systems are uprooted, only for them to be reterritorialized and rerooted through the new time-spaces of national representation of nonhuman life. This is the contemporaneity of the laboratory and the molecular, of the international network of laboratories and the novel subnational relations between previously discrete biological beings. A rearrangement of the national and the natural occurs as novel objects of national representation emerge: a novel chronotope of genetic sovereignty becomes discernible. It is only within this chronotope, and the generative relations it consists of, that the Alexander becomes its figuration as a genetic being, as a national genetic resource, as a national embodiment of genetic sovereignty. Genetic sovereignty, then, is a new assemblage of the natural and the cultural, here of novel calculation between the nonhuman genetic beings and Finnish society—a new ethical plateau and complex terrain of scientific decision making.

In this chapter we have seen how novel objects come into being with practices that occur in a very particular field of relations of genetic sovereignty. The next chapter takes a closer look at how the laboratory practices themselves are not only warranted by the politics of the CBD but also traversed by new rationalities reconfiguring economic, ecological, and national considerations. In the case of the Alexander, we have seen how the in situ condition paradoxically does not root the new genetic entities in their native soil and how, instead, complex spatio-temporal rearrangements are necessary for doing so. Similarly, when one considers genetic resources ex situ, or in the particular mode of their being that is usually called the gene bank, a complex articulation between economic, ecological, and national practices comes to the fore: a thematic variation of biopolitics presents itself and calls into question some of the old ways of capitalizing on nonhuman life. This new biopolitics in the post-CBD world relies on a form of rationality that I analyze in the next chapter, indicating the emergence of a novel vital corporeality and biobanking infrastructure via the technique of cryopreservation.

CHAPTER 3 stilled life: animal gene banks and new infrastructures of life

Where would biotechnology be if after being spliced or frozen or fused or extracted from its original environment, the cell or organism just up and died?

—HANNAH LANDECKER, "CULTURING LIFE"

These technical matters are never socially neutral. . . . Considerations of harvesting, biovaluable engineering, storage, and distribution are also political considerations.

—CATHY WALDBY AND ROBERT MITCHELL, *TISSUE ECONOMIES*

PREPARATIONS FOR A FIELD TRIP

I was arranging my field notes at the office when the phone rang. I barely had time to say hello before I heard an enthusiastic voice exclaim through the earpiece, "All the equipment I was waiting for has finally arrived! We should leave tomorrow." Before I could get a word in, the caller continued, "Let's meet at the office tomorrow morning at eight sharp, and you can to help me pack the car." On the other end of the line was Juha Kantanen, the coordinator of Finland's Animal Genetic Resources Programme, and the invitation was to join him in gathering material for the national sheep biobank. The excitement on his end was understandable; this would be the first ever trip for the biobanking of sheep material, and he would get to test his new biobanking field kit. For me, this collection journey turned out to be one of the key moments in my fieldwork: I would witness some of the intricate technical arrangements that had become accepted as reality and various reconfigurations of living materials that were needed to form animal biobanks in a project, all nested within a complex territory traversed by technical ecological considerations and global economic rationalities intersecting with national body politics.

Nonhuman life, plant and animal, is witnessing another reconfiguration of its corporeal existence. Perhaps one of the most prominent claims today is that of the informational character of genetic information. The current discourse of popularized life sciences regularly speaks of life as something calculable in its basic components; the base pairs found in the genome of any living organism provide for the easy counting of variations in the "book of life" (see Kay 2000 and others). It has not always been this way, and these developments are rippling through the epistemology of the informational paradigm with what has also been called the molecularization of life. As a result of these developments, Nikolas Rose, among others, claims, we have reached and passed the threshold of "life itself" becoming the object of "decision and choice" (Rose 2007, 40).[1]

Beneath the well-known surface of that claim are currents of other, equally radical reconfigurations that have been flowing within new global politics over nature in the past fifty years. Its seemingly simple words reveal several of the concomitant reconfigurations if only we stop to consider them: What ecological niche does the biobanked life we take for granted technically occupy? What economic considerations does it embody? And how does it all fit into a field of decisions aimed at the conservation of native national biological material? They also help us find parallels to new arrangements of human-derived materials of research and exchange (even beyond tissues of all kinds).[2] Hannah Landecker, for example, has noted how very much it is taken for granted that, thanks to the development of biotechnology, living matter is kept alive outside the body. Our wonder has been directed toward foregrounded genome-level research. She claims, "These disembodied, productive, replicating cells that are derived from human bodies but live in laboratories are new but also newly normal. It takes an anthropologist in the laboratory to note the strangeness of what has become quickly routinized or banal to its practitioner" (Landecker 2007, 3).

The first strangeness that we can point to in new laboratories with their new techniques lies in the way that biological substances are separated from bodies and inserted into new biotechnological envelopes that are capable of transcending spatio-temporal limitations of the original bodies. Generating this newly normal biological state of being requires advanced technical expertise and experience in taking the living substance out of its original context and keeping it alive outside those living bodies. These knowledge practices routinely go unnoticed today, for they are considered normal. The roots of these changes are found in the development of agricultural technologies, such as now-standard practices in animal breeding, which are themselves serving as baseline models for current reproductive technologies such as in vitro fertilization (IVF) within human animals (Clarke 1998; Franklin and Ragoné 1998; Franklin and Lock 2003). These reconfigurations are not locked within an information-based paradigm (that of genetic code); instead, they involve motion and mobility as central indicators of valuable life. They bring in what can be called intracellular and extracellular modalities of life. Here, motion and mobility are taken as objects of knowledge within the sciences of reproduction and as corporeal targets of related biotechnological interventions entangled with modern biopolitics of nonhuman life. Today, life—whether plant, animal, or cell life—is undergoing a transformation from being animation to being a cessation of this animation (Hayden 2003a; Landecker 2003; Lock 2003), suspension of the very essence of what was once considered to be living both at a corporeal level and in the politics targeting it. The cessation of animation in biobanking practice signals an important potential: it indicates the freezability of biological material. Freezability, in turn, enables the transformation of a biological substance into a technically managed, standardized, and easily circulated genetic commodity. This is a new modality of vital nonhuman corporealities, *a stilled life*, and a novel bio-object. It is material for a number of agro-bio-technological knowledge practices on the global scale. The cessation of animation is nowhere more present than in the genetic resources and their banking.

The second strangeness in these newly normalized bodies and practices—and the reason to pay closer attention to these kinds of biotechnological reconfigurations—is that many biological operations that are considered to be of value today would not be possible without living biobanked substances. What is captured in stills, a collection of microscope slides, can be reanimated largely as desired and can potentially be exchanged within the circuits of novel bioeconomies. Catherine Waldby and Robert Mitchell have succinctly described what makes such a difference when life is treated as informatics rather than as living substance and why the latter is such an important and valuable asset. They claim that "unlike genetic information, which can be stored and manipulated in the durable form of computer data, . . . tissues are an exhaustible resource, whose value or utility could be lost with poor management. They require marshalling and oversight, economy in the archaic sense of 'husbandry'" (Waldby and Mitchell 2006, 33). Further, value that is derived from living materialities and bodily substances is dependent on the economic infrastructure in which they are inserted as bodies that are capable of generating and sustaining value through various networks of circulation where exchanges are made. Hence, Waldby and Mitchell continue, "these technical matters are never socially neutral" in that matters of "harvesting, biovaluable engineering, storage, and distribution are also political considerations" (Waldby and Mitchell 2006, 33). This is also true for genetic resources falling under the aegis of the CBD and the Nagoya Protocol.

At an economic level, recent transformations in the bioeconomies based on gene-banked forms of life and its governance are well noted in the ongoing arguments about biovalue and biowealth in the larger discourses of (human) biopolitics and related forms of governmentality (e.g., Sunder Rajan 2006; Gottweis and Petersen 2008; Santoro 2009). Here, one of the major transformations has been described as a shift from the actuality to the potentiality of life,[3] or from simple biological beings that are capable of being and reproducing to beings that are capable of both novel biological and cultural generation. I claim that within earlier discourses the transformation was understood mainly as a nonmattering generative potentiality as expectations and/or symbolic value (Martin et al. 2006; N. Brown et al. 2006; N. Brown 2007), a capitalist form of creating virtual value for new forms of life through the expected breakthroughs, the gaming of stock markets, and the exploitation of other volatile mechanisms of transforming biowealth into capital. In other words, not only current biological research but also recent social and cultural analysis has tended to treat disembodied bio-objects and related knowledge practices as newly normal. The interactions between new disembodied vital substances, their innovated technical ecologies, and complex politically infused economic mechanisms in the *coproduction* of novel bioeconomies have been left largely unexplored at the empirical level. This is why new configurations of disembodied corporealities and the knowledge practices that go into producing them need to be brought back into focus and taken as a starting point for the analysis of how bioeconomies work today. Without technically managed biological substances, bioeconomies would not exist in the first place. The question of bioeconomic value generation therefore becomes articulated in a new way—how does the potential value of genetic resources get actualized in the corporeality of the gene-banked material, and how is this value conditioned by the political economy surrounding it?

Finally, however important these economic mechanisms at large are, they do not suffice for explaining how it is that new corporeal configurations of life-under-management, or forms of nature "enterprised-up" (Strathern 1993), are generated in the post-CBD world. The third strangeness is that the rationality behind creating national biobanks within genetic-resource conservation programs that are operating with the mandate of the CBD cannot be reduced to purely technical ecological considerations nor to the maximization of economic processes as once suggested by Foucault, whose argument has been amplified by recent inquiry into new forms of biowealth (e.g., Heller and Escobar 2003; Sunder Rajan 2006; S. Franklin 2007b). Instead, the rationality is also based on the maximization of pure difference within nonhuman life in the name of conserving the unique natural genetic components of the nation in its territory.

Within these three intersecting rationalities, the economic, the ecological, and the national are translated to strategies, justifications, and concrete practices that together constitute gene banking within genetic-resource programs. These dovetailing rationalities also enact corporeal changes, or, more precisely, a number of variations, in the quasi-natural figure of the natural (nonhuman) populations that constitute nations. Outside the corporeal, the intersecting rationalities have significant effects on how the derivation of value from these new populations can (or cannot) take place with genetic material that is considered native to a nation.

The core observations in this chapter come from the empirical work I did on that first national gene-banking trip back in 2005. The life to be arrested was of Finnsheep, a native sheep breed of Finland. As with Finncattle, the Finnsheep has been one of the symbols of national life and natural grounding for national identity. The trip was part of a project to construct the first gene bank of Finnsheep from the very best national genetic material available. In this chapter, I look in detail at the practices through which life causes the kind of novel national bio-object described above to come to life within the intersecting rationalities. How are the rationalities of the individual truth regimes that are anchored in ecology, economy, and nation articulated within each other in the very corporeality of the conserved reproductive matter itself?

My aim is to show how the intertwining fields of rationalities involved in biodiversity conservation are transposed in connection with the material interests and become embodied in the genetic resources themselves while also uncovering how their creation is traversed by these all the way down to the biobanking techniques themselves. The rationalities—fields of reasoning in which certain aims, methods, and ends are seen as better than others—are not themselves given or static but are constantly negotiated in relation to other mobilized justifications (the reasons and interests behind them) for conserving particular species of nonhuman life in diverse corporeal forms.[4] In simpler terms, in gene banking the Finnsheep breed undergoes a signification transformation in its mode of being. Its very beingness as a form of nonhuman animal life changes in important ways (see Lynch 1988) when it is translated from its in situ condition to being an ex situ resource of the nation.[5] It becomes biologically a new form of life, a stilled life, whose very corporeality as a being becomes inseparably woven into the social, into the politicized technoscientific infrastructure that creates it and is aimed at producing various (and not only biocapitalist) generative effects through the reconfiguration of life as animality.

The chapter is an inquiry into the complexities of current practices and the resulting curiosity about the theoretical ways in which gene banking within conservation programs could be best described and understood. I believe, as do writers examining other contexts of new biology, that we require new analytical tools in order to disentangle the many threads that tie into the current understanding of nonhuman biopolitics. These should render us able to examine the engagements and rationalities behind the practices related to today's new forms of reproductive matter in all their complexity. These tools, largely missing in the context of gene banking in national conservation programs, are something we must create if we are to understand the unfolding future.

THE VALUE OF FINNSHEEP

On a cold Wednesday morning displaying the gray weather typical of a Finnish November, I arrive at the front doors of the rectangular building of the Animal Breeding Research Group (EJA) at MTT headquarters in Jokioinen. The group's car is parked with its trunk open just outside the doors. One of the group's scientists is packing it and hollers from the back of the car that I should go directly into the office. Walking through the entrance reveals that the preparations for the field trip have transformed the research group's facilities into chaos: instruments of various shapes and sizes, pieces of luggage, and brown boxes are piled in the hallway. I step into one of the offices and meet Dr. Kantanen, who is sitting behind his desk to compose some last-minute emails. "Hi," he hollers. "It's going to be an exciting week with sheep! Let me introduce you to my colleague." He is referring to Maciej Murawski, a seasoned conservation scientist who has done sperm banking for years. He will join us for the trip to teach and to oversee the technical tricks of the banking business.

The preparations have left more than the group's office space in disarray. The other members of the team seem a bit stressed, too—there is always somebody knocking on the door to ask for last-minute instructions. The overall atmosphere is one of excitement because this field trip is to be the first of its kind ever made in Finland's genetic-resource programs. The aim for the field work is to collect Finnish genetic material in a form that has never been collected before on a large scale: the gametes of Finnsheep rams. These sperm cells will be the first to acquire the status of officially banked Finnsheep genes and will represent the very purest national genetic patrimony in the form of frozen reproductive matter. They will act as the foundational material for the first national sheep gene bank.

I ask the reasons behind the gene banking, and Dr. Kantanen tells me to take a look at the brochures in the brown boxes. "They've just come from the printers," he says. He continues, smiling, "They're our PR leaflets." I take a fresh-smelling brochure from one of the boxes that is blocking the hallway as it waits to be loaded into the car. The top of the brochure reads in large letters, "FinnSheep. A Northern Speciality" (MTT 2005). Flipping through its four pages reveals some key aspects of the underlying rationalities for the establishment of a national sheep gene bank. For one thing, the brochure is marketing material directed to and disseminated through relevant stakeholders in the Finnsheep network: the sheep breeders, restaurants buying the animals' meat, the wool industry, and the larger public interested in the breed. But it is also an internal marketing exercise aimed at the higher-level political decision makers within the genetic-resource programs in that it stresses the patrimonial value of the sheep breed, one that is native to Finnish nature. To make one of its main points, the brochure says, "The Finnsheep is the native sheep breed of Finland. Over thousands of years, it has adapted to the rough climate of its Northern home country. The Finnsheep is part of the national memory, identity, and culture of Finland."

Historically, the idea and creation of Finnish sheep followed the same ideological trajectories as Finncattle—ecological and economic arguments intertwined and were used to legitimate the national agenda. The first thoughts surrounding Finnish landrace sheep, though, were expressed around the mid-nineteenth century when the Finnish local breeds were evaluated against the imported breeds used by the nobility. In 1850, for example, the newspaper *Countryman's Friend*, whose explicit mission was to publish agricultural news and research and to spread the Finnish national spirit to fellow countrymen, reviewed the state of Finnish sheep farming. The article stated that national difference is easily spotted and that the Finnish sheep should not be confused with others, especially not with the sheep of the nobility, which stand in contrast to the real "countrymen's" sheep:

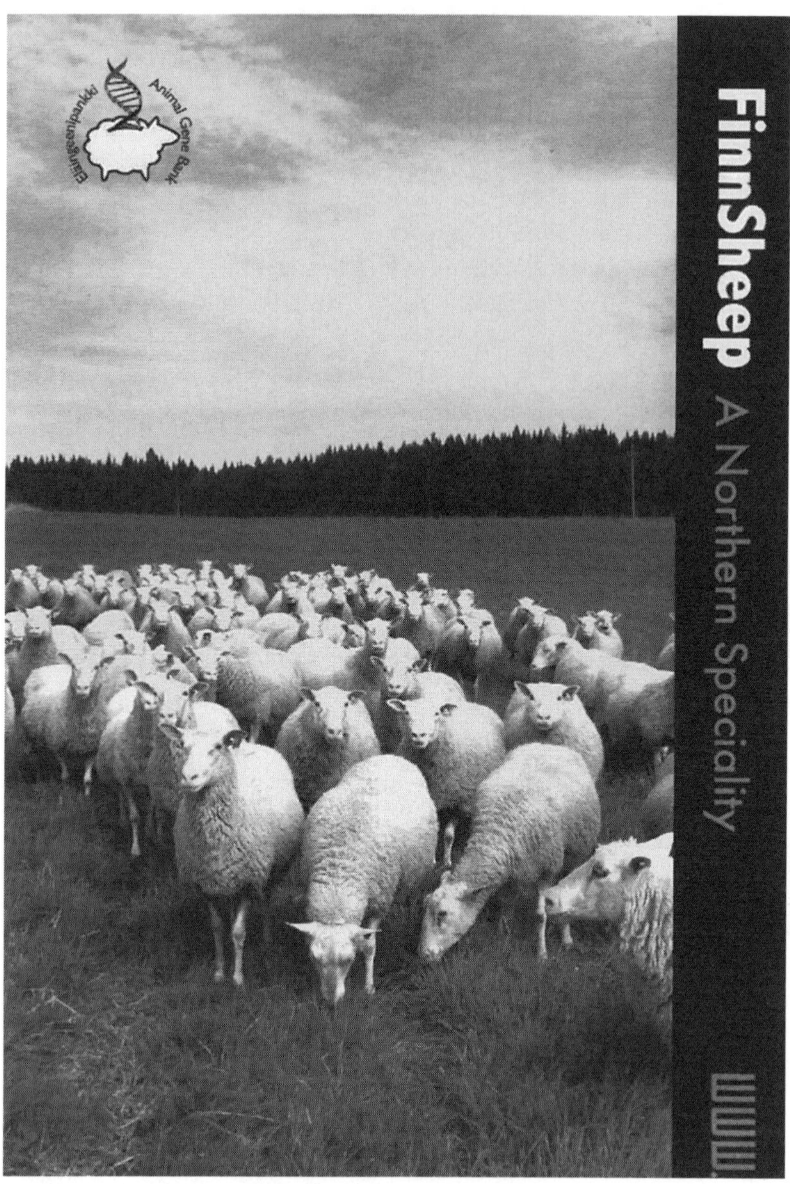

FIGURE 3.1 The front page of the Finnsheep brochure.

> In Finland, sheep divide into two different breeds. The first one is more or less sturdy, with straight and long wool. These are normally sheared twice a year and are called the Finnish sheep in normal speech. The second has finer, shorter, and curlier wool and is called German, although sheep belonging to this category are not only German but also Spanish and sometimes even British. However, you encounter the latter only at the manors of the nobility.[6]

The Finnish sheep- and goat-breeding society was established in 1918 (shortly after the country's independence) with the aim of advancing the agricultural economy through the breeding of better animals. In selecting the main breed for Finland in its first few years, the society recognized that foreign sheep were more productive with regard to various important traits: fertility, body structure, wool generation, and wool quality, among others. Yet the ideal sheep that the society chose as the recommended breed was the one that would serve the overall national interests of those who raised sheep in Finland: it was to thrive well in the Finnish climate and have low fodder consumption. In a parallel with the Finncattle of chapter 1, there is an echo permeating the theories of the way in which contemporary ideas of breeding science propagated national ideologies.

And if carefully bred foreign breeds did better on some dimensions of performance, this only demonstrated that the nonbred landrace breed must have hidden potential that had not yet been unleashed by systematic breeding practices since the breed most likely contained malleable breeding material that served the purpose of the common Finnish farmers (not only the nobility). The official, native Finnsheep pedigree was then established in 1921 (Sawela 1919; SLSY 1921).[7]

The nativity of the Finnsheep—in both natural and cultural terms—is not expressed only by its clearly evocative name. It is backed up by powerful political and scientific claims. Beyond the claims made in the brochure, the Finnsheep is one of the nine officially recognized animal breeds included in the Finnish genetic-resource conservation programs. Once a ubiquitous fixture of the farms and landscapes of the Finnish countryside, this breed had been declining in population steadily, dropping from 1.7 million in 1920 to 1 million in 1950 and falling sharply to 150,000 by 1967. In the forty years that followed, the population saw further reduction to a national collection of only 1,100 sheep as a result of changes in economic structure similar to those that affected Finncattle (Maijala 1971; Soini 2007).[8]

It is also one of the twenty or so sheep breeds that has been identified as native to Northern Europe, and its genetic origins are considered Finnish, which is evidenced by various historical documents. In addition, Finnish population scientists working with the breed argue that it is genetically different enough to claim its nativity to Finland (see, for instance, Tapio et al. 2006a; 2006b). Accordingly, the breed can be considered not only historically but also genetically Finnish. Here, the national identification process has broadly been similar to the one described for the case of the Alexander apple tree in the last chapter.

Unlike with the trees, however, one of the explicit goals of the national programs, as stated by the special genetic-resource group within the Ministry of Agriculture and Forestry in charge of the work, was to establish an ex situ collection—a gene bank—of Finnsheep genes. Diverse conflicting rationalities at various levels and derived from different temporal trajectories have made this task a national imperative, but it has been difficult to operationalize on a national scale. The reasons found in official documents can be roughly divided into three categories that correspond to particular fields of interests: the ecological, the economic, and the national.[9] I start with the ecological and its mobilization as a rational argument both to justify the national gene bank and to gain access to the national herd, which is mostly in the possession of individual farmers scattered around the country.

The worry about the destruction of viable populations of nonhuman (national) life by human activities has prompted action since the early twentieth century and became a global concern after the Green Revolution (see the introduction and chapter 1 and the history of plant genetic-resource movements provided by authors such as Pistorius 1997; for animals, see Barker 1994). The reason usually cited in the literature supporting genetic conservation is the impact of human action on the biosphere, which is characterized by the "growing proportion of unusual ecosystems which have substantially lower species diversity with lower genetic variation than most of the natural systems. In other words, there is a global loss of both species and their genetic diversity" (Vida 1994, 9). The first international considerations pertaining to strategies for the conservation of animal genetic resources (AnGRs) were voiced to the public by a panel of experts appointed by the United Nations Food and Agriculture Organization in Rome in 1983. In the panel's report the three major reasons for conserving AnGRs were all about radical changes in ecosystems. According to the report, these changes were brought about by the introduction of genetically homogeneous high-production animals together with the "indiscriminate introduction of exotic breeds" (FAO 1984, 5). Additionally, there exist large areas on the planet where challenging environmental conditions such as extreme temperatures and humidity render it impossible to use high-yield animals. Recognizing these geographical conditions, the experts argued that small animal populations that are ecologically adapted to harsh environments (FAO 1984, 6) should be taken as objects of conservation because they embody significant potentials of genetic diversity.

The Finnsheep, as the national brochure states, is one of these ecologically well-adapted breeds. In corporeal terms, however, the problem with Finnsheep as an embodiment of biodiversity is palpable in the fleeting nature of the sheep's presence: only five thousand individuals are living today, representing ten purebred lines. Because of the small size of the national population, the Finnsheep, both as an animal breed and as a source of national and international genetic diversity, is rapidly approaching ecological peril.[10] For conservation scientists, this means a twofold challenge. A large enough live, or effective, population must be kept alive to avoid inbreeding—genetic combinations between excessively close relatives, which results in an increase in the expression of recessive traits within the population—and to guarantee its genetic diversity through the sexual reproduction of viable offspring.

At the same time, however, the breed must remain pure via controlled reproduction, which sets limits to the phenotypes of the animals that are counted as members of the breed in a manner similar to what we saw in the chapter dealing with population-management practices for Finncattle. Thus, the contradictory conditions set by the purity requirement for deeming Finnsheep a purebred animal breed and the maintenance of a desirable level of genetic diversity are managed through strict population-management practices. But the biological life of any widely dispersed animal breed such as Finnsheep is hard to sustain. The breed's normal farm ecology—barns, sheep pens, and dedicated grazing areas—is disappearing at a rapid pace because of three interlinked economic problems that cause a big headache for the conservation scientists working with Finnsheep within the national genetic-resource programs, as they do for the whole international community of conservation scientists.

The first FAO report on AnGRs' banking, cited above, puts the problem like this: "The concept of conservation by gene banks is complex. One can think of live animals, being preserved *in situ*, or in some semi-artificial situation; alternatively one may think of cryogenic storage of sperm or fertilized ova or other tissues or gene segments. The economic problems are difficult with both live animals and . . . haploid or diploid cells. Who is to pay? There are also questions of how many to preserve, for how long, and where" (FAO 1984, 3). Subsequent global strategies were published by the

FAO in 1999 and in a follow-up in 2007. All have pondered the economic problems related to conservation in similar terms. The dwindling of ecological environments that are suitable for native breeds leads inevitably to tricky questions of agricultural economy.

First, because of the ecological conditions needed for maintaining a native herd, not just anyone can keep live sheep. They need constant care plus expertise in sheep breeding, all of which is currently very expensive if applied for the sole purpose of conservation. Agricultural policies in Finland have changed rapidly over the past few decades, especially with its accession to the EU, which abolished domestic subsidies to sheep breeders. Also, market prices for all agricultural products were cut by 30–70 percent (MAF 2003). Therefore sheep breeding has become an unprofitable form of business for most of the farmers, who hence, in the changing agricultural economy, abandoned the sheep for more economical animals (e.g., bovine species). The new political economy linked to national and international subsidy policies has devastated the agricultural niche of Finnsheep, contributing to their nearing extinction. The private farmers, individuals whom Dr. Kantanen calls "the guardians of the national herd," are abandoning their commitment and will continue to do so unless the Finnsheep proves to be an animal of economic interest in the none-too-distant future.

Second, as the coordinator of the national Animal Genetic Resources Programme, Dr. Kantanen had to address questions about the economic ordering of conservation priorities in the management of nonhuman populations, where budget is taken as a national economic mechanism creating the conditions for successful nonhuman biopolitics (see also Collier 2005). The yearly budget for the entire animal genetic-resource program, including all nine native animal species it encompasses, is quite limited (at around €50,000). In practical terms, this means that keeping a sufficient population of sheep in a dedicated ex situ live gene bank, a farm that would keep the Finnsheep true through sustained breeding efforts, financed by the government is not an economically viable option in Finland. The number of animals needed for such a bank would be too great to match these budgetary constraints: of the five thousand Finnsheep, only around three hundred are kept on a state-operated farm, such as the prison farms of Pelso and Sukeva encountered in the chapter about Finncattle, and this number of animals is not enough to keep the genetic variability at the desired levels for their conservation. Quite simply, maintaining an acceptable level of Finnsheep genetic diversity embodied in live animals is currently too costly a business for the farmers and conservation scientists alike.

Finally, the decline in the live population and the genetic diversity it embodies is an economic problem in a third sense. To safeguard sheep production globally, a certain level of genetic variation should be available so as to make future animal breeding possible and to keep industrial animal husbandry alive. Here, the question is not of keeping any one local herd alive but of harvesting most of its genetic diversity for animal-breeding purposes. The "Global Strategy for the Management of Farm Animal Genetic Resources," a joint declaration that the FAO and the Initiative for Domestic Animal Diversity (iDad) made in 1999, illustrates this point well. It casts the genetic variation in terms of both ecological necessity and agricultural commodity. The document states, "Locally adapted breeds also tend to retain significant genetic diversity, which provides for adaptability over time to changing environmental conditions and provides options for farmers to select for characteristics in response to changes in the marketplace" (FAO 1999, 8). According to international declarations, the upkeep of the ecology for Finnsheep is also a question of international agricultural economy.

The same is true for all animals in general and for Finnsheep in particular. Even if the value of live animals has generally sunk with the professionalized animal industry, the Finnsheep's local—ecological—adaptation in terms of special genetic characteristics provides farmers with the potential to adapt to changing national and global agricultural markets. The Finnsheep breed is unique in that it has long been considered a superior breed that is well known to sheep farmers around the world for one of its special characteristics. It has what is called an unusual fertility gene (e.g., Owen 1976; Brackett et al. 1981; MAF 2003). This gene (most likely a gene complex in actuality) makes the breed highly prolific even in the harsh climatic conditions of Finland. Additionally, these fertility genes help the sheep gestate at any time of the year—a rare quality among the sheep breeds of the world. Thanks to its special genes, it is highly sought after for crossbreeding and is thus a very valuable sheep breed for reproductive purposes.[11] This local genetic variation has the potential to become a lucrative form of biocapital in the international animal industry for Finnish farmers.

It is here that the ecological, economic, and national rationalities are articulated with each other at the first level—the three together form highly interlinked and perfused rationalities for conserving the Finnsheep as a national genetic resource. The differing rationalities for conserving Finnsheep genetics are articulated as a problem of value (of diversity, the useful gene, and cultural history) embodied in the corporeality of animal life. Living Finnsheep animals are a form of life whose ecological niche is being destroyed since it has lost much of its agricultural value in the changing markets over the two past decades. The ecological rationalities—of the protection of an ecological niche—behind conservation science are exactly the opposite of the rationalities driving the agricultural economy to eradicate Finnsheep as a nonproductive form of life. The national rationality behind conservation, in turn, is intertwined with both because of the double temporality employed in national thinking: the importance of conserving an embodiment of living cultural history is knitted into a tight weave with the promised future potentials that the fertility genes indicate through the corporeal existence of the national animal. Interestingly, then, the three rationalities converge in the idea of maximizing genetic difference. This difference provides for ecological adaptability, economic potentiality, and national uniqueness in relation to other sheep breeds.

The brochure that I quickly paged through was intended as a rhetorical intervention to mediate the opposing rationalities and to convince the stakeholders involved in the conservation work to arrive at this conclusion. It illustrates well the complex relations and leaky borders between different rationalities, ones that seem to implode in the processes of valuation. There is no value in an animal beyond its inherent links to the (ecological and economic) thinking that conservation science and agricultural economy mobilize in various ways within their intersecting fields of rationality. I place the leaflet back in the box and help others pack the car, and about an hour after my arrival everything seems ready for starting the field work. The trunk is filled with brown boxes and various instruments, and the staff members are buckled in. Dr. Kantanen, now "Juha" in our shared endeavor, starts off, steering the car toward the highway that leads to the first collection site. It is a private farm in southern Finland, about two hours' drive away, that still keeps Finnsheep in situ. The first vital matter contributing to the construction of the national Finnsheep gene bank will be found there.

HOMOGENIZATION IN ANIMAL (RE)PRODUCTION AND THE CONSERVATION OF GENETIC DIVERSITY

As we cruise over long, straight roads bordering the large farmed fields of the rural Finnish landscape, I wonder aloud about the upcoming set of collection procedures and how I should orient myself to it. Juha responds that he is the apprentice here: he has not done cryopreservation before. It is Maciej who will run the process, with us as extra sets of hands. Juha also explains that Maciej has given some preparatory instructions, which were communicated to the farmer in advance. These directions, sent by email, were simple: (1) the rams must have ejaculated two to three times weekly in the time leading up to the semen collection, with their last ejaculation no later than four days prior to the collection date; (2) the rams selected for the procedure must be accustomed to humans and not shy around new people; and (3) two ewes in heat must be available for the collection process (the ewes are used to entice the rams, and the sperm will be collected as the rams try to mount them). I continue by asking about the criteria for the initial selection of rams. Whose sperm does he want to collect? In what they consider to be total agreement, Juha and Maciej start explaining the basic criteria: only the best individuals as identified by pedigree and the fittest animals in terms of health, structure, and color (pure white) are to be chosen. It will not be that simple, though—as we will see later, the practical work of collection beyond this starting point entails much more detailed criteria for suitable animals and their genetic material.

While we are discussing the criteria, we reach the farm. The arrival does not go unnoticed. When Juha stops the car next to the sheep farm's large barn, the door opens immediately. A heavily built man in blue farmer's overalls and traditional Nokia rubber boots emerges and walks over to us. "We have been waiting for you," he says and asks us to join him for midday coffee before unpacking and starting to work: "Just leave the car here and follow me." The coffee is served in the building opposite the animal shelters, an old agricultural school now renovated to accommodate visitors. The farm is owned by a larger private foundation that has for the past decade or so concentrated solely on the breeding of Finnsheep. "The fact is that we're now the best breeders of white Finnsheep in the world," the farmer states, not at all in the typical self-effacing Finnish manner. He continues that they are excited to have Juha's team there: "We're happy to help. And we are very interested in seeing how this freezing thing works."

After a while, the discussion turns toward sheep farming and its economic conditions in Finland. It is in this discussion that the economic furrows of our field site begin to be revealed. The man starts by telling us the story of Finnsheep breeding on the farm. He recalls that it started at almost the worst possible time—only a few years before Finland's accession to the European Union in 1995. "That was a bad time for us," he says, then elaborates on why:

> The sheep markets in Finland collapsed almost overnight as European lamb meat could be imported and the domestic subsidy policy changed radically, reducing the monetary compensation for sheep to almost nothing. At the same time, someone had the idea that Finnsheep should be done away with since, for some reason, they would not be as good as the foreign Texel and Oxford Down breeds. So sheep breeders

> imported semen and embryos of those with huge amounts of money; about a million or so they spent on it. And they were meant to crossbreed, or to enhance the Finnsheep . . . with foreign qualities. I just couldn't believe it! There's nothing wrong with Finnsheep; they are actually better in many ways than the Texels and Oxfords!

Everybody at the table agrees that these decisions by the farmers were inimical to Finnsheep as a breed. "But we've managed this far; we've built ten lines, and our sheep are the best white Finnsheep in the world today. Their genealogies are well managed, we have kept the lines pure, and the animals are performing well," our host emphasizes.

Little wonder, then, that this farmer is interested in cryotechnology and its possibilities. This is illustrative of the intertwined rationalities that serve as conditions of possibility for enrolling private farmers in the work that is aimed at establishing a nationalized gene bank based on the reproductive matter derived from their animals. Industrial animal husbandry has been highly dependent on various technological innovations ever since Robert Bakewell's experiments with selective breeding. Managing reproductive processes is what makes the derivation of value from animals possible—Bakewell and his disciples already understood the interlinked nature of reproduction and capital in the mid-eighteenth century and capitalized on superior animals by loaning them out for the breeding season for use by other breeders (Walton 1986; Ritvo 1995). The reproductive powers of one superior male animal became an economic asset first for Bakewell and then for others who were capable of demonstrating the reproductive superiority of their sires: stallions, bulls, and rams. Male animals were considered capable of fertilizing females in large numbers, thereby keeping the herd patrilineally manageable and identifiable. The key here was ratification of the breed in the language and a linguistic codification for pedigreed lineage of pure animals of a desired type (Derry 2003)—a principle of animal production that is still in use, as I have analyzed in more detail in the chapter on Finncattle.

Herd books and good animals, or lineage records and good reproductive material, are important because animal breeding depends not on individual animals but on the successful management of their reproductive processes and, through them, better pedigrees embodied in individual animals. Keeping with the trajectory of Bakewell's techniques in the provision of sires and its coupling of reproduction and economic interests, subsequent research has concentrated heavily on extending the reproductive powers of male animals and, more specifically, on the male reproductive material:

sperm. The twentieth century witnessed important advances in the management of reproductive processes, made principally through artificial-insemination innovations. These steadily eliminated the need for the male animal to be physically present in all phases of animal reproduction. The reconfiguration of the processes of reproduction quickly led to further innovations and to the rise of a large-scale animal industry that was capable of a new level of industrialization and capitalization on animal (re)production (Foote 1983; Rasbech 1993; Clarke 1998), making it an internationally lucrative business.

The large range of material apparatuses and practical protocols required for successful AI also provided for a new ecology for sperm. The fundamental problem to be addressed was the short temporal window of vitality of the sperm outside the animal body: without any artificial technique, the sperm cells were dead within hours or minutes depending on the surrounding conditions. But many years of research led to the perfection of an artificial environment where the sperm could survive long after ejaculation. Steadily, the reproductive vitality of sperm was extended from a few hours to several days in suitable liquid mediums: fresh semen could be preserved for days either in egg yolk or in milk-based substances before fertility was lost and the cells died. In a complementary fashion, the development of sperm dilutants—appropriately known as extenders—allowed more than one insemination to take place with one ejaculate. The initial volume could be divided into numerous batches of less vitally concentrated liquid mixes, which extended the reproductive force of a superior animal (Salamon and Maxwell 1995a; Foote 2002).

It was only the well-known chance observation of the possibility of keeping sperm cells vital and mostly unharmed at very low temperatures within a glycerol mixture, made in the mid-twentieth century, that radically changed both the pace and the scope of the breeding work. This observation was made by Christopher Polge and his group working at Cambridge University's Animal Research Station. The observation and the group behind it ushered in the era of cryopreservation and, perhaps more importantly, that of cryobiologically assisted artificial insemination in animal breeding (Polge et al. 1949, 666). Cryopreservation as a new technique of reproduction gave the breeders a high level of control over the temporal and spatial dimensions of their animals' reproductive powers. It did away with the constraints imposed by cellular decay by literally stopping the biological clock of the cell via extremely low temperatures. The novel potentiality of life that such an operation generates is twofold. What normally would indicate a potentially viable sperm batch—the amount of mobility (overall mobility within the sample volume) and the motility of spermatozoids (movement of individual cells)—is complemented with its reverse potentiality within the techniques of cryopreservation. The frozen vital material is viable only insofar as all signs of life-as-mobility are gone and the cessation of animation within the sample is complete. Frozen life is a form of life at absolute rest, arrested life at the level of cellular processes.

First, this technique allowed the temporal cycle of natural conception to be broken. Time between sperm extraction and insemination was no longer merely stretched. The new technique also allowed the biological processes of the reproductive material to be arrested and restarted at will. This extended the possibilities of old principles of selective breeding in an important way. For example, the sperm of a selected genetically superior male could be used to fertilize several generations in a row: the inbreeding practiced by Bakewell could be extended far more than with live animals as long as it was deemed appropriate and an enhancement of the breed's lineage. This also reorganized the way of marking the genealogies and kinship structures of animals: genealogical kinship relations involving identified individuals in linear herd books gave way to a more important marker of relationship that was calculated by the heritability of traits, genetic distance, and—with these—composite representations of estimated breeding values (see chapter 1, and Holloway and Morris 2008). It also made possible the rapid narrowing of genetic variance in a breed lineage by keeping the patrilineal descent constant. Breeding with cryotechnologically assisted AI worked well as a general technique of homogenizing genetic variance; it was a clear and direct response to the aims of the industrialized animal industry to produce more predictable and profitable offspring (e.g., Owen 1976; Derry 2003; S. Franklin 2007b).

The suspension of cellular processes opens up not only a new temporal but also a new spatial scope. This yields extracellular mobility, too: an animal's reproductive powers could be extended from a local farm to global agricultural business. The sperm of superior animals could be transported virtually anywhere in the world to meet the great demand as long as it was kept within a certain ecology—an unbroken cold chain providing the suspension of cell life in a frozen state. The genetic information embodied in sperm changed from a local into a global product in a very short time. It is simple-to-use and cheap technology for fast genetic enhancement and is easy to circulate around the world for various animals such as cattle.[12] Before long, its popularity had widened the spatial scope for the cryopreserved reproductive material enormously and created a novel global economy of frozen reproductive material (Cole and Cupps 1977; Brackett et al. 1981; King 1993; Foote 2002; Wilmot 2007).

At present, this is the world's most widely used biological technology in livestock farming. Globally, more than 100 million AI procedures in cattle, 40 million in pigs, 3.3 million in sheep, and half a million in goats are performed annually. Of these, only about 4.5 percent are carried out with fresh semen. The vast majority is cryostored, making AI synonymous with cryopreservation in most cases (Thibier and Wagner 2002).[13]

However, no large-scale Finnsheep ram sperm markets have emerged for two reasons: for a long time, no well-functioning cryopreservation protocols for sheep were available even though their study began soon after the Cambridge group's breakthrough (see, for example, First et al. 1961; Salamon 1967). The problem has long been a decrease in the fertility of frozen sperm: even if cryopreservation with glycerin extenders protects from most of the damage, the sheep's living sperm cells suffer readily from cold shock when frozen to extreme temperatures. In consequence, some of the cells eventually die in the process of freezing, and thawing reduces their reproductive capabilities (Salamon and Maxwell 1995a). Hence, conception rates have remained low until recent years since each species and sheep breed needs specifically optimized protocols if the cryopreservation is to be performed correctly such that the fertility of the frozen sperm batch does not suffer and the breeding process is not too costly (and ultimately uneconomical) as a breeding practice. Second, farmers themselves seldom have the time or expertise to perform this optimization; they would need expert advice in order to develop breed-specific protocols themselves. This is why the technique's profitability has been questioned from the start; the economic margins of sheep farming are small. The two benefits achieved with cryo-bio-technologically assisted AI—speeding up the development of higher fertility in lambing in ewes and better meat production in flocks—have been too costly for individual sheep farmers, who still favor the easy and low-cost selective breeding techniques invented by Bakewell and perfected by his followers (Inskeep and Peters 1981; Rasbech 1993; Salamon and Maxwell 1995a; 1995b).

In view of this technological trajectory and the direct economic links to agricultural animal production and the resultant loss of genetic diversity, it is interesting that the proponents of animal genetic conservation embraced the cryopreservation technique as one viable potential strategy from very early on (see FAO 1984). Only recently, however, as the international animal genetic-resource movement has gathered more momentum, has the technique been reevaluated and put to practical use (e.g., Boa-Amponsem and Minozzi 2006). According to S. J. Hiemstra, T. van der Lende, and H. Woelders (2006), for example, this technique of conservation has the benefit of allowing the "virtually indefinite storage of biological material without deterioration over a time scale of at least several thousands of years but probably much longer." However, their evaluation has resonance with the economic problems of using it in the animal-conservation business. These scientists claimed, "In general, cryopreservation and associated reproductive technologies are costly; the main limitations for extensive development of ex situ collections are high costs of collection and limited use of preserved material" (Hiemstra et al. 2006, 46–53).

While cryopreservation serves the conservation of biodiversity, it simultaneously serves the opposite interests of industrialized animal production in its use as an efficient tool for the genetic homogenization of breeds. Additionally, while the technique is an economic problem at large for conservation practices, for the agricultural industry this is seen as a new and interesting technoscientific ecology for trading and circulating the vitality of animal matter, quite literally a new market space for the matter that is vital to reproducing animal life. The Finnish Animal Genetic Resources Programme has adopted cryopreservation as a crucial strategy to save Finnsheep from extinction while attempting to solve the related economic problem by aligning sheep farmers' interests with its own.

The farmers who were contacted by Juha in his capacity as AnGR program coordinator agreed to provide access to their herds since they were interested in witnessing the viability of the cryopreservation technique for sheep. This was because its successful performance with their rams would multiply their value and provide a possible opening to larger (national and international) markets. One standard sperm dose from a superior Finnsheep ram—and with the right technique, anywhere from ten to twenty batches can be produced from one ejaculate—could fetch as much as €200, almost as much as a single live animal on the market. With the cryopreserved reproductive material, the economic value of a pedigreed ram could then be multiplied many times. The producers of cryopreserved sperm could carve out an entirely new economic niche for themselves in the worldwide animal-reproduction industry while simultaneously helping the government at home in its efforts to conserve the breed. The scientists, on the other hand, are interested in extracting sperm from the animals in the possession of the individual farmers because their animals constitute the national herd—the sum of all registered Finnsheep animals of Finland ought to be conserved as national genetic resources.

Here, the field site begins to be articulated on one of its more visible dimensions. Sheep breeding is an economically oriented activity, interwoven with developments in technologies of reproduction. This is where the economic rationalities of the international animal industry, the cryopreservation technology developed by it, the local farmers, and the reasoning behind the national conservation program come together again in the local context of Finnsheep gene banking and traverse the practical arrangements related to it. The two problems—ecological and economic—related to the conservation of Finnsheep would be solved if cryopreservation of the breed's sperm were possible. It would allow the indefinite storage of the animal sperm in ex situ gene banks while at the same time making the Finnsheep a viable form of agricultural economy for Finnsheep farmers. Thereby, the in situ (in vivo) preservation of Finnsheep would also gain new viability, and the continued maintenance of Finnsheep in their living corporeal form would be in the interests of the farmers. Thus, the farmers' enrollment and the possibilities for the national program for Finnsheep genetic conservation are heavily dependent on successful cryopreservation practices. We will see how these work when we head to the barn after coffee at the guesthouse. Although most of the remaining action will unfold in the barn, this is only after Maciej and Juha rearrange the barn into a cryobiology station allowing for biobanking of Finnsheep gametes.

BUILDING THE BIOBANKING INFRASTRUCTURE: SHIFTING SHEEP ECOLOGIES

After coffee, we thank our hosts and start to unpack the car. Over the next two hours or so, Juha and Maciej use numerous boxes, canisters, and instruments to transform the space in the barn into a temporary cryopreservation station. The necessary equipment consists of surprisingly basic technical objects.

Maciej directs Juha and me in how to position the equipment for as convenient a workflow as possible in an office space and in the small cold room next to it. "Let's keep the cold stuff in the cold room. Nitrogen canisters should be placed there. Oh, and the centrifuge too. It'll be best to centrifuge the sperm in cool temperatures. Let's put the microscope, extenders, chicken eggs, and other stuff on this office table here," he says. A centrifuge, two liquid-nitrogen containers, and a Styrofoam box with a tube rack serving as an ad hoc prefreezing apparatus are set up in the cold room, which, at 4°C is normally used only to store slaughtered sheep until they are processed further. This transforms a space for the preservation of dead bodies into a center for the preservation of the cells generating life.

As this field infrastructure takes shape, numerous technical boundaries and passage points emerge. In the delineation between the various areas of the barn, parts of the spatial order are reordered in line with the

FIGURE 3.2 Equipment for the mobile collection station: microscope, extenders, chicken eggs (yolk), centrifuge, nitrogen canisters, Styrofoam box with tubes, etc. Photo by the author.

detailed protocol described below. The passage from the sheep pens (the animal area) to the office (the human area) is now restricted to only particular kinds of living materials (the collected sperm and the humans), and this material must be transformed further (into sperm diluted with other liquids) before passing from the control room into the cold room.

Even the order of the barn's animal area is not left untouched. Interestingly, the rearrangement of the sheep and their pens is directly related to the way biological processes of reproduction must be arranged if the biobanking protocol is to be followed successfully. Isolating the rams from the flock for a few days in advance will have increased the quality of their sperm since they have not been able to ejaculate. Also, the two ewes mentioned in the email have been isolated from the group, and their biological processes have been reordered more directly. They were injected with a special hormone (prostaglandin PGF2α) two days before we arrived at the farm.[14] This hormone disrupts their normal estrous cycle and catalyzes the ewes' reproductive system (bringing them into heat), thereby making them a good tease for the rams whose sperm will be collected.

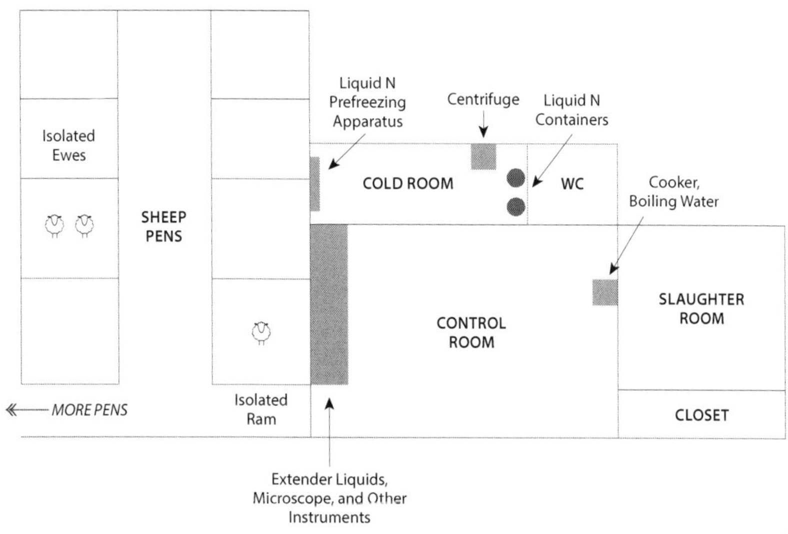

FIGURE 3.3 The layout of the makeshift collection station. Diagram by the author.

This spatial and biological formatting of the barn has followed the instructions that Maciej and Juha gave the farmer earlier. The only sign that betrays the change to the animals' social order—or the abnormality of the rams' and ewes' isolation from the usual flock—is the boards hanging over the pens (each with several selected ewes). These boards contain the ram's name together with a dozen digits: the identification numbers of the other flock members that are usually present. These chalk marks point to a new social-biological order that was created in the barn even before the makeshift biobank infrastructure was constructed. Several infrastructural devices used in that ordering (such as the pens) have helped Juha and Maciej in setting up the gene-banking station. Clearly, the order is not simply created from disorder; this is reordering.

Once the equipment is set up, Maciej starts to prepare the most important material for the successful freezing of the biological material. In fact, the entire reorganization of social-biological order described above is aimed at supporting the standardized cryopreservation protocol that is to be applied after the collection of spermatozoa. The most important element in the protocol after the sperm is the extender. Since its invention, described above, numerous extender components, including various cryoprotective agents, have been perfected, and a working mixture has been found for almost every domesticated animal (and human) breed. The site is still not fully domesticated, though. However finely honed, any cryopreservation

FIGURES 3.4 AND 3.5
Two juxtaposed orders, with the chalk marks implying the normal order of the barn. Photos by the author.

procedure still needs to be adapted to local conditions, though, and Maciej prepares the extender accordingly. It includes a nutrition source for the spermatozoids and various antibiotics to kill any bacteria that is accidentally introduced either in the extender liquid's cooking process or during the collection of the sperm.

Once the extenders are prepared, Maciej moves on to the last task before the collection can start: the preparation of artificial vaginas. They are a central instrument for the whole field trip. Maciej stops in his tracks. He is puzzled at first—these vaginas are different from what he is used to. They are bigger, the temperature isolation is different, and the sperm container is not as visible as he is accustomed to. He also complains that they are not equipped with an external air or water container to allow easy, steady, and—above all—controllable cooling of the sperm after collection without external water beds. Juha shrugs his shoulders and states that these vaginas were ordered from Germany. He did not know that there would be so many differences in artificial vaginas from one manufacturer to the next: "How could I have known? I have never bought an artificial vagina before!"

Maciej starts to put together the vaginas from pieces on the table and says that a water bed is needed for cooling down the material collected. He fills one of the flasks on the table with water, checks the temperature with a thermometer, and says that this will serve as the cooling device. Returning to the vaginas, he notices that they have a partition to allow filling an internal area with water for easy control of the temperature within. "Good that we have at least this feature here—it is very important," explains Maciej, "as the actual collection is very invasive for the ram: the temperature must be just right; otherwise, the ram won't ejaculate at all, meaning we will not have any sperm to work with." According to him, the temperature must be around 42–45°C for the best results. After some tinkering, the parts of the artificial vaginas are now assembled. A black plastic tube with a removable rubber liner leads to a small glass container. All we need now is some lubricant inside. He applies that to the rubber, and we are ready: "Let's start freezing!"

Above, we set cryopreservation-based biobanking in contrast against the traditional management of nonhuman life represented by the order of barns and farms. Setting up the complex technical infrastructure that is necessary marks or mirrors a total change in the object of knowledge and material interest. However, the farm is already an interesting form of hybrid natural-social order, with a whole ecology of its own sort: a special human-made arrangement of relationships between the sheep and their environment. The spatial arrangements of fields for grazing, the pens with identifying markings hanging over them for sheep, the separation of various human (and animal) spaces into control rooms and sheep pens and dedicated spaces in which the sheep live (copulating, giving birth, and carrying on their day-to-day life) and die (the slaughter room) are all outcomes of thousands of years of the architectural coconstruction of human-animal relations and their boundary-making processes as well as the ordering of the biological life of the animals.[15] In other words, our work on the farm began with a layout that resembles a laboratory in its organization of spaces for controlling naturally occurring events: the nonhuman life of the sheep flocks.

The rearrangement of infrastructure under the same tenets of control enables an unproblematic move from the animals to their reproductive material and provides a new ecological niche for the cryopreserved genetic material. The path is prepared for the total reconfiguration of the ontology of the Finnsheep breed as it moves from in situ to ex situ. In practice, the ecological environment of this novel genetic resource is completely different from the farms, barns, and herds required for the Finnsheep's survival in vivo. The first aspect of bridging we can point to in cryo-biotechnologically assisted suspension of the sheep's reproductive life is a radical change in the scale of operations. A Finnsheep is big, with an adult ewe weighing 65–75 kg, a ram 85–105 kg. A gamete is microscopic. The sheep is reduced to its reproductive cells only if it manages to pass through a long transformation process starting with the extraction of the material from sheep themselves.

NATURAL CONTINGENCIES AND NEGOTIATING THE BIOBANKING CRITERIA

Now that our makeshift technical infrastructure is ready, the farmer takes us on a tour of the barn to see the ingredients: the Finnsheep population he is in charge of, about 120 ewes and 10 rams. Juha fetches one of the ewes in heat. He holds the skittish animal steady in the passageway between the pens while the farmer approaches with the first ram, Rabbe. After being released and smelling the ewe, Rabbe considers for a few seconds and then decides to mount her. At this point, Maciej interposes the artificial vagina between the animals. The event is over a few seconds later. He makes sure the tube contains more than 1 mL of semen, the sheep are returned to their isolated pens, and we return to the control room to process the batch of sperm.

In the control room, the freezing of the collected substance, in contrast to the fifteen minutes of constructing the laboratory and the few minutes to collect the raw material, is time consuming. It takes around four hours to process one batch of gametes as the freezing follows a set protocol. The protocol Maciej will be following is one form of standardized workflow that science and technology scholars are already familiar with (e.g., Cambrosio and Keating 1988; Jordan and Lynch 1998; Lynch 2002). These are professional resources describing the right sequence of actions for a desired outcome, a standard of action. The implementation of a protocol should generally reproduce a successful experiment or work as a path to follow in order to unfold a desired laboratory event—in this case, the cryopreservation of Finnsheep sperm. But any standardization is subject to contingencies, which render parts of the recipe useless without a localized interpretation and tinkering. Contingencies are more the rule than an exception to the protocol on the way to successful cryopreservation, as we will soon see. No wonder, then, that Maciej refers to his own "cooking recipe": it is with his recipe and all the practical work going into the local implementation that the Finnsheep will be baked into a novel form of genetic resource.

An important contingency is highlighted here: not all gamete material is capable of sustaining life in the difficult passage from in vivo to in vitro, from in situ animal to ex situ genetic resource. This journey, not one easily made by living matter, imposes a novel kind of selection process for the sperm—the protocol is not the natural one involving rams' judgments in a larger pattern or the more traditional processes of selective breeding. Hiemstra and colleagues (2006), for instance, noted in their analysis of cryopreservation as a means of genetic conservation that "there may be considerable differences between breeds and between males in the 'freezability' of the semen. As a consequence, frozen semen of some genetically interesting breeds or males may not be suitable as a gene bank resource, or can be used only with . . . poor efficiency" (Hiemstra et al. 2006, 47). Freezability is itself a contingent and contestable category behind the selection process and works as the key criterion for the sperm that is to be biobanked. Only freezable gametes are capable of surviving in the new ecological niche created by the technical infrastructure of cryopreservation. This consideration translates first into a set of criteria imposed for the extracted sperm then becomes naturalized through banked semen material.

The first phase in freezability assessment is the visual evaluation of the collected sperm's vitality with the aid of a microscope. The evaluation leading to visual judgment of the material's quality is a complex process, but as a seasoned biobanker, Maciej has a few tricks up his sleeve for working around the seemingly difficult task. He uses his training to see and identify certain qualities in the genetic material along with some physical aids—standardized scales—as a guide and to manipulate both the perceptual field and the form of the sample material. To help with his visual assessment of the motility and direction, Maciej uses an evaluation standard. This is a photocopy from his field manual showing paradigmatic diagrams for each of the categories of movement and direction. It is a list for orienting the vision to search for certain kinds of patterns in the sperm under the microscope, where the slide otherwise displays vibrant chaotic movement. Thereby, it performs a task similar to birdwatchers' manuals as John Law and Michael Lynch (1988) described them: it provides the descriptive organization of vision by making visible possible patterns of identification within the material.

With the assistance of the paradigmatic diagrams next to the microscope, the evaluation of the sperm becomes intelligible—literally readable—for not only Maciej (who probably would not actually need the diagrams anymore since he has already internalized them) but also Juha. The picture of the sperm offered by the microscope is now legible as an indicator of their overall vitality as the diagram directs the gaze to identify certain patterns of movement. In the first step, visually confirmed wave motility in the sample is taken as the first sign of the spermatozoids' vitality. The more movement seen, the more vital the sperm are taken to be. Next, the motility of this sample is evaluated on the basis of the direction of movement—according to the standard, a large number of spermatozoids moving in the same direction forms an easily recognizable visual fingerprint whereas individuals' scattered movement is visible only as hectic and random chaos under the microscope's enhanced vision.

The calculation procedure proceeds with the sperm batch being assigned a discrete value from one to five and a symbolic notation consisting of between one and five plus signs (+). If the sperm batch is judged to have up to 20 percent motility, it is assigned the number one; if over 40 percent, it will be in category two; and so on, with five indicating the best quality possible for material displaying at least 80 percent motility with a good direction of overall movement. The pluses, meanwhile, are used for evaluating the direction of the movement: if most sperm cells are moving in the same direction in many waves, the symbol assigned will be five pluses (+ + + + +), and the number of plus signs decreases as the number of rivers in the sample decreases.

Sitting at the microscope, Maciej dictates to Juha the outcome of his evaluation: "It's a four with two pluses. Write that down for Rabbe." Juha stands beside him and notes the numbers and the pluses in his notepad under the heading "Rabbe." The documentation of these visual evaluations

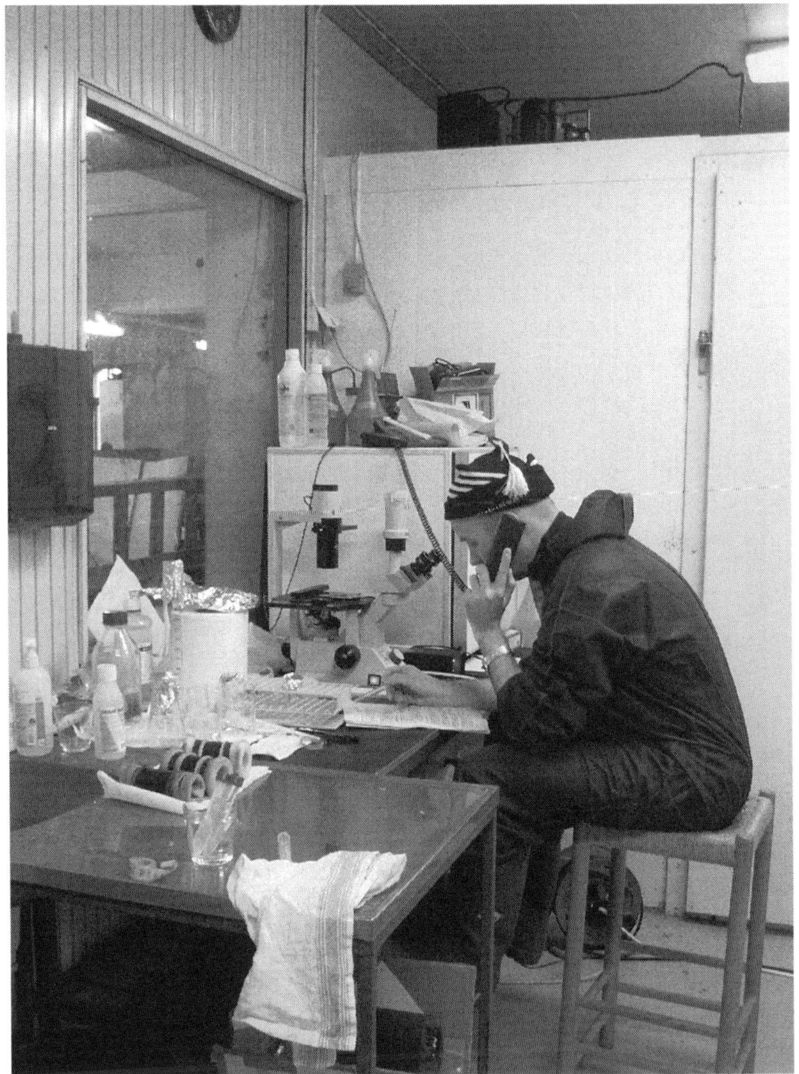

FIGURE 3.6 Dr. Kantanen performing visual judgments and vitality assessments. Photo by the author.

is an inscription trail that is visible in Juha's notations, and it is mirrored on the test tubes and microscope slides that embody the material, all of which ultimately composes a table for comparing performances across the various materials (see table 3.1). This particular batch, while receiving high scores on the numeric dimension of the evaluation, fares poorly on the second dimension. This worries Maciej. Something is wrong with the sample. Maciej muses, "There is a small number of immobile spermatozoids already, which is quite strange. I have to study those later back at home in the labs. I want to see whether they are naturally deformed or what's the problem!" He takes a small sample of the sperm and seals it between two glass plates, then writes "Rabbe" on the sample. He wants to perform a morphological analysis of the sample at the home lab. He explains in more detail:

> Some of the spermatozoids are naturally deformed and will not be able to move like the others—for example, if their tail is not suitable for swimming. That's why they seem dead. They're not moving. Some others may be really dead for other, unknown reasons, but we will have to check that later. Movement-wise, the sperm material is quite good. But there's something wrong here with the sperm moving in strange directions, which I really did not expect. That's why it got only two pluses, and that's really a bad result. There is a chance that this batch will not survive the freezing.

The movement and its direction are here taken as a direct signifier of the vitality of the cells—morphologically deformed sperm might be alive, but they are not vital enough to withstand the freezing process. Maciej and Juha take a minute to discuss what to do now that the batch seems to be unsuitable for continuing the protocol. All the practical knowledge that has been accumulated by breeders indicates that Finnsheep should be the most fertile sheep breed in the world. This should have, in their opinion, translated into vital sperm. Does that apparent knowledge exaggerate the fertility qualities of the breed? Or is it just Rabbe whose reproductive capacities are somehow impaired? Did something go wrong in the collection process?

After pondering these issues from several points of view, they conclude that there are only two possible reasons for the sperm quality being too low: the sperm quality of the individual is a problem, or Rabbe was not isolated as early as he should have been for the spermatozoids to mature enough for a higher number of points on the scale. They decide to ask the farmer more about Rabbe's isolation. When exactly was the ram isolated from his flock? He finally reveals that this ram had not been isolated at all; indeed, he was with the flock the whole time. "That's the reason! We have to put Rabbe into isolation for a couple of days to let his sperm mature and try again after that. Do we have any rams that would have been isolated early enough?" asks Maciej.

The farmer points to the pen where a ram named Pamppu is isolated. He continues, "Pamppu was isolated two days ago. Is that good enough for you?" Maciej nods and says that we will try with Pamppu then. The collection process starts again from the first step: Juha fetches the ewe in heat, and the farmer releases the ram to mount her. Maciej collects the sperm, he checks the volume (more than 1 mL), the ewe and Pamppu are returned to their pens, and everyone returns to the control room.

After the small detour for the collection, we are all back at the microscope to perform visual judgment of the batch. "This one's far better already. Yes, Juha, write down five and five pluses. Pamppu's sperm are very good!" Then Maciej proceeds to the next step of the protocol. It consists of diluting the sperm with the first liquid (extender 1, as Maciej calls it) and letting the mixture settle to room temperature for about half an hour. Next, the mixture and the four of us go to the cold room to let it cool to 4°C in preparation for the next steps. "We don't have a thermometer here, so let's just count on the equilibrating effect of the cold room," says Maciej. "I checked that it was exactly four degrees in the room before we came in from the small display above the door. It shouldn't take more than half an hour to cool down." Maciej and Juha continue talking about Finnsheep fertility and sheep in general.

Half an hour later, Maciej opens the door and fetches the second cryopreservative liquid (extender 2) and a bottle of 7 percent glycerol lying on the control room table. On his return to the cold room, he takes a peek at the temperature display over the door and sighs loudly. He explains, "We may have another problem here. It seems that the temperature in the room has risen to nine degrees, probably because of our body heat. Let's hope that has not affected the process by cooling down the mixture too slowly. Let's all leave the room and let it cool down again to four degrees." The rest of us exit the cold room, and Juha asks whether we can continue the protocol. "We can. But this might affect the sperm batch's resistance to the freezing effects. But let's continue and see what happens," Maciej responds.

After the temperature has dropped to 4°C, Maciej enters to dilute the mixture with extender 2 and glycerol. "OK, now we have to wait two hours for the whole mixture to cool down again," he says. He and Juha start cleaning up the control room—various tubes, flasks, and pipettes that have been used in the protocol thus far are sterilized in boiling water and prepared for the next batch of sperm. When the cleaning is done, the farmer asks us to join him in the main building for coffee in the meantime.

TECHNICAL STANDARDIZATION OF THE REPRODUCTIVE MATERIAL

After two hours and several cups of coffee, we return to the barn laboratory to continue with the protocol. "Good, we're almost halfway done now.

All we need to do is to centrifuge, put it in straws, and freeze this batch," Maciej tells us. The protocol, however, faces another obstacle at this point: the centrifuge that Juha has brought is not the type that Maciej uses back home. "So what we would like to have in here is four hundred g or about fourteen hundred rpm, depending on the size or length of the arms of the centrifuge, for fifteen minutes," he says. But this model has no such controls. Instead, it has a power-control dial ranging from 0 to 100 percent. "How much power do I have to put here, Juha?" he asks.

Juha replies, "Hmm, I actually don't know about this model either. I took it because it wasn't in use at the lab, and I thought it'll do."

Maciej says, "OK, no problem. Let's try this, then." He adjusts the dial to 50 percent, puts the tube with the liquid mixture into the machine, and turns it on.

Fifteen minutes later, he stops the spinning: "Let's see whether that was enough." Maciej takes the glass tube out of the machine and holds it up to the ceiling lights so that he can visually check the contents. The force applied to the mixture of fluids seems to have done its job: two layers of liquid material are now easily distinguishable. The liquid components of the mixture, the supernatant, float on top of a much denser white fluid, which has been forced to the bottom during the spinning. "Now let's check if that was good enough—we want to have all the spermatozoids compressed to the bottom, so there should not be too many of them in the supernatant," Maciej says. He pipettes a drop of the supernatant on a glass plate and places that under the microscope. "Oh, there are too many swimmers. I'll give them another spin," he concludes. An evaluation after the second spin shows that all is good. "It's a bit of a hassle today, but at least now we know how much we want to spin the mixture. I hope that the spermatozoids are not too dizzy after these two spins. I mean, normally we want it done only once, since we don't want to kill them," he concludes.

After the second trip in the centrifuge, Maciej removes the unwanted supernatant—now free of swimmers—by pipetting it away, and he begins the next step in the protocol. For even sperm quality and standard distribution across the Cassou straws in which the material is eventually to be cryopreserved, another visual judgment of the batch's quality has to be performed. Maciej notes the volume of the mixture remaining in the glass tube and explains, "Now we have to calculate the number of individual spermatozoids in the concentrated material, because we want to have an even concentration of two hundred million spermatozoa in the straws, which have a volume of twenty-five milliliters. So first we calculate how many individual swimmers we have here, dilute the concentrate with the extenders to the desired volume so we have that two hundred million per twenty-five milliliters, and then just pack the straws with that."

At this point, another problematic aspect of the practical work is highlighted. How can one assess how many individual spermatozoids are actually present in the remaining material? Visual judgment for such a large number of individual moving cells is impossible for one person, even one with infinite patience and the enhanced sight provided by a powerful microscope—a successful sample is defined as about two billion spermatozoids with most sheep breeds, even more for Finnsheep. There has to be another solution available. This consists of a trust in the probability of a normal distribution and in what Latour (1990, x) called optical consistency: "The two-dimensional character of inscriptions allow them to merge with geometry. . . . Because of this optical consistency, everything, no matter where it comes from, can be converted into diagrams and numbers." Optical consistency is provided by a special microscope slide that allows a crucial transformation to take place: the three-dimensional volume of the concentrated liquid is rendered two-dimensional. For the calculation, we use a slide engraved with geometric shapes, called a graticule, or, more familiarly to people working in laboratories, a Brucker slide.

This slide assists with visual calculation in a different way from what we saw with the paradigmatic guide for assessing the sperm's motility and direction of movement. Whereas the usefulness of the latter visual aid lies in its capability of representing a simplified graphic similitude with the object of evaluation, the engraved geometry we use now provides for dimensional translation of the object under the calculative gaze; the volume of spermatozoids is superimposed on visible rectangular areas, which render them calculable within simple two-dimensional geometric spaces. The chaotic movement is reduced not to patterns of movement but to its smallest components—the spermatozoids—within the geometric space. The individual cells are now geometrically bounded by an easily recognizable area. Their calculation has become much easier.

Maciej has already noted the volume of the concentrated sperm. He pipettes 1 mL onto the special slide and begins to count the number of spermatozoids within the squares. From these totals he calculates a mean in his notepad. He reads out the result to Juha and declares, "It's very good. We have here about three-point-three billion spermatozoids in the whole ejaculation. It's almost one and a half times the norm for other breeds. This batch will make us sixteen Cassou straws to pack. We have to have sixteen times twenty-five milliliters of the mixture, then, so we have to add some extenders to the concentrate now to reach that volume. How much is it . . . ? About four hundred milliliters of the diluted, cryopreservable sperm mixture in total. Did you write that down, Juha?"

Maciej then adds the extenders. The entire extender 1 volume is added immediately, and, after another two hours of waiting as the protocol prescribes, the mixture goes into the cold room. At this point, extender 2 is added to the mixture in three parts, at ten-minute intervals, and the resulting liquid is sucked into the final containers, the small-volume plastic tubes that are suitable for cryopreservation. These straws are sealed by rolling the ends in stopping powder.

ASSESSING THE MATERIAL VALUE WITH THE NOTION OF FREEZABILITY

"We are now ready to finally start the freezing process. Juha, could you help me with this and pour some nitrogen in the Styrofoam box?" Taking the proffered container, Juha pours some liquid nitrogen into the box in which Maciej has installed a tube rack. Maciej explains, "Now we have to gradually cool this material down. We can't just stick these into the containers; otherwise, they'll easily die." He places the straws one by one in the rack, about 3 cm above the cold liquid, explaining, "We'll let them freeze slowly there for about ten minutes. It's already negative one hundred twenty degrees there. After that, we're almost done with the freezing. We'll just place the straws in the container, and with luck we'll have ourselves the first batch of frozen Finnsheep sperm in the gene bank!" Ten minutes later, he removes the straws from the rack and gently places them in the final repository for the standardized genetic material: the metal liquid-nitrogen-filled container equipped with special holders inside for raising the straws as needed. He declares the first batch done, explaining, "All we have to check now is how much motility they have after we thaw them in a couple of hours." Maciej closes the lid and lets the straws slide into their sleep.

About two hours later all return to assess the motility of the material after thawing. It is here that affirmation of the banked material's freezability takes place: the frozen batch must live up to the set motility standards if it is to be *accepted as national* biobanked genetic material. No amount of tinkering will make a difference anymore—no technical aids, application of standards, or adding of other materials will wake this vital material if it has died during the lengthy process of freezing. To assess the freezability of the material, Maciej takes one of the straws from the container and starts to thaw it slowly, using warm water beds. After thawing, he breaks the sealed end of the straw, lets some of the thawed liquid dribble slowly onto a slide, and looks under the microscope. "We would like to have at least forty percent motility; otherwise, the material is too weak to be effectively used in artificial insemination of any kind," he says. It is this threshold set by AI praxis—based on experience and local criteria rather than strict scientific norms—that the sperm must pass in order to become valuable frozen material. In barn conditions, freezability is taken as the ultimate heuristic notion and as a proxy for the value of the batch, which is otherwise impossible to evaluate in situ at extraction sites.[16] All the standardized straws belonging to unfreezable batches are taken from the container and thrown away. This is the last assessment in the long series of visual judgments by which the normal and the pathological (Canguilhem 2007) of cryopreserved sperm are decided on. With certain local thresholds, the figures for viability (related to morphological characteristics of sperm), the motility of the whole sperm population, and the forward mobility exhibited by individual spermatozoids are added up. The sum is judged to indicate freezability, and the sperm is thus suitable and of good enough quality for ascension to the national Finnsheep ex situ gene bank.

Maciej adjusts the microscope lenses and the slide a few times to make sure he can see the action on the slide clearly. "No, I think we have to discard this batch. Too little motility. But let's wait another ten minutes and see whether some more of them will wake up," he says. Time elapses, and the diagnosis is confirmed: "A little more motility, but still not much. All we have is about ten to twenty percent. That's too few to save this batch." Maciej and Juha both are visibly disappointed. All this work and the result turns out to be nonviable sperm for the ex situ bank. The entire batch will not make it into the final collection. Maciej considers:

> We have many possible reasons for this. What first enters my mind is that we had to calibrate the centrifuge by giving the batch two spins. It might have been too much for the spermatozoids. And then the first equilibration temperature was not optimal: it was nine degrees in the cold room when it was supposed to be only four degrees. And then it might be that Pamppu's sperm just are not viable for freezing, so we have many reasons there. But the good thing now is that we got to calibrate all the laboratory with this batch; we know how many g's the centrifuge gives at a certain percentage marked on the dial, we know the equilibrium times in the cold room and that we can't all be in there while we are doing it, and we put the first ram into isolation so that we can use it in a few days' time. We'll just follow the protocol again tomorrow with these things in our minds, and I'm sure we can make it work.

Though we lost the batch derived from Pamppu, something very valuable was achieved with the many hours of work described above. The infrastructure was adjusted to field conditions. The protocol had been tried and tested. The freezability assessments were performed successfully. Problematic field-site contingencies were identified and, to the extent possible, eliminated. The first day, although riddled with biobanking challenges, ended with positive feelings among all participants.

With technical know-how and empirical testing, a fully working collection site for biobanking was put together, and the next four days of the field trip saw seven rams put through the protocol. Of the seven, the sperm of four were judged to perform well enough to be cryopreserved in the gene bank (see table 3.1 for details of the results). The three not passing the hurdles had exhibited excessively low freezability—vitality of the freeze-thawed sperm—and, incidentally, one of these was Pamppu. He had gone through the protocol again three days later, but still the freezability of the gamete material was too low to be included in the national Finnsheep gene bank.

Over the five days on the farm, the scientists and the farmers achieved smooth following of the protocol, and they were happy as the banking sped up after the first day's tinkering work involving the instruments and their relations in the makeshift biobanking site. "Quite a good end result," says Juha at the end of the week. He sums up, "This is the basic reserve of our gene bank now" (see table 3.1). The collection, standardization, and banking work to extract, select, and process the Finnsheep breed is complete. It is transformed from a biological animal breed into reproductive materials, with all the consequences that accompany this.

The most important material consequence is that only certain genetic material embedded in the sperm is selected for the gene bank. Pamppu's material—the ingredients of a purebred Finnsheep—did not make it even though this ram is otherwise considered an elite representative of the breed. This is because Pamppu's material was not freezable. Acceptance to the national biobank depends on gametes' resistance in the freezing protocols and the moves between the cessation of animation and resumption of movement once thawed. The national similarity among the banked rams' gametes is therefore defined not through genetic similarity but via the successful alteration of ratios of movement in different mediums and temperatures, of stopping the intracellular clock and restarting it in accordance with the will of conservation scientists. Here, a novel technoscientific normalization process (Foucault 1985) occurs, the end result of which is a new population of frozen sperm batches, which together form the national gene

TABLE 3.1 A comparison of performances across the genetic materials of Finnsheep. The collection results represented as a table of performance of rams and their sperm accepted to the national gene bank

						Fresh Sperm					
Ram	ID	Farm ID	Born	Color	Date of Collection	Vol (ml)	Motility and Direction	Spermatozoids in Ejaculate (mrd)	Straws	Vitality of Thawed Sperm	Other
Nyyperi	246/375062	LS	6.3.99	W	16.11.05	1.5	+5/100	5.835	26	40–50%	Centrifuged two times, nonoptimum temperature in cold room.
					18.11.05	1.8	+4/80	4.644	21	50%	
Pamppu	1077/405356	LS	8.3.01	W	16.11.05	1.1	+5/100	3.320	16	10–20%	Centrifuged two times, nonoptimum temperature in cold room. Bad freeze resistance.
					19.11.05	1.7	+5/90	5.780	29	10%	Bad freeze resistance.
Rinssi	1731/540721	LS	17.3.02	W	17.11.05	1.0	+5/100	2.670	16	60%	Go Mosse!
Mosse	36/374711	LS	2.3.98	W	17.11.05	1.3	+5/100	3.390	22	50–60%	
					19.11.05	1.5	+4/100	4.380	19	>50%	
Taito	23/407279	LS	11.03.04	W	18.11.05	1.1	+4/100	4.100	18	>50%	Bad freeze resistance.
Tuomari	2770/689526	LS	29.4.04	W	18.11.05	1.4	+4/80	3.770	17	n. 10%	
Rabbe	9008/398659	LS	24.3.01	W	19.11.05	1	+3/60	1.290	5	50%	

bank of Finnsheep. In the end, national genetics is, quite literally, cellular movement that is capable of being arrested—an embodiment of stilled life. With the characters in our story now written, however stubbornly, these new forms of materiality can be mobilized and demobilized in various contexts and new ecologies while embedded in the new technical infrastructure of national life.

OWNERSHIP RIGHTS AND THE COMMONS

Through the gene-banking work of Maciej and Juha, the sperm became technologically naturalized as the representative material of Finnish Finnsheep genetics. Interestingly, by the very same work it is also brought into the society and made subject to its politics. "Naturalization" has two meanings here, pointing to the bidirectional relationship between nature and society. While with cryopreservation the gametes are rendered as national genetics in a new form, by the same token the cultural identity of "Finnishness" extends over and is articulated materially as Finnsheep gametes. Finnish nature and culture fuse together in the mundane materiality of diluted sperm inside a few felt-pen-marked Cassou straws in containers of liquid nitrogen. This nationally mattering relationship is open to reconfigurations: the national population consisting of cryopreserved, suspended nonhuman life is open to a new practical definition every time a new collection is successfully carried out. The list indicating the Finnish genetic material in the bank (see table 3.1) is not closed but extendable ad infinitum given pure Finnsheep and proper cryopreservation protocols.

Within the process, other relationships are also rearranged. The reduction of Finnsheep to their reproductive material and suspension of life at intracellular level is what generates the lucrative potential by allowing easy and fast mobilization and circulation at the extracellular level. This new form, however, problematizes the previously stabilized ownership relations between the individual citizens and the nation as a sovereign state. The stilled life throws relationships into motion. Writing on new reproductive technologies, Sarah Franklin has observed that "the capacity to own, to market, and to sell the reproductive powers of animals has changed quite dramatically over time, and has done so in close association with redefinition of other forms of property, such as intellectual property. Moreover, the reconceptualization of property is itself technologically assisted, through inventions such as studbooks, pedigrees and patents" (S. Franklin 2007b, 355).

Clearly, the reproductive capabilities of animals have been recently reinvented via techniques such as the cell-nucleus transfer that was used with Dolly the sheep,[17] thereby displacing many of the prerequisites for sexual reproduction (most notably, the rams that are so central to the AI techniques); reversing the sexual politics of procreation; and largely complicating issues of identity, life, and reproduction in general (see S. Franklin 2001; 2003; 2007b). However, contemporary sheep-breeding work still operates with older techniques such as selective breeding and AI. The astonishing experimental technique used with Dolly is extremely laborious and requires costly equipment and special skills, and while it has redefined some aspects of biology, it has yet to prove itself as a viable large-scale technique of animal (re)production. Compared to this novel technology that holds out promises, cryo-bio-technologically assisted AI is one that has already lived up to its promises with most animals, and with the right protocols it can now be extended to Finnsheep production. It is also a technology that, since the CBD arrived on the scene, has been articulated with the global politics of nature as a technology that has the potential to mobilize the local genetics for the economic purposes of sheep breeders. While it is an old technology for enhancing animals' reproductive powers, its newfound use as one of the main conservation strategies for ecologically endangered species also redefines the political relations embodied in its operational objects, the cryopreserved cells.

In July 2007, about eight months after the field trip, the problem of reconfigured relations was addressed in Finland's main national daily newspaper for agriculturalists, *Maaseudun Tulevaisuus*, also the third-biggest paper in Finland. A front-page article bore the headline "Finnsheep in Demand for Export—the Government Needs to Decide on the Export Permissions for Sperm." Under this banner the paper discussed Finnsheep sperm export as a way to boost the sheep business's profitability in Finland. Meat production, according to the article, is not profitable since the market value of animals in that context is very low. In contrast, the article went on to explain, the best breeding animals, especially their sperm, could become lucrative business for sheep farmers, replacing meat production as the main source of income.

In a familiar manner, the article turned to the farm that was the destination of that first gene-banking trip. Reminding readers that this is the globally leading breeding farm for the white Finnsheep, the piece stated that said farm is ready to export its semen if only the government would define the directives for the business. The farm worker who had welcomed us with coffee commented on the problem in an interview for the article:

> There are large sums of money revolving around the best breeding animals globally. The sperm material can be easily frozen with the same

MAANANTAINA 10. HEINÄKUUTA 2006 | www.maaseuduntulevaisuus.fi | NRO 77 - PERUSTETTU 1916

MAASEUDUN TULE

Laajalti helteistä

Männyn hinta nousi.

PÄÄKIRJOITUS Taimikonhoidossa riittää töitä

YLIÖ Maaseutu hyvä kasvuympäristö

www.maaseuduntulevaisuus.fi Kärsitkö helteestä?

Hallinnolta kaivataan päätöstä sperman vientiluvan perusteista

Suomenlampaalla kysyntää viennissä

Suomenlampaan vientinäkymät ovat lupaavia, sillä se on yksi maailman kysytyimmistä lammasroduista. Hyvän hedelmällisyyden ansiosta suomalaisrodun perimää halutaan hyödyntää maailmalla jalostettavissa uusissa lammasroduissa.

Elävien eläinten vienti on jo viriämässä, mutta nyt kaivattaisiin hallinnolta päätöksiä sperman vientilupaan liittyvistä perusteista.

Maa- ja metsätalousministeriössä tulisi tehdä selkeät ohjeet vientiluvan ehdoista eli siitä, kuinka sperma pitää ottaa, mitä tutkimuksia tarvitaan ja millaista terveydentilaa edellytetään täyttääkseen eri maiden vaatimat vientivaatimukset, sanoo suomenlampaita jalostavan Lihasulan tilanhoitaja Matti Koivisto.

Lihasulan tilaa kiinnostaisi kuitenkin ennen kaikkea sperman vienti. Tilan pässeistä otettiin spermaa talteen viime vuonna perustettuun pysyvään kansalliseen geenipankkiin.

Samalla tekniikalla pystyttäisiin ottamaan spermaa myös vientiä varten, Koivisto sanoo. Ilman viranomaisten laatimia ohjeita se ei kuitenkaan onnistu.

Suomen ainoa virallinen valkoisen suomenlampaan jalostustila Lihasula on saanut jo lukuisia kyselyjä jalostusaineksen ostomahdollisuuksista ympäri maailman.

Sivu 6

Hedelmällisellä suomenlampaalla olisi menekkiä maailmalla.

FIGURE 3.7 The daily *Maaseudun Tulevaisuus* (Agricultural future) newspaper, proclaiming "Finnsheep in Demand for Export" on its front page.

protocol it was collected with for the national gene bank last year. With one mount, one could collect about twenty straws of sperm, worth €200 each. In that way, even one mount would increase the overall value of one ram to €4,000. We've had inquiries all around the world, all the way from Brazil and Egypt, but could not sell anything because we are lacking any clear directives from the Ministry of Agriculture and Forestry on how to proceed.

This highlights two problems related to capitalization on the new genetic potentiality. The first is related to the lack of procedures and permissions from the Finnish Food Safety Authority (EVIRA) addressing how the sperm should be collected and what kinds of safety measures should be taken in order to prevent the possible spread of contagious animal diseases through the material. Issues of biosafety in the management of populations—especially after the large-scale epidemics of foot-and-mouth disease and other contagious animal diseases (e.g., Law 2008; Nimmo 2008; Skarstad 2008)—are a crucial matter of concern for many countries that are dependent on agricultural trade. In Finland, however, because markets for ram sperm were nonexistent before the inspiration gained from the gene banking, no procedures or permits for it existed at national level. Only laws, statutes, and procedures for live animals' import and export crossing the national borders exist; regulation of sheep gametes is still missing, thereby making it virtually impossible to export the material legally outside the nation's borders.

This is the first, and more acute, source of frustration for the sheep farmer. Even if well-functioning protocols for gene banking are now in place, the questions of health related to these new frozen populations of sheep gametes are not readily answered by the official organs of the state. Without technologies of health associated with these new populations, the circulation and trading of the new reproductive materials remain at a standstill for reasons of biosafety related to these technologically created forms of life. This is a rationality that is broadly derived from the ecological perspective on species-level management and governance with attempts to determine what kinds of processes and modes of life guarantee the animals' health and minimize the risks of diseases and pathogens embedded in their corporeality.

While the missing techniques of health management for these new reproductive materials are crucial for the trade, the issue may be easier to resolve via expert work than the bigger problem behind the noncirculation of ram sperm. That bigger problem, related to the ownership of animal life, becomes pronouncedly manifested in the context of these newly formed populations. For farms such as the one in our story, the question is not only a theoretical pondering of the social contract and its constitutive rights of citizens to new kinds of natural properties. It is also a very practical question of business opportunities and economic rationalities. If the Finnish ex situ gene bank now practically defines "genetic material" as cryopreserved sperm, how are the ownership rights and the capitalization possibilities that go with it defined? If Finnsheep breeders start to sell the cryopreserved sperm in worldwide markets, is this sperm material also identified as containing the genetic patrimony of Finland, thereby making it the property of the nation instead of the farmers? Or are the samples derived from the animals just single instances of genetic resources? The question is at once both philosophical and legal. It is a philosophical one in the sense of the ontological definition of frozen sperm: Is the matter biological and cellular or, rather, genetic and informational in essence? This is a vexing legal question since the legislative provisions pertaining to animals and the trade of them apply to the biological but not informational realm of living entities. Should Finnsheep sperm be regulated as a biological or instead as an informational object? Currently in Finland and many other states domesticated animals are treated as property similar to nonliving objects. Their practical and legal regulation is clear-cut. But an information-oriented understanding and definition of the reproductive material would call for other legal spheres and interpretations in order to make sense of how to regulate the exchange and reuse of the information embodied within the sperm cells. The state's undecidedness in terms of assigning a clear legal definition to this form of life, mainly because of the ontological instability and questions associated with that, has also prevented the state from providing farmers with licenses for capitalizing on the sperm.

Given that working protocols for sheep species and the know-how of the conservation scientists form the keys to the creation of ex situ banks—both biologically, for translating the breed to its reproductive materials, and socially, because the relationship to farmers must be configured in particular ways to include them in the conservation work—the technoscientific cessation of the national AnGRs' animation at the intracellular level is, with these problematic questions, complemented with the cessation of mobility at the extracellular level. While, at a very practical level, the nation's farmers are included in the conservation of the valuable breed, these unresolved questions currently exclude them from deriving any value from this new lucrative material before they are answered through the development of clear procedures and legal relationships within official political decision making.

Problems with ownership issues and compensation systems related to these and other kinds of new natures abound and have been discussed in recent decades at both international and local levels (e.g., Kloppenburg 1988; Strathern 1996; M. Brown et al. 1998; Parry 2001; Kamau et al. 2011; Vogel et al. 2011). One thing is clear, however: whatever promise the cryopreserved sperm, translated as genetic resources, might have, the multiple rationalities that are crossing in the gene-banking work and pulling in different directions threaten to dilute these generative potentialities. Interestingly, while most research on ownership rights has examined rights in cases of bioprospecting originating from a biodiversity-poor country of the North and targeting the biodiversity hot spots of the South, here the redefinition of ownership rights related to frozen sperm that are considered to be genetic resources happens at a subnational level, between the nation's state and the individuals who compose that very nation.

These kinds of ownership questions (and others that are just as problematic) remain vexing for the whole international community of signatories to the CBD. When the signatory nations gained sovereign rights over their native patrimonial genetic materials, they were largely disconnected from the global networks, allowing only some distinct and separately specified ex situ banks to stay operational within the networks of trade and research (Parry 2001; Whatmore 2002). The variety in the many international and national regulations, with no supranational organization to oversee the circulation of nonhuman genetic materials, has combined with the right for every nation to devise its own regulatory frameworks. One result is a muddled map of ownership rights and compensation systems pertaining to genetic resources.

The genetic sovereignty that was enacted with the CBD rearticulated national boundaries to the circulation of nonhuman life, thereby demobilizing genetic resources and banning international genetic transfer without due material-transfer agreements (MTAs) between parties to the still-only-potential transaction. Through this, the intracellularly arrested life that was stored in national ex situ gene banks was removed from the international machinery of animal (and plant) production for national conservation purposes. Within this process, the extracellular motion of frozen reproductive materials that were considered native was arrested, too, by national interventions to the neoliberal trade resulting from deep-rooted agricultural and pharmaceutical interests in these materials. The pure economic rationality was interrupted by the ecological and, most importantly, by national interests in dealing with genetic resources. This is why frozen gametes, as particular material embodiments of genetic resources, have become both intracellularly and extracellularly a stilled life.

STILLED LIFE?

I started out by claiming that current discussions of new forms of life focus a great deal on the promised value of biological substances as economic commodities—as potential sources for the creation of biovalue and the accumulation of biowealth—and as yet they have not taken a detailed enough look at the material practices by which any biological substance is made a commodity (or, as in most cases, is not). This is especially true in the context of gene banking in the conservation programs that are on their way within the nations that are signatory to the CBD. The potentiality generated within the banking process cannot be reduced to pure expectations and promissory values articulated through capital interests. It should be seen instead as a more complex generation of potentialities at both the intra- and extracellular levels of operation. This generation, I have suggested, is dependent on freezability—the successful seizure of animation happening within a novel field of reasoning, where the economic, the ecological, and the national intersect, converge, and finally diffuse into each other.

At the corporeal level, the complex situation becomes articulated by the gene-banked matter embodying these complicated relations. The material interests of all—economy, ecology, and nation—are best served by cryotechnology that is capable of arresting movement at the intracellular level. However, the same technology that generates the potentiality of biocapital by creating biovalue out of reproductive matter also generates a new articulation between the corporeal matter, of whatever nature, and the nation. Here, in the national genetic-resource programs, cryopreservation is used to arrest animation in order to maximize national biodiversity, which is translated as the pure genetic difference found in nature itself.

At the same time, the arresting of motion at the intracellular level actualizes the potentiality of the Finnsheep's reproductive matter for extracellular circulation through global agricultural networks of animal production and biocapital. This actualization of potentiality is based on the promise of the easy accumulation of added value for sheep sperm via its circulation beyond territorial boundaries. However, it is precisely the ban on exports and extracellular circulation that actualizes the nation through its new nonhuman population, which is found stored within the ex situ banks. The nation interpolates the reproductive matter and constitutes it as both ecologically native and economically viable genetic resources through the mediation of cryopreservation technologies—technologies that themselves have a long genealogy of agricultural striving toward control and capitalization of reproductive forces. Perhaps surprisingly, at the level of material practices and corporeal substances, the generation of potentialities in the context of genetic resources leads to the actualization of the nation through a new life form that becomes a politically charged form of life—a stilled life.

Similar surprises related to genetic resources can be found at the level of political texts and their articulated interests. It is true, as recent commentators such as Corinne Hayden (2003b) and Geoffrey C. Bowker (2000) have posited, that bioprospecting of biodiversity is heavily and with increasing volume made to speak through the idiom of markets. However, as should be obvious after the analysis presented above, the mobilization of economic arguments for the interest of conserving genetic difference cannot be reduced to a global striving for *only* the generation of biovalue that is potentially economically capitalizable based on these materials within the larger agricultural markets. In gene-banking work operating under national conservation programs, this idiom does not stand alone and in relation only to the processes of capitalization on the new biology or to economics. Instead, other underlying and perfused rationalities are at play here. These mobilize the economic argument for other purposes and aims than capitalization on new genetic matter, be it gametes such as sperm or other materialities embodying materials that are native to a country.

For example, economic arguments are increasingly made within conservation science with the aim of justifying ex situ strategies that are enabled by cryotechnologies to maintain genetic difference in a cheap and efficient manner, especially in cases wherein the possibility for conserving live animals in situ is limited. Here, the argument mobilizing an interest in the genetic resources should then be read as using economic reasoning to justify the particular means of technoscientific maximization of biodiversity, not straightforwardly implying an argument in favor of the immediate creation of biocapital out of it through the technology used. Here, intermingling discourses of economy and ecology lie behind the apparently similar arguments but cannot be immediately truncated to one or the other. One cannot be understood without the other, however strong and prevalent the economic rationality field might look at the outset in the practices of genetic conservation sciences.

This is why I have argued in this chapter that the network comprising the collection, identification, standardization, and banking work that goes into the making of national gene banks operates within a very special imploded (in Haraway's sense) space of economic and ecological rationalities, which the question of the national cuts across at many levels and in many ways. It might not be very off point, either, to mention that the words "ecological" and "economic" are derived from the same Greek root, *oikos*—they are both the art and rationality of governing the home (for a recent analysis of this etymological similarity, see Latour 2004a, 130–83). I have attempted to show how the two rationalities that these words represent are not only etymologically but also at very practical levels entangled and articulated with the interests of preserving a particular type of cultural identity (taking care of a nonhuman population of Finnsheep in their homeland). This is a form of nonhuman biopower that is aimed at optimizing and capitalizing on vital processes of the national herd of Finnsheep.

Quite interestingly, writing back in the 1980s, Raymond Williams urged readers to consider the relationship between the economic and the ecological, Man and Nature, in a novel way. He argued, "It will be ironic if one of the last forms of the separation between abstracted Man and abstracted Nature is an intellectual separation between economics and ecology. It will be a sign that we are beginning to think in some necessary ways when we can conceive [of] these becoming, as they ought to become, a single discipline" (Williams 1980, 84). With the Finnsheep case, I have attempted to show how ecological and economic interests, as Williams might say, traverse each other at multiple levels, get materially articulated in the context of national gene banks, and are finally embodied as national genetic resources in gene banks of all sorts that currently hold the nonhuman genetic heritage of nations. The contemporary articulation and the multiple foldings of the economic and ecological, translated to and empirically witnessed in the material interests and corporeal substance of national genetic resources, are inseparable and without clear boundaries. Instead they are perfused, porous, and complex rationalities, all inextricably linked to the new business of conservation science and related ex situ strategies. The "location of culture" (Bhabha 1994) is embodied in a new form of arrested life within ex situ gene banks. These gene banks, as new locations of national culture, also enact literally a form of nontemporality, the timeless time of the nation (Benjamin 1968; B. Anderson [1983] 1991): a national life that is conditioned by liquid nitrogen stopping the cellular clock and bringing biological processes to a standstill.

The question of nation and of the political naturalization of genetic resources links now to the "national order of things" (Malkki 1992), and its institutionalized governance (N. Brown and Michael 2004) is still partly unresolved in Finland, although a national law on genetic resources has recently been passed. With the next chapter, I strive to answer why this problem is so troubling. Chapter 4 therefore takes us to the heart of political ordering of the nation and the questions surrounding the limits of its sovereignty over national natures. To see how these issues are unfolding in Finland, we have to explore the site where the political decisions about this novel form of life are made, the ministerial body working on these questions, a special group with the Ministry of the Environment's mandate, and in the corridors of the Ministry of Agriculture and Forestry. Accordingly, I will next examine how the institutional arrangements and juridical problems related to ownership rights over genetic resources were worked on as political problems within the Board for Genetic Resources at that ministry between 2004 and 2007. Considering this part of Finnish governance of nature, I discuss what is revealed in the more recent preparation and reception of the aforementioned draft law on genetic resources in 2014–17.

CHAPTER 4

experimental administration: genetic sovereignty and the institutional (bio)politics of nonhuman nationhood

The ministry meeting room is like any other—a long wooden table for accommodating two dozen experts with comfortable chairs and a side table for refreshments. The smell of fresh coffee and sandwiches fills the air. They are needed to keep the experts on stage going during the meeting, one that repeats mundane patterns and soon becomes the soothing sounds of a lullaby for the participant-observer. One expert proposes that ownership issues related to genetic resources should be addressed in Finland according to the Bonn Guidelines. Silence as others are thinking. Then a long comment about the possible problems of the proposition advanced. Someone opposes both the arguments because of a third. More silence indicating more speculative thinking. Only noises from midday traffic outside this building at the heart of the city disrupt the speakers from time to time. The meeting lasts, as usual, about two hours, and no conclusion is reached among the participants. Instead, a new meeting time is scheduled for within the next few months.

—MY FIELD NOTES FROM JUNE 2006

Settings of this sort provided the backdrop for the long discussions I followed for two years at the Ministry of Agriculture and Forestry about the ways in which genetic resources could and should become new objects of Finnish nature and institutionalized subjects of national governance. As an ordinary way of organizing discussion around a political topic, it is not that unique an arrangement of social interaction. In fact, as a social setting, this scene represents a normal element of meeting procedure—negotiations take place among the expert parties gathered around the table. This is one particular form of political reasoning, a form of thinking within the society for the society itself. This is the institutional place for imagining Finnish nature-culture configurations with and by particular political and juridical structures—ones that genetic resources as objects of knowledge and subjects of governance challenged and rearranged in a process extending between 2004 and 2006, which had an echo in further rearrangement carried out in 2013–14 when national draft legislation on genetic resources was being prepared and yet again after it was passed in 2016.

One interesting aspect of this institutionalized, expert-driven imagination of possible configurations of a nation's natural order stems from its location within the larger national topography of official political decision-making processes. The event that my field notes describe above was one of the many official meetings of a political body called the Working Group for Access and Benefit Sharing Issues (or ABS group). This was an interim subgroup created by the Advisory Board on Genetic Resources (ABGR), another expert body that was initially composed to guide and oversee the work done in national genetic-resources programs.

As far as institutionalized political powers are concerned, the ABGR as an overseeing body is granted the highest political powers over genetic resources in Finland as long as the issues related to them remain within the official topography of its vertical mandate. This vertical mandate comes about from the fact that it is institutionally enveloped within the Ministry of Agriculture and Forestry and the proper political powers over nature that the ministry holds in practical operationalizations of the administrative powers that the civil servants themselves call "sectoral responsibility." In its work on genetic resources, the ABS group challenged any strict separation of powers between administrative branches and national governance over nature by its institutional positioning within the national institutional space of political decision making. As in other work on new natures (e.g., Sharp 2002; Walsh and Goodman 2002; Faulkner et al. 2003; N. Brown and Michael 2004; Metzler 2007) and especially on their governance with established administrative structures, the analysis presented in this chapter shows how "these new spaces of politics initially exist in an *institutional void*: there are no pre-given rules that determine who is responsible, who has authority over whom, what sort of accountability is expected" (Hajer and Wagenaar 2003, 9; emphasis in original). New natures such as genetic resources hardly fit with the existing structures of power and consequently call the limits of institutionalized sovereignty of nation-states into question.

The main focus of interest in analyses of the politics of nature (or with regard to political decision making in general) is usually on its articulated contents—the various means of agenda setting and the weighing of issues and their prioritization as supported by related discourse plays between various stakeholders (in the context of new natures, see, for example, Gottweis 1998; Knoppers 2003; Jasanoff 2004; Gottweis and Petersen 2008). No matter all the hard work that goes into making this activity possible, the daily work and the institutional contexts in which civil servants and experts enrolled in it act are usually left unanalyzed.[1]

This chapter is a detailed analysis of the formation of institutional biopolitics (Foucault 1985; 2003), a politics that takes nonhuman life as its objects within national spheres of administration, and of the rearrangement and modeling of institutional powers of the state and their administrative boundaries in the face of new genetic natures.

This lens is not applied for an academic exercise in picking at threads of political maneuverings and minutiae. Rather, the analysis demonstrates the paradoxical relations of nonhumans to the nation-state as constitutive to the governance of any modern state. It does this first by turning to the delineation created in national inscriptions of genetics, which entail creating an institutional picture that must take sides in its conceptualizations of natural resources: Are the identities to be linked to the realm of production (under the agriculture and forestry ministry) or that of conservation (on environmental turf)? The ensuing articulation work in Finland proved able to create an institutional identity that seemed to circumvent the paradoxes that were attendant to genetic resources; however, the protocols that followed the CBD brought the second paradox, of missions, to center stage. Boundary work in a new politics over nature had to address life that had been left outside the drawn borders but that fell very much within institutional mandates. Ultimately, the work to assert political representation for the bodies of nature at issue even entailed reframing the Constitution of Finland and broaching its amendment.

This might seem somewhat extreme until we consider that the doggedness of Finland's attempts at coherent implementation betrays far more than national desires to maintain a sense of credible leadership on the domestic and international stages. There is also a keen awareness that these positionings are important for the interplay of powerful economic forces (e.g., agricultural and biotech players), political powers worldwide, and scientific actors. Perhaps more importantly still, they are constitutive of relations among the elements of the nation—the state as sovereign, the people from whom the sovereignty is derived, and one or more national natures that have continued to resist ready categorization.

More recently, various organs of the state have detected the acute third paradox, between commons and sovereignty. As we will see, it ended up "bracketed out," with the picture of national bodies not yet fleshed out. It remains to be seen how long this can continue. After all, the various organs of the state do not operate in a void. They are part of a worldwide experimental process of determining who is the sovereign, in patterns through which entire societies are re-formed and natures are reconceived.

What is experimental here is not to be found in the ways policy processes are unfolding. They are conducted by the book as far as administrative work goes. Rather, the experimental aspect involves the necessary institutional fluidity and negotiations over the meaning of genetic resources as objects of administrative, institutionalized governance. As biotechnological innovations keep on pushing the boundaries of the possible in extracting, shaping, and synthesizing biomaterialities, thereby rendering them available to new uses that had not even been imagined barely a few years ago, the key to understanding the regulation-linked challenges hinges on the question of value. This is the jumping-off point for the discussion that follows. The CBD defines genetic resources as actually or potentially valuable genetic material, and biotechnological innovations rearticulate the meaning of genetic resources every time new value (or a new type of value) and use, actual or imaginary, can be attached to those resources through a particular innovation. This is why the local level in Finland but also the regional and global levels have already become stages on which biotechnological developments continue revisiting the definition of genetic resources as an object of national governance (especially in connection with issues of access, benefit sharing, and ownership). These motions are in tandem with the reidentification of the location that is most suitable (for various purposes) in the national and international political infrastructure in recent decades.

Even if the globe-spanning networks of novel bioeconomies themselves are growing more visible, with the CBD and the Nagoya Protocol being perfect examples of the new politics over these networks and redefining global relations, my argument in this chapter goes further. I contend that the same global process is re-forming the very societies that take part in this global exercise by forcing them to recount what the society—the body of each respective nation-state—is made of and which kinds of orders it should impose over its natural members. I am interested in how novel objects of nature, national genetic resources, are carved out (N. Brown and Michael 2004) by their identification within national governing bodies and in how this identification itself allows for renaturalization of Finnish society in the corporeality of nonhuman genes.

INSTITUTIONAL INSCRIPTIONS

The protracted process by which the precise wording of the CBD's text was molded (e.g., Kloppenburg 1988; Shiva 1993; Pistorius 1997; Parry 2001) did not involve politically adopting a commons perspective (as was explained in the introduction), although it did entail noting that conservation of biological diversity is a "common concern of humankind."[2] Instead, the text reasserted the signatory nations' sovereign power over their biological resources, including the genetic material one might find within these. For making this right explicit to all parties, almost as if to express subtle worry that some parties might not get this point, the CBD reaffirmed the right's legitimacy several times throughout its text—for example, in the preamble, in article 3, and in article 15.

The running definition of genetic resources that is applied for convenience is given in article 2, "Use of Terms," in which they are nested within the definition of "genetic material." The latter is defined as "any material of plant, animal, microbial or other origin containing functional units of heredity." After this, "genetic resources" gets its definition as "genetic material of actual or potential value." In other words, the idea of genetic resources is directly linked to value judgments about genetic materials. Accordingly, the Convention on Biological Diversity left the operational definition of genetic resources aside, rendering it a task of governmental exercise that was open to national specification of what constitutes valuable genetic materials. Described more precisely, because the nationally claimed value of these materials could be either actual or potential, much interpretative room was left for the parties to the CBD. They could choose their claims about their genetic resources and decide how they would politically identify and manage the various types of value as the source for national identification. The signatory countries, each in its own way, indeed proceeded to address the issue in line with their own political procedures, though adhering to certain patterns. At the same time, though, a potential interpretation of genetic resources as "human genetic resources" did get excluded in article 22 and at later meetings of the Conference of the Parties (for example, in decision II/11, made at the second meeting in 1995). The most noteworthy exclusions were that the rights and responsibilities related to genetic resources as described in the CBD do not extend to agriculturally important plant breeds or life forms addressed in prior international treaties such as the the International Treaty on Plant Genetic Resources for Food and Agriculture (IT PGRFA—for more detailed analysis of these, see Whatmore 2002, 91–116). Otherwise, it left their definition to the countries themselves.

In the discussion below, I will analyze the institutional identification of national genetic resources in Finland as one of these and the way this process has unfolded within those resources' administration via experimenting with the meaning of genetic resources—suggesting, freezing, and unfreezing materials and notions—within national nature governance.

The most obvious work early in the process was an official Council of State Decision-in-Principle issued by the Finnish Council of State in the final days of 1995. The overt objective of this move was to lay out measures aiding with biodiversity research and conservation with the specific mechanisms focused on the government level: encouraging interministry cooperation and specifying the responsibilities of the individual ministries in the national implementation efforts. Each ministry was declared responsible for the conservation and sustainable use of biological diversity within its jurisdiction. At the same time, importantly, the CBD-related work was to be spearheaded by the Ministry of the Environment: the Decision-in-Principle appointed that ministry to be in charge of overseeing the implementation work.

Accordingly, within a little more than three months, the Ministry of the Environment had appointed a broad-based body composed of representatives from all the ministries, key sectors of trade and industry, and environment-focused organizations. This body, the National Commission for Biological Diversity, had drafted Finland's first national action plan for biological diversity by the end of the year, as had been mandated by the Decision-in-Principle. Alongside several action points for the implementation of the CBD, it identified a concept of responsibility in the management of biological diversity that followed on from what it presented as the Decision-in-Principle's description of ministries' respective duties: "Each ministry is responsible for the conservation and sustainable use of biological diversity within its field of jurisdiction, as well as for making proposals for measures promoting biodiversity" in line with the guiding principle of "sectoral responsibility" (Kangas et al. 1997/8, 6). Tasks were to be handled sector-specifically, each by the ministry linked most closely to the task's subject matter. This key political principle served as a boundary infrastructure between the ministerial bodies, where boundary infrastructures do "the work that is required to keep things moving along. Because they deal in regimes and networks of boundary objects (and not of unitary, well-defined objects), boundary infrastructures have sufficient play to allow for local variation together with sufficient consistent structure to allow for the full array of bureaucratic tools (forms, statistics, and so forth) to be applied," in the words of Geoffrey Bowker and Susan Leigh Star (2002, 313–14). It was adopted for ensuring tasks' legitimate distribution among the various bodies and their respective spheres of administration in the implementation of the CBD. The concept thereby served as a pillar for building the national institutional ecology in genetic governance; it provided a framework within which the national tasks related to the implementation of the CBD's three main objectives were spread in a legitimated manner across quite distinct-seeming national spheres of administration.

For those objectives (conservation of biological diversity, sustainable use of its components, and fair and equitable sharing of the benefits arising from the use of genetic resources), the commission set forth 124 action points and, relying on the "sectoral responsibility" principle, identified the administrative bodies responsible for each. Of these action points, three pertained directly to genetic resources. In these three points, it was implicit that national plant and animal genetic-resource programs would be needed for identifying and organizing native Finnish genetic material and thereby safeguarding the genetic diversity of Finland's plants and animals. As for carving up this work territory in line with sectoral responsibility, the commission determined that the actions under all three items lie within the mandate of the Ministry of Agriculture and Forestry (MAF). An additional element proposed was that national legislation addressing the patenting of genetic resources and related rights of ownership should be kept up to date with respect to international developments, but no single governance entity was pinpointed as responsible for this task. In line with the mandate specifically identified as belonging to it, the MAF began slowly preparing programs for two kingdoms of nonhuman life: plant and animal genetic-resource strategies were drafted within plant and animal working groups operating under the ministry's aegis. These were ready by 2001 and 2003, respectively, and the ministry delegated their realization to a large research institute under its control, Agrifood Research Finland, and to the Finnish Forest Institute. These institutions started their programs in 2003 (for plant and forestry elements) and 2004 (for animals). A final piece of the brickwork was laid when the national Board for Genetic Resources was established by law to oversee and guide the work done within the two programs. Comprising experts in diverse areas, the board was to operate under MAF control.

These institutional arrangements may be cast as self-evident in discourse of sectoral responsibility, but there is an important interpretative element here: a decision was made in initially interpreting and identifying genetic material in one particular way rather than others in the Finnish administration of nature and in how the national political epistemology works at the upper levels in the Finnish governance of nature. In judging that genetic resources belong under the responsibility of the MAF, the national commission made a particular reading of their nature. The responsibilities of the MAF are set as steering policy on sustainably using natural resources "as part of the Finnish Government and the EU institutions and decision making," with that task validated by dint of that ministry's administrative sector, including "agriculture and horticulture, rural development, forestry, veterinary services, control of foodstuffs of animal origin, fisheries, game and reindeer husbandry, use of water resources and land surveying" (MAF public description of institutional responsibilities 2012). This institutional recognition of responsibilities entails the coconstruction of political power over specific activities of specific parts of nature and the delineation of power to define their identity.

Within this joint construction project, the above description of the MAF's administrative sector constructs its elements of governance under the figures of natural referents, the objects of nature that lack their own voice. Those offering the description, then, are able to act as a representative for these mute entities or give/assign them a voice in Finnish nature politics. The objects of nature were taken as a bundle with this institutional identification—the commission interpreted all genetic resources as belonging to the MAF's administrative realm by dint of the MAF's handling of specific aspects of nature: only those of (1) cultivated plants and forests and

(2) domesticated animals. Imposing the lines between two kingdoms and making others excluded or residual followed divisions that were already in place. It is for the same reason that the aims for the national genetic-resource programs that were prepared under that jurisdiction follow a parallel division. "In its work, the group decided to limit the program now presented to only the genetic resources pertaining to agriculture, horticulture, and forestry," the MAF (2002, 6) explained matter-of-factly, and this declaration followed within a couple of years: "The working group for animal genetic resources decided in the meeting on 5 Sep. 2001 that the preparation of the report should be extended to preparing the national program for farm animal genetic resources. Of the farm animal species, the working group defined the program to deal with bees, cattle, chickens, dogs, animals raised for their fur, goats, horses, pigs, reindeer, and sheep" (MAF 2004, 4).

At this juncture, one might wish to stop and think about this list in a bit more depth for what it reveals of politico-juridical institutions' role as interfaces between nature and culture. What exactly do agricultural plants, bees, and fur animals have in common? The answer to this important question is, of course, that they are linked only by their biological status as life forms or by their genetic makeup as understood in a traditional or day-to-day sense or in administrative governance. In taxonomic terms, they do not even belong together at the most general level in the standard Linnaean taxonomy, that of kingdoms (plant versus animal), let alone that of phyla (bees in the phylum Arthropoda versus reindeer in Chordata). Nor do they possess a singular Finnish genetic condition (whether a gene or a gene complex) that would connect them together and at the same time set them apart from other nonhuman living beings found within the national territory. So what *is* the connecting element here?

What all the animals in this list share is their institutional location as agricultural species falling under the MAF's political jurisdiction. That is, being agricultural objects of nature is what connects them as national genetic resources. What confers this identity on them is an inherently economic relation that is given voice politically here. Whereas they already occupied certain positions in the social-economic order as heterogeneous forms of nonhuman life in the biological sense-making practice between taxa, these steps took them further: the boundary infrastructure enacted in the wake of the CBD through sectoral responsibility, initially effected by the political decision of the Council of State, brought them together under the figure of genetic resources.

This new horizontal connection that cuts across biological categories is fundamentally derived from the preexisting economic relations to the

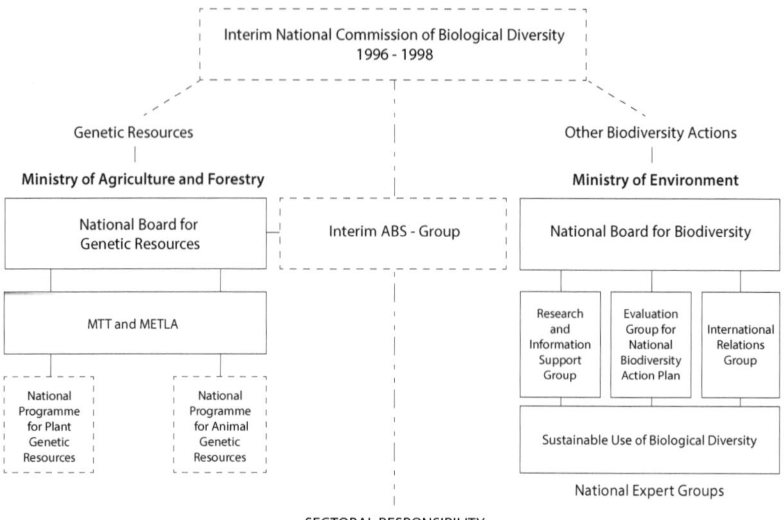

FIGURE 4.1 The initial institutional topography in the implementation of the CBD (later rearranged). Genetic resources were delegated to the Ministry of Agriculture and Forestry and actions related to biodiversity in other realms to the Ministry of the Environment, which set up its own expert bodies focusing on other issues.

national order of things. It is precisely the underlying economic relationship between nature and culture that draws the collection of species that is listed together under a new ontological status of national genetic resources. That is, this underlying relationship, which characterizes the essence of the MAF's administrative sphere, delimits these species as a new political assembly of nonhuman life. This institutional identification does more: by becoming Finland's natural resources, they are brought under the rule of the sovereign. In this, they literally became part of the body of the state and its political life. These genetic resources, a form of life that enjoys the state's protection,[3] are now a *political* form of novel nonhuman life—the novel nonhuman life becomes a political concept (Agamben 2000, 7) that is fitted to the institutional requirements of Finnish politics of nature. This is something that belongs much more to the world of politics than to the corporeality of genetic resources themselves (i.e., as attested to through the knowledge practices of biological sciences prior to their overt exploitation for political ends). This was the first move in defining the issue of genetic resources as a matter of nonhuman nativity.

We can now turn to what followed in the process of nativization. As soon as the genetic resources (living in forests, held in pens, and buzzing about flowers) gained a relatively stable temporal identity as beings of domesticated nature, their institutional interpretation was ready for use by the ministerial bodies that were tasked with their further governance. Once the identity and institutional location of genetic resources had gained relative fixity, they were manageable as part of the national nature, and more work could be done with them.

CONTINUING THE BOUNDARY WORK AND MANAGING NEW SPACES OF POLITICS

While genetic resources were seemingly frozen for political projects, stabilized as objects of governance, this would not be the case for long. They remained naturalized nonhuman forms of life for only nine years (1996–2005), between the launching of the national biodiversity program in its initial form and the drafting of the genetic-resource programs. Soon after this, they started to unravel as clearly defined objects found in the national nature as they began to problematize both their institutional location and governance based on this. One might recall Bowker and Star's words here: "Objects exist, with respect to a community, along a trajectory of naturalization. This trajectory has elements of both ambiguity and duration. It is not predetermined whether an object will ever become naturalized, or how long it will remain so" (2002, 299).

This problematization, and the accordant destabilizing, began when genetic resources and the experts acting as their representatives in the institutional structures refused to accept their identity as purely agricultural beings. Their inclusion in Finnish society purely through an economic relationship was called into question. The once-naturalized national articulation between nature and culture was ruptured with new identities yet to be crafted for genetic resources.

Picking apart the chain of disruptive events on the road to the reinterpretation of genetic resources, one finds that the first was the issuing of the Bonn Guidelines by the signatory nations to the CBD. Fruit of the six Conference of the Parties meetings held in 2002 in The Hague (by decision COP VI/24), these were created to serve as nonbinding guidance in the interpretation and implementation of the CBD at a national level, with special focus on issues of accessing genetic resources and sharing the ensuing benefits.

The second key disruptive event leading to the reinterpretation in Finland was the development with which I began the chapter, the subsequent establishment of a new interim institutional body, the national ABS group (more formally the Working Group for Access and Benefit Sharing Issues). This group, which the National Advisory Board on Genetic Resources deemed necessary for dealing with the issues raised in the Bonn Guidelines, was ultimately not an ideal match for the national political topography and the distribution of powers over issues of nature that had been clearly identified and set in place within it. It had been determined that proper implementation of the CBD in line with the Bonn Guidelines would require that those problematic ABS questions that were deemed mostly political be resolved alongside the scientific identification of the new genetic corporealities. It was in line with this that in 2003 the national board proposed that the ministry set up a working group under the national board to examine these issues—such as who in Finland can legitimately own and use genetic resources that are identified as native and how the related benefit sharing should be officially arranged.

This proposal was accepted later in the year, with the ABS group mandated to operate for two years from 2005 to 2006. The ministry's mandate to the working group states its aims, areas of action, and obligations. The key language was the following specification of tasks (Mandate of the ABS Group, Dnro 580/041/2003[4]):

- to deal with the aims of the Bonn Guidelines and related national implementation, including the development of legislation;
- to clarify the roles and liabilities related to access and benefit sharing issues according to article 15 of the Convention on Biological Diversity and liabilities stemming from other contracts (*WTO/TRIPS*, *WIPO*, *UPOV*, *FAO/IT*)[5] as needed;
- to prepare a proposal for a national strategy or action plan on the access and benefit sharing issues related to hereditary materials, and other provisions and tasks.

Technically, the Bonn Guidelines are not a strongly binding international document,[6] but it is clear from the wording of this mandate that the ministry has defined them as binding with regard to the requirements for the working group. While the signatory nation-states are not interpreted as legally bound to act on the guidelines' terms, the ministry performed an operation typical of politico-juridical institutions: it altered the nonbinding modality of the guidelines to legitimate the work of the ABS group and to foster the intertextual connection between national and international documents and the institutions in charge of genetic resources. By changing the interpretation of the national weight of the document, the ministry obliged the group to examine the provisions of the CBD through the lens of the Bonn Guidelines and to relate the outcome of its work (a proposal, strategy, or national action plan) directly to biodiversity actions in Finland. In political practice, the wording of the mandate turned the Bonn Guidelines into a nationally binding document. Reinterpretation was thick in the air.

While the CBD itself, in its definition of genetic resources, stresses national sovereignty, the Finnish reality was that national interpretations and actions based on them now had to mesh with the Bonn Guidelines and a host of other international agreements. In simple terms, the tasks of the working group encompassed reviewing national legislation but also considering the various ways in which the national implementation could be harmonized with the Bonn Guidelines and the network of international agreements to which they refer.[7] Alongside the role of the ministerial institutions as interfaces articulating the appropriate relationship between national nature and culture, another mediating role became explicit: the working group would need to articulate the national institutions and legislation for supranational institutions and the various international agreements for which they act in supervisory capacity. My fieldwork led me to an up-close view of the articulation work that was started in October 2004 by this buffering entity.

The boundaries in question began to emerge as the working group started to reexamine the definition of genetic resources. I was granted silent-observer access to the Advisory Board on Genetic Resources, the ABS working group's meetings, and the documents produced early the following spring. One of the first questions I began to ponder was how the institutional division of labor affected the work. It soon became clear that the action plan's positioning of genetic resources within the sphere of agriculture and forestry had the consequence of bifurcating Finnish nature. With genetic resources having been placed under the MAF's political powers, the nature administered by the Ministry of the Environment (MENV) was excluded from their possible definitions.

This is where the ripple effects, obvious and less so, of the early demarcation decisions become apparent. The boundary infrastructure enacted via the principle of sectoral responsibility dictated that the parts of nature under MENV administration could not be defined as nonhuman life forms found in their natural state in the environment or beings of a wild and undomesticated nature.[8] The members of the working group on ABS issues were well aware of the issues following from the division of tasks and responsibilities between the two institutions from the outset. The attendant division into two administrative natures served as the very starting point of the work. In an interview conducted while the group was active in its work, its secretary commented on this division of labor thus:

> The Ministry of the Environment is the ministry politically in charge of the issues pertaining to the CBD, and, for example, it organizes the national consultations in Finland that are to be represented at the EU-level meetings and consults all ministries affected by the issues somehow. And then when we have this national Board for Genetic Resources and its ABS group, they are located under the Ministry of Agriculture and Forestry. This is why we are not specifically concerned about wild plants and life forms. Rather, we concentrate on cultivated plants and domesticated animals.[9]

While the members were keenly aware of the borders, it grew clearer and clearer to them that working within those bounds rendered the review work and further articulations problematic. They saw the institutional location of genetic resources in Finland as being at odds with full implementation of the Bonn Guidelines, which required national strategies to cover all genetic resources (apart from human genetics, as stated in their clause c9). Addressing only those belonging to agriculture would not suffice. While the vertical responsibility of the ABGR entailed limiting its administrative sphere to agricultural species (see fig. 4.1 and the definition of the board's administrative powers above), the mandate given to the ABS group would necessarily transcend any clear political dichotomy of nature following the national political topography on account of the definitions in the Bonn Guidelines. A contradiction emerged: for the ABS group to implement (what had become for Finland) the requirements of the guidelines nationally, its operational mandate would extend beyond that given to its parent body, the Advisory Board on Genetic Resources, which supervised the ABS group's work. The secretary continued her comments about the national-level separation of administrative powers over spheres of nature by saying, "This ABS subgroup is situated on the borderlines [of sectoral responsibilities]. It includes both the cultivars and domesticated animals, but also these wild . . . well, we will be considering all these issues in the national strategy. Or there are usually four categories: they are cultivars, domesticated animals, forests, and then wild plants and species. Of these, three are in the MAF mandate, and the wild ones belong to MENV." It was abundantly clear that the group's mandate extended horizontally beyond the ministry's sectoral responsibilities to spheres of nature that were considered to be the administrative realm of MENV. Also wild resources as found in nature had to be considered in the ABS strategy. The definition of genetic resources found in the Bonn Guidelines could not be ignored.

What was the solution to be? With this interpretation of the ABS group's mandate as a given, it found itself in a liminal space of politics between two ministries—that responsible for agriculture and forestry and that managing the environment—while operating under only the political powers of, and accountable only to, the ABGR. In practice the ABS group gained a diagonal mandate that required an unofficial trust relationship between the two ministries. For the Ministry of the Environment to take into account the findings from a strategy produced outside its political boundaries and by another ministry, the borders in keeping with sectoral responsibility had to be crossed via unofficial routes by trusted experts and civil servants and their personal relations with the officials working within MENV.

While a diagonal mandate of this sort is not unheard of in institutionalized decision making, it is important to recognize both that it enables a new way of politics and that this form of politics has been characterized as operating within an institutional void for a limited time (see Hajer and Wagenaar 2003, 9). With this pragmatic mandate, the working group could draft its final report. Released on September 1, 2006,[10] the final ABS report extended the definition of genetic resources by including life forms in their natural state. Under the heading "Wild Life Forms," that report acknowledges,

> Organisms in their natural state form a large heterogeneous group, including wild plants, excluding the family of wild plants related to cultivated species listed in Annex 1 of the IT treaty,[11] wild animals, most of the sea creatures, and microorganisms. Most of the life forms of this group are unknown, and their economic value is hard to evaluate as their mapping is not exercised in Finland in a systematic manner. This group of life forms belongs under the CBD, and the Bonn Guidelines are targeted especially to help create governance of this group. (MAF 2007, 24)

With this piece of text, new boundaries were drawn. The initial post-CBD national identification of genetic resources was dismantled. They were no longer limited to purely agricultural forms of nonhuman life.

Genetic resources gained a new textual representation here with the report specifying that Finnish genetic resources cut through the national political topography and related institutionalized spheres of administration. As subjects of governance, the natural resources themselves called into question the bifurcation of nature that was wrought through institutional politics over nature. Although the limiting division into distinct spheres of agricultural nature and nature as in its natural state, or between domesticated and wild nature, was no more, the new representation did not bring change to their political or corporeal representation within the national politics of nature. Another contradiction-rife situation resulted.

Finnish genetic resources had been redefined to encompass all native forms of life, wild or not, but at the same time official ways of making them into objects of national politics were absent. The ABS report was a relatively lightweight political document. Perhaps partially in order to tame its diagonal mandate, even its cover page classed it as only a "working group background memo" (at odds with the essence of a national action plan or strategy with the political weight that was ostensibly intended). This might not be so surprising since the Ministry of Agriculture and Forestry lacked the institutional powers to represent the newly defined genetics, including wild ones, within national politics.

Accordingly, it also lacked the powers to address the other question raised by the ABS report: mapping of the known-unknown wild national bodies. The corporeal identification programs were initially delegated to the two research institutes operating directly under that ministry (MTT and Metla, the Finnish Forest Research Institute). However, their genetic-resource programs, again, could only target agricultural native species according to the principle of sectoral responsibility with the vertical boundary thereby established between set categories of life forms under the institutionalized politics that legitimated and funded the research. The chair of the Advisory Board on Genetic Resources commented on this institutionally enacted problem of corporeal identification on March 7, 2007, by considering an example from plant-genetics programs, which she bemoaned as no longer being systematic, continuing,

> Well, we have systematized our gene bank for cultivated plants well. . . . It is in-built in breeding work that the materials that are not used anymore [i.e., the known unknowns, whose further potential is not evident] will be sent to the gene bank, which conserves them. And then we have in some kind of order the horticultural plants, apples, cherries, pears, currants, rhubarb, shallots, and a very small number of other plants. . . . All the others are in a gray area.

She identified familiar and concretely named corporeal forms of life, known genetic resources, as being in contrast to known-unknown life forms that were left in the gray area—life forms that are known to exist but that lack inscription in the scientific instruments as corporeal objects of nature and textual materialization as lists of varieties or breeds (as in the case of the

Alexander). In her comments they were linked mostly to the potential of wild, uncultivated varieties. As the above extract illustrates, the civil servants in the ministry (most of whom are themselves former biologists) are amid the known that they do not know.

While the corporeal identification programs are only taking their first steps, it is abundantly clear that they are hampered considerably by the problematic national division of labor between the ministries that are in charge of the governance of the new genetic objects of nature. The problems were not solved by the interim ABS working group and its liminal institutional location within the larger political topology. These had made it possible to define genetic resources in a way that carved out space by transgressing the principle of sectoral responsibility, but at the same time the move complicated enactment within the existing space, the institutional infrastructure in charge of governing Finnish nature. Full implementation of the suggestions presented in the group's background memo would seem to require the institutional duplication of genetic resources. That is, letting the wild genetics enter the national politics of nature with explicitly legitimated institutional representations and corporeal identification programs requires the space that is created by placing them under both MAF and MENV mandate.

The principle of sectoral responsibility had initially been suggested for creating a clear-boundary infrastructure guiding the division of political labor and for keeping things moving along. It transpired that this principle actually arrested the political movement required for the issue's resolution. Neither the ABS group nor the ABGR could articulate the textual, political, and corporeal representation of national genetic resources in a coherent enough manner. In consequence, there were now two quite different political definitions of Finnish genetic resources: one allowing for legitimate national institutional representation through the Ministry of Agriculture and Forestry alone and the second (presented in the ABS group's somewhat toothless final report) enabling the articulation of national genetic resources with the complex network of international agreements and institutions. In this contradiction, the complex agency of genetic resources as subjects of governance rears its head. These recalcitrant and highly unstable beings of nature may leave us wondering exactly how many natures could emerge in human attempts to manage them.

NEW INTERPRETATIONS OF THE CONSTITUTIONAL ORDER

The complication brought about by the various genetic resources reached even the constitution, for institutional positioning, political definition, and corporeal identification were not the only matters problematized with the ABS group's report. The other task under the group's mandate was to suggest any legislative changes necessary for bringing the relevant genetic resources under the sovereign rule of the Finnish nation. In the course of its far-reaching review of national and international legislation surrounding natural objects and property, work that took two years, the ABS group reached the conclusion that it was challenging and perhaps even untenable to bring these new objects under national jurisdiction as specified in the CBD—by which, again, every signatory nation gained sovereignty over its native genetic resources and thereby gained sovereign power to decide on their governance within the context of national legislation. Their rightful governance with the legislation that was already in force was not possible, and several challenges had to be addressed to enable the exercise of national sovereignty in this domain.

Because genetic resources in this connection are novel objects of nature, key questions about legitimate ownership claims and their fair use were not directly addressed in the existing national laws. To complete its mission, therefore, the group had to come up with suggestions for how national legislation addressing genetic resources could be developed through taking into account the (national and international) regulations that were already in place. Reflecting on the work carried out, the chair of the ABS working group said the following in an interview only a few months before the final report on ABS issues was released:

> Our mandate was, of course, relatively clear—to deal with the Bonn Guidelines and to foster cooperation with other Nordic countries with regard to genetic resources and also to the review of the limits of our current system. We also had to look at the administrative and juridical issues and how they work with our national structures. . . . I built the process in such a way that we looked at all international agreements from the point of view of genetic resources. To work this way also meant that, in addition to the international agreements, we have had to go through all the national agreements, laws, and statutes at the same time. We have looked through all the national legislation concerning the spheres of both the agricultural and the environmental ministry. This means that we have examined in detail, for example, the environmental regulations as well as the game and forestry governance in place, from the point of view of genetic resources, and we have tried to identify possible holes or overlaps in governance or the elements in which these holes exist.[12]

The question of ownership claims and relations seemed simple when the first National Action Plan was released in 1998. It took the stance that the genetic resources do not necessitate legislative development. The explanation offered was that "legally speaking, [ownership] does not present a real problem. Although the Convention contains certain obligations concerning the distribution of benefit from genetic resources, these obligations only have legal effect between the Contracting Parties, in compliance with the international law. None of the stipulations of the Convention requires changes to national property laws" (Kangas et al. 1997/8, 85). However, when sifting through the network of related international agreements and comparing them to the national legislation in force,[13] the working group came to a contrary conclusion. Genetic resources are not inscribed in the national legislation as objects of ownership—no Finnish legislation in force identifies them as a possible form of natural property. Therefore they cannot legally be claimed as objects of governance either by private individuals or by the institutions of the state.

This made things trickier for two interconnected reasons. The first problem was that section 15 of the Constitution of Finland guarantees citizens very strong legal protection of ownership with regard to objects that are traditionally called "natural": nonhuman life in biological beings such as cows or trees. In addition, the Finnish legal system acknowledges some basic rights, such as that of collecting certain natural objects for personal use (e.g., berries and mushrooms from all forests, privately owned or not). One logical consequence of this acknowledgment is that if genetic resources are legally defined as traditional nature comprising biologically identifiable nonhuman species, state sovereignty would be undermined: the state's arms of governance would lose much of their administrative power (and thereby operationalized sovereignty) in favor of the private citizens possessing the native biological matter. Clearly, defining genetic resources within this interpretative frame would be impossible if the claim of sovereignty over them in the CBD and the Bonn Guidelines were to be enshrined in Finland. Inversely, in the absence of national legislation recognizing genetic resources as juridical objects, neither the state nor private citizens can lay any legitimate ownership claims to them. The senior adviser from the Ministry of Justice who was a member of the working group described the situation thus:

> The problem is that if we are talking about genetic material, even if it is connected to certain biological material that itself can be subjected to ownership, and this biological material—for example, animals or

> plants or a collection of bacteria—can be exchanged, then from the viewpoint of the current legal system in force, it is unclear whether it is possible for private persons to exchange the genetic material that is included in these biological materials. At the moment, we cannot really use traditional property laws fruitfully to solve this problem.[14]

The second hurdle for the working group, which was related to the first problem, stemmed from the problematic corporeal form of genetic resources as a potential object of ownership and governance that is always already included within biological matter. It was not enough for the group to find these problems with current legislation (holes of governance, as the chair termed them); its mandate also required considering possible ways of tackling these problems. One possible solution was suggested in early 2006. In all its simplicity, it involved a juridical bifurcation of nature into biological and genetic natures, with the former consisting of known biological beings (trees, reindeer, bees, etc.) and the latter including only the hereditary material that makes biological beings possible: genetic resources. The secretary of the ABS group clarified this possible solution for me, with its two further natures, a few months before the release of the final document:

> You could put it this way: if a tree grows in the forest and I'm the forest owner, then I can make use of the biological matter by cutting down the tree and selling it to a paper factory and make money out of it. Or then I can . . . pick a pine cone from that tree and use the biological matter—for example, burning it in a campfire. Or then you can collect some mushrooms growing in the forest and extract a valuable gene from them and do whatever you like with that—for example, use it in breeding work. And the problematics related to the issue are now culminating in the question of whether we should separate these two. If a private citizen owns the tree, then that person would not own the genetic resources embodied in the pine cone; those would be owned by the nation. At the moment, anybody can come and take the cone and make money out of it in any imaginable way. But the open question now is are we going to interpret the owner of the biological matter also as the owner of the genetic matter, or should we separate these two ownerships? This is the big issue we are considering at the moment.[15]

The working group suspected that even if juridical separation between two natures could be considered a possible solution to the ownership problem, such a suggestion was bound to pose political problems. First, it would be difficult to justify the rearrangement of ownership relations between the citizens and the state, especially with regard to land and forest owners. Even trickier would be to inscribe this new ownership relation for genetic resources in national legislation because that would require huge changes—an amendment to the constitution, section 15 of which guarantees such powerful protection of private ownership that even the exercise of sovereignty by vesting authority to decide on ownership issues related to genetic resources in the Finnish state would require changing or even rewriting portions.[16] The possible politico-juridical problems were many. Nonetheless, the working group did hint toward this as possibly being workable in the final report.

The proposal of resolving the jurisdictional system's problematic status by creating two separate natures, one biological and the other genetic, is inscribed in the report with the following wording:

> If the system is to be extended both to the organisms in the state of nature and to the public and private collections including live organisms, the realization of the system would probably require legislative action pertaining to at least the content of the contracts, the involvement of relevant stakeholders, a mechanism of prior informed consent, and administrative redress. In this case, the questions related to the Constitution must be taken into account, as must, for example, the regulations dealing with everyman's right [the common citizen's right to pick berries, etc., for personal use]. (MAF 2007, 17)

The message within this politically sophisticated language is not manifestly apparent. The working group here reinterprets the first action plan's stance on genetic resources as nonproblematic objects of national governance and objects of legal ownership relations. Going further, it suggests radical action to bring native nonhuman genetics under national governance and to legally naturalize them as parts of Finnish nature.

The question about the number of natures in Finland that was prompted by the novel objects of genetic governance is still unresolved today. While this has remained an open question, the report has had an impact on the politics of genetic resources. Perhaps the most visible change is that the report underwent a transformation in modality from background memo to central text in the intervening years. It has become a founding document in the official politics in that it is now woven into an intertextual network that is wider than that of any other Finnish official document on genetic resources (see table 4.1). As the chair of the ABS group said, in a discussion that crystallized the aims and uses of the memo for me, it "creates a base for the continuation of the work. And it is a justificatory document for all the actions of the future." In the years following its release, this document traveled higher in institutional circles, and it quickly became integrated into the official plan for future action on biodiversity issues. In a new Decision-in-Principle document issued on December 21, 2006, the Council of State decided to launch a biodiversity program called Saving Nature for People for 2006–2016. The memo drafted by the ABS group has been connected to this by the questions raised about the status of genetic resources as political objects. The new Decision-in-Principle, while not pinning down the number of natures that is suitable, states that genetic resources, the actions related to them, and the ministries responsible for their representation in the politics of nature will be worked on with a slightly different national configuration. For measure 58, it states,

> On the basis of the background report prepared by the subcommittee of the Genetic Resources Committee, the next steps for implementing the Bonn Guidelines in Finland will be examined, including the need for action on essential legislative issues and the development of administrative practices in accordance with Article 15 of the CBD, having regard where necessary also to obligations arising from other international agreements. The Genetic Resources Committee, which deals with issues related to genetic resources in agriculture under the supervision of the Ministry of Agriculture and Forestry, will examine Finland's national obligations related to the implementation of the International Treaty on Plant Genetic Resources for Food and Agriculture and the Bonn Guidelines with regard to agricultural genetic resources.—[the ministries in charge] MENV, MAF, 2006–7. (Heikkinen et al. 2007, 105)

The issue of genetic resources and their political representation has been once more redelegated, with two branches of administration again involved. For the next decade, both MENV and MAF were placed in charge of the political and juridical issues related to them. A new biopolitical formation arose once more between the ministries around the issue of politics working with the national question of genetic resources. What may be new here remains to be seen, but it seems clear already that the corporeal identification of the genetic resources remains unsystematic: no new programs of genetic identification were mentioned in the new national action plan and strategy, and the problematic juridical issues, including the ABS group's suggestion on the bifurcation of nature, did not get addressed in the plan. The genetic resources are still a novel multitude of national genetics, a problematic collection of nonhuman life and matters of muddled biopolitics of the state.

DRAFTING THE NATIONAL LAW AND BRACKETING OUT BIOGENETIC PARADOXES

After a few years' bureaucratic circulation of the document produced, implementation of the Bonn Guidelines was put on hold, and the legal issues identified with the latter agreement were finally replaced with the Nagoya Protocol and its provisions, signed in 2011 by Finland and most signatories to the CBD (see also the introduction). The new protocol, originally meant to clarify the access and benefit-sharing issues arising from the original CBD text and the Bonn Guidelines, brought new aspects of global agreement into national preparation. Furthermore, it was not only individual countries that signed the document but also the European Parliament,[17] enforcing elements of minimum compliance such as designating specific national authorities on genetic resources and focal contact points for information dissemination and thereby imposing community pressure on the national politics of European Union members such as Finland for implementing the new protocol by the date of its agreed entry into force, October 12, 2014.

The Nagoya Protocol was designed as a response to many issues that had been left unresolved by the CBD either through unclear or wholly absent definition or by divergent interpretation of its articles. The protocol was designed to rectify the contentious political issues related to one of the three aims stated for the CBD, "the fair and equitable sharing of benefits arising out of the utilization of genetic resources,"[18] by providing a clear legal framework for that sharing. The keystones of this framework consist of newly articulated obligations for parties to define certain, clear, and transparent procedures for *access* (e.g., by nationally reiterating the need for prior informed consent by the party providing access) and *benefit sharing* (by obliging parties to the convention to take legislative, administrative, and policy measures to ensure "fair and equitable sharing" and define "mutually agreed terms" for this) and also to specify what the utilization of genetic resources means in the context of grounds for benefit sharing—for example, research and development related to genetic and/or biochemical composition of the genetic resources. Another obligation is that of working on *compliance* measures and setting up mechanisms for *monitoring* adherence (Nagoya Protocol 2010; see also Kamau et al. 2011; Greiber et al. 2012).

The main Finnish government response to the Nagoya Protocol was to perform a review of the protocol to reveal what implications it would have with regard to national implementation. The report issued in June 2012 on the review identified three key areas of focus and suggested actions: establishment of a system that allows the monitoring and identification of the country of origin for genetic resources imported to Finland, the creation of a system that allows for the protection of national interests for genetic resources exported from Finland, and compliance with the minimum demands of the Nagoya Protocol as backed by EU regulation. This compliance entailed setting up a governmental system with a national institution that was designated to act as the Finnish "competent authority," identifying a "National Focal Point" for granting access and for international coordination, and sharing information about the national ABS regulation.

Interestingly, the report also identified a key challenge in enacting the protocol and its national implementation. This is related to the definition of genetic resources. The report stated the following:

> Because [national] genetic resources are regulated by the ABS [system of the Nagoya Protocol] . . . and regardless of the way in which their governance or ownership is organized, it will be relevant to define what is meant by genetic resources in the [Finnish] legislation. This is needed also because the national actors will need to comply [with the ABS terms by informing the national authorities with information about the import and use of a foreign genetic resource], even if the access to [that] genetic resource in the country of origin will be determined by the national legislation. (Hollo 2012, 39)

The report thus raised an important point about the enforcement of a global agreement: if genetic resources are to be regulated, one should know what they are. This goes for both imported and exported genetic resources.

In April 2013 the Ministry of the Environment appointed a new working group, which it mandated to prepare the national implementation of the Nagoya Protocol by the end of 2014. Although the group was institutionally situated firmly under the political mandate of the MAF this time, the composition of this group, too, was cross-sectorial, bringing in participants from various ministries. In the group's fifteen meetings during its assigned work period, it discussed, evaluated, and debated a broad range of issues from the aims for the new protocol to the current state of valuable Finnish genetic resources. It ultimately produced a draft text for genetic-resource legislation and national implementation of the Nagoya Protocol.

When I interviewed the senior officer for legal affairs who was tasked with coordination of the working group's efforts, their completion, and their presentation to the parliamentary expert council, some key points of contention, which had already been evident from the work done several years earlier with the review of the Bonn Guidelines, emerged again as "bracketed issues" (Riles 2006)—that is, issues isolated as contested elements that were to be subject to later negotiation, studiously ignored, or directly addressed on account of their ramifications or the alignments they signal:

> We had to make a choice between drafting entirely new and extensive genetic-resources legislation or implementing only the needed compliance measures and codifying them in the national legislation. During the work, we agreed that we are going to concentrate on the minimum required implementation of Nagoya. This includes setting up the system to monitor the use of imported genetic resources. This does not, of course, include full consideration of genetic resources and ownership and so on at a national level. And regarding access to national genetic resources, the group was quite univocal that we do not really need to regulate that up front with new bureaucratic maneuvers such as prior informed consent; instead, we will rely on usage declaration from those who have taken and used Finnish genetic resources for research or development purposes.[19]

In this case, the form of bracketing that was chosen was to bracket out the problematic elements. The implementation of the minimum compliance measures—most importantly, designating the "competent authority" and "National Focal Point" for genetic resources—was what the officer quoted above called a pragmatic choice since the group was under time pressure to review and agree on legislative and policy measures to be taken nationally within a space of roughly eighteen months. Comparing this work and the scope of the work explained above to the output of the ABS working group from several years earlier, one can see how the issue of genetic resources has again mutated and how they have been bracketed out from the legislation implementing the Nagoya Protocol because they are considered too complex to govern.

Between 2013 and 2014 genetic resources were not the main objects of the draft legislation. Central status was given instead to *access* to them and deciding on *compliance* measures. And, by implication, access to national genetic resources and compliance measures refer to informing other countries and other interested parties about the policy for access to Finnish genetic resources and safeguarding imported genetic resources. The key object in creating the policy and drafting the legislation was other nations' genetic resources, and rather than national genetic resources being codified by means of the legislation, the policy and legislative work set the access policy for Finnish resources and established the local mechanisms to protect imported ones from misuse.

In a follow-up discussion with the MENV official responsible for the draft legislation, I asked whether the group had ever considered defining national genetic resources and specifying their ownership as part of this Nagoya Protocol implementation work.

> Yes, we did. For this, we even commissioned a review about valuable Finnish genetic resources that was completed in 2015. Accordingly, there are two categories of them that might be valuable to Finland: microbes found in nature, because they might have all sorts of interesting features, such as freezing resistance, and also endangered species or breeds [that] are valuable to us. But we could not, within this period of time, start to consider these in a broader context and include them in legislation in any special way. They can be freely accessed as they've always been.[20]

As can be seen from the quote above, the group started to approach the problems in definition of genetic resources from the CBD's perspective—in terms of actual and potential value. The identification of nationally valuable genetic resources was now based on an evaluation report issued by the Finnish Environment Institute, a research entity under MAF institutional mandate. In the report, "microbes (archaea, bacteria, microalgae, fungi including molds and yeasts, viruses, protozoans) were identified as the most economically significant organism group in Finland. Further, such endangered species that are not fully protected are taken up as important organisms as well, since they are a vital [*sic*] for the protection of the genetic resources" (Fitzgerald et al. 2015, 95). Hereby, the review recognized two distinct categories of "nationally valuable genetic material." First, microbes as a biological category were now accorded potential economic value since they might in the future prove to embody valuable features. Additionally, endangered species and breeds were identified as valuable because they are critical for conservation in a category of value that is not based on biological taxonomy but builds on the evaluation and status of endangeredness (referring to national breeds such as Finncattle, analyzed in chapter 1). This is yet another new interpretation of national genetic resources, one that creates a dichotomy between two new (not previously existing) types. Although this definition was not incorporated in any codified manner into the draft national legislation that was to follow, it was mentioned in the background memo attached to the draft as one way to define the objects of governance.

When the draft of the new legislation was ready and had been submitted for a round of comments to ministries and NGOs represented in the working group or parties to its work (in March 2015), major criticism was levied against it by one ministry, the Ministry of Agriculture and Forestry. The ministry's official statement on the draft legislation from early April 2015 started with this claim: "According to the Ministry of Agriculture and Forestry, the draft legislation should not be handed in [to parliament] in its current form that was sent for a comment round. The preparations and drafting process for the legislation for genetic resources should be continued in collaboration between ministries [MENV and MAF] according to the notes below" (MAF 2015, 1). Why such a total rejection of the draft text? The reason becomes clear when one dives into the details of the seven-page commentary, which raised the following problematic issues with the draft: the general reasoning for the legislation and its scope, the matter of access to genetic resources, the question of traditional knowledge, and national authorities.

> First, the ministerial comments mounted a critique against the reasons explicitly stated for implementing the national legislation, whose underpinnings were the idea of the Nagoya Protocol correcting the many years of biopiracy and historical wrongdoing against biodiversity-rich countries that began in the imperialist era. The statement noted that Finland has never been an imperialistic country and argued that basing the national legislation on this kind of moral reasoning would be untenable and would need to be rethought. Then the commentary made lengthy criticism of the article dealing with the scope of the law. While the draft explicitly states that it covers only those genetic resources that fall under the Nagoya Protocol, the commentary pointed out that there are several ways in which the protocol's scope can be interpreted and that the legislation needs further definitions with regard to its scope, especially in relation to plant genetic resources used in agriculture. (MAF 2015, 1)

Continuing the critique, the MAF submission then considered shortcomings in the parts of the legislation dealing with access to Finnish genetic resources. The draft text defined Finnish genetic resources as those that are "freely" accessible. This, according to the ministry, brought in a problematic term, since "freely," in its legal sense, could be interpreted in such a way that Finland does not seek compensation for the use of national genetic resources. Accordingly, the MAF argued, provisions for access to genetic resources would need to be articulated differently.

Another question, much deeper and more vexing, arises in relation to the idea of access. This ties in directly with the form of genetic resources analyzed in chapter 3: frozen Finnsheep sperm. The draft legislation noted that natural resources traditionally fall within the sphere of property rights but that genetic resources are problematic to regulate in the realm of property law because it is the genetic information that is the valuable aspect of genetic resources. Yet the draft does not suggest a resolution to this. The MAF letter of comment identified this problem, too, in the legislation draft and stated,

> Agricultural genetic resources per se always have also the physical, organismic form. According to the article currently dealing with the issue in the draft text, it remains unclear, for example, how the legislation will interpret and govern access to collected and cryopreserved sperm by private actors. Collected sperm is not only genetic material but also material property that falls under the property rights legislation, and [we note that], depending on the animal, the value of frozen sperm batches can be considerable. (MAF 2015, 3)

Thus, the criticism highlighted that there is still no resolution to the problem surrounding ownership and access to genetic resources—which had been unresolved since early on and was so clearly evident when I witnessed the first sperm banking of Finnsheep. In late 2015 I interviewed a senior official from the Ministry of Agriculture and Forestry who was a member of the working group about the critique of the legislation. The official spontaneously raised as one of the key issues a problem that I had seen beleaguering the formation of the governance system for genetic resources from the very beginning of the work on the Bonn Guidelines and that, more recently, had been pointed to in the first national review on the Nagoya Protocol's implications (cited above):

> In the draft legislation, and in the work throughout 2013–14, we can see that the problem is that we haven't defined which are the things we're protecting and governing access to. Is it biological organisms or genetic information? What are the genetic resources we are legislating

here for? We haven't really touched this fundamental problem in the work we did, nor have we solved it in the draft legislation.[21]

The ministry also commented on two other aspects of the draft. The draft identified traditional knowledge, one of the key concepts and elements addressed in both the CBD and the Nagoya Protocol, as being synonymous with the traditional knowledge of the indigenous Sami people of Finland. The commentary questioned this, and the senior official commented on this matter in the interview: "Why should we legislate only for Sami people? We noted in the commentary that the idea of traditional knowledge should be interpreted more broadly and, in line with the Nagoya Protocol, include not only indigenous people but also the traditional-knowledge of local communities, such as plant-breeders and so on."[22] This comment points to a huge issue with the CBD's and the Nagoya Protocol's lack of a clear definition of traditional knowledge. What is it, or what does it consist of; who possesses it; and how should it be addressed in legislation at a national level? Interestingly, we saw in chapter 2 on the Alexander apple that traditional knowledge about apple trees held regionally by pomologists (apple-breeding professionals and hobbyists alike) has been of the utmost importance in tracking down apple varieties. Would this type of traditional knowledge be covered by the Finnish legislation envisioned? That issue, too, was left unresolved in the draft.

The final criticism made by the Ministry of Agriculture and Forestry pertained to national authority over genetic resources, which was initially assigned to the Finnish Environment Institute operating under the auspices of the Ministry of the Environment. This designation was not considered appropriate given the bureaucratic principle of sectoral responsibility for particular parts of nature. Consequently, the comments suggested that the national authority that was responsible for agricultural genetic resources be subject to the Natural Resources Institute operating under the Ministry of Agriculture and Forestry.

In the criticism of the draft national legislation, not all the issues raised were technical and political in nature (such as designating the authorities handling genetic resources). Others had to do with the questions that have been constantly stressed and negotiated in the global arena over the decades as well. The definition of national genetic resources and of access to them remained open in the draft legislation with no apparent intent to address these fundamental shortcomings immediately. In my most recent interview, the senior official from MAF explained the next steps in the legislative process:

TABLE 4.1 The political issue and material object of national genetic resources in its various forms in the course of the political process as it is mediated through different representation techniques—political institutions, corporeal identification, and textual definition in Finland. Over the years, the textual complexity of these has grown more rapidly than their political or corporeal beingness, on account of political decision-making processes that have not been able to fully articulate the textual complexity with politico-juridical representation or with corporeal identification programs.

Years	National Genetic Resources Interpreted as . . .	Political Representation by Institutional Location	Corporeal Representation	Textual Definition
1992–1996	Valuable or potentially valuable genetic material	Biodiversity Commission (1995)		CBD
1996–2003	Agricultural form of nonhuman life	MAF	MTT + Metla Plant Program (2001) + Animal program (2003)	CBD + first national action plan + Plant GR (genetic resources) Program (2001)
2003–2006	Genetic resources under review: bifurcation into knowns and known unknowns	MAF + ABGR + ABS group (2005–2006)	MTT + Metla Plant GR Program (2001) + Animal GR Program (2003)	CBD + first national action plan + Plant GR Program 2001 + Bonn Guidelines + Animal GR Program 2004
2006–2014	Genetic resources as ambiguous objects: corporeally known and known unknowns; Finnish nature possibly divided into biological and genetic beings	MAF + ABGR + MENV	MTT + Metla Plant Program (2001) + Animal Program (2003)	CBD + first national action plan + Plant GR program 2001 + Bonn Guidelines + Animal GR Program 2004 + ABS report + second national action plan
2015–	Not fully settled, with new reports hinting that these might include microbes, endangered species, and digital sequence data	National Resources Institute Finland (under MAF) + MENV	?	CBD + Nagoya Protocol + EU legislation + national legislation

> We [the Ministry of Agriculture and Forestry] had our comments on the draft legislation, but we did come to an agreement that this legislation now is only about the implementation of the Nagoya Protocol. It is not full or general national legislation on all genetic resources in Finland. So we will most likely be bringing this draft to the parliamentary approval process with minor adjustments. For example, the idea and language for "free access" was dropped, and the national authority for genetic resources will be split under the two ministries as suggested.

Accordingly, it appeared highly likely that implementation of the Nagoya Protocol via the legislation described briefly above would be ratified in Finland before 2016 was out. Yet it was clear, too, that even with implementation of the new legislation and with it the protocol, national genetic resources in Finland—as corporeal objects of native genetics, as political objects of institutional representation, and as legal objects of governance—are going to remain a complex, ambivalent form of national life.

POSTLAW UNCERTAINTIES

Irrespective of the concerns detailed above, very few changes were made to the draft legislation, and the Finnish act on the implementation of the Nagoya Protocol was passed by the parliament. After more than a decade of work preparing policy and legislation, it entered into force on September 1, 2016. Once the dust had settled, I returned to interview the senior officials who had represented the national competent authorities and focal points in that work. In the interviews in the summer of 2017, I asked them how they now saw the policy and legislative infrastructure in the wake of the first legislative act. The representative of the national authority responsible for Finnish implementation of the Nagoya protocol under the auspices of the Ministry of Agriculture and Forestry commented on the legislation thus:

> We now have the first legal framework for the genetic resources that follows closely the idea of the Nagoya Protocol. If we are more specific, this legislation does not really apply to Finnish genetic resources so much as to the imported ones. Now we have an obligation and right to do checks for the utilization of other countries' genetic resources, to monitor the national users that may have imported materials for their use. But we are not really talking about regulating Finnish resources here, since they are not really regulated under the legislation implemented.

These musings make it clear that the ownership of national genetic resources is still not resolved after many years of uncertainty. And ownership is still only one arena of uncertainty. The Nagoya Protocol is a multilateral treaty that is based on trust among the signatory parties to implement it in terms of practice and in a legally codified framework at national level. Each country should regulate the use of imported genetic resources within its respective territory. Today many have yet to implement the protocol in law at national level, and although all parties can view the current state of the multilateral system through the ABS clearinghouse (a public website meant to digitally mediate the communication and tensions between parties),[23] it is up to all parties sovereignly to decide how they will implement the Nagoya framework within their sovereign territory.

When I probed further on the questions that remain unresolved or have not even been subject to debate yet, the issue of ownership lingers in the air without easy resolution in sight. In fact, the question might be still more muddled as new biotechnical innovations and practices emerge and spread. While the access and use of genetic resources falling under the Nagoya Protocol are subject to codes of conduct and a legal framework, the old question about ownership remains. On this elephant in the room, the interviewee quoted above continued,

> Well, we haven't really touched upon the question of genetic resources' ownership yet. Access and benefit sharing for genetic resources under the Nagoya Protocol, yes. But it still is not clear who would own the genetic information contained in the biological material. It's a complex question. We will need to consider this in our continuing work with genetic resources here in the ministry and also elsewhere, but for now it is uncertain whether we will ever reach an easy conclusion with that. At the same time, there are new challenges related to ownership of sequenced data—it's a hot debate right now globally. Nobody really knows how to deal with that in the future.

The question about digital sequence data on genetic resources did get raised recently on the larger stage at the thirteenth meeting of the Conference of the Parties to the CBD in Cancún, Mexico.[24] On that occasion, in December 2016, the conference parties decided to establish an ad hoc group of technical experts "to consider at its fourteenth meeting any potential implications of the use of digital sequence information on genetic resources." Digital data emerging out of the ever-increasing sequencing performed for research and development purposes, along with the easy circulation of said data, was recognized in the meeting as a cross-cutting issue, one with potential to undermine the whole idea of the CBD. As synthetic biology and related technologies that could use the data to synthesize any valuable gene or genome have advanced rapidly, the issue has grown into an international concern.

Accordingly, before the ink has dried on national legal implementation of the CBD's Nagoya framework, new regulation challenges are rearing their head, and old ones are taking new shapes, filling the gaps in the systems. Genetic resources are continually reconfigured through biotechnologies that conceptually question their definition and limits as a legal concept and object of regulation. As long as there remain undercurrents of unresolved issues related to the political economy of the nation (such as the question of ownership) and emerging challenges presented by innovations (such as the digital sequence data), the biogenetic paradoxes of the state will evolve, mutate, and recombine—in the future, too. Just as life resists any easy ordering in the first place.

GENETIC RESOURCES AND INSTITUTIONAL BIOPOLITICS OF THE STATE

This chapter has been an empirical inquiry into institutionalized political processes and related elements with regard to new beings of nature—genetic resources—in Finland. I have shown how these new objects of nature have had a historical trajectory that has carved out the new genetic beings in particular ways with regard to national and international events, encompassing agreements, bodies of governance, and technoscientific enterprises. At the level of the Finnish state, in turn, the national biopolitics works through institutional structures, ones that may (or may not) legitimate the striving to bring particular life forms into the sphere of politics and to turn these into collective forms of national life.

Within these processes, as I have been arguing, both the institutional structures and the objects of their governance are alive and in constant interaction through diverse strategies of mediation, representation, and intervention such as the political documents and their modality shifts. This is the process of institutional biopolitics in action. Through these historical trajectories, institutional biopolitics, and new forms of institutional biosociality, the state attempts to articulate the nativity of nonhuman genetic matter with the sovereignty of the nation in a process of naturalization and nativization of genetic resources.

This chapter therefore is not and should not be read as a critical analysis of the shortcomings of the institutionalized politics with regard to new natures. As seen throughout the chapter, the question about identifying national genetic resources points to serious challenges for their national governance: what life forms—plants, animals, microbes, and others—are encompassed by the national community? What is the actual object of governance with regard to these forms of life? We could pose the question the other way around: What is the essence of genetic resources? Should genetic resources be seen as the live-organism form of the plant or animal or microbe, with the regulation being focused, accordingly, on access to these and their usage? Or should the national governance see genetic resources instead as composed of genetic information and hence legislate the use of information and access to it rather than the living matter of organisms? Each of these questions, if it is to be answered, will require a very different approach from the government for true governing of these new objects of national nature, genetic resources. This is true no matter what answer comes for each. Meanwhile, the questions go unanswered, and the associated governance challenges remain unresolved. Even the implementation of the Nagoya Protocol in the form of the new national legislation that entered into force in 2016 has not changed this.

To be fair, the system works as well as it is designed to work for particular purposes. Every governance structure has its shortcomings, holes, and gray areas, and this is especially true in the context of new natural beings and innovated natures such as genetic resources and other quasi-objects (Sharp 2002; Walsh and Goodman 2002; Whatmore 2002; Faulkner et al. 2003; N. Brown and Michael 2004). This does not strike me as a particularly strange situation since the very task of politico-juridical institutions of the state is to maintain order by constant work to correct these shortcomings, the stabilization and the naturalization of national order with the means available to it within its infrastructures and political topographies—the constantly renegotiated reconstitution of the sovereignty and the body of the nation.

The more theoretical aim of this chapter has been to point out how the empirical analysis of the genetic resources is relevant to the academic theory of nation. Instead of offering a critique of governmental practices, then, I have attempted to show how the issue of genetic resources opens the possibility of not only imagining a nation (B. Anderson [1983] 1991) but politically, juridically, and materially reconfiguring Finnish society in a new way. With the questions of sovereignty over nature and the commons, the citizen's relationship to the state as expressed through work with Finland's nature has the potential to shift radically, even more powerfully as the nation and nationalism were once crystallized through Finncattle. The questions about natural order (how many realms of nature are there?), of what nonhuman life forms national natures consist of, and about the articulation of social relations to the different possibilities of natural configurations (how ownership relations can be established with old and new natural objects and in what way) are all problematized. And these are, as has become apparent, fundamentally political questions about the ways in which it is possible and desirable to assemble a nation's nonhuman life through institutional and constitutional changes. This question is not resolvable by resorting to external reality of true national nature because the very composition of this nature is questioned alongside other problems related to the Finnish constitution.

Today the questions of the definition, ownership, and future of Finnish genetic resources remain unresolved and subject to ongoing political wrangling. As one of the experts put it in an interview, "It is now, of course, a matter of politics what kind of stance to these issues is taken." If this is, then, a matter of national biopolitics—of politics taking life as its object—what kind of national politics of life is this? By considering the institutional and constitutional problems that genetic resources pose for the Finnish state, I want to point to the question that Agamben (2000, 7) has presented for any analysis of biopolitics: "Foucault's thesis—according to which 'what is at stake today is life' and hence politics has become biopolitics—is, in this sense substantially correct. What is decisive, however, is the way in which one understands the sense of this transformation. What is left unquestioned in the contemporary debates on bioethics and biopolitics, in fact, is precisely what would deserve to be questioned before anything else, that is, the very biological concept of life." He argues that this concept, "which today presents itself under the guise of a scientific notion," is actually a political one, no longer sacrosanct within pure objective science.

The question about life extends here to the political separation of national and nonnational genes. Genetic nonhuman nationhood is a thoroughly political form of life in which the nonhuman genes brought under the *bios* are recognized as a naturalized part/body of the sovereign political community of nation-states while those considered to be *zoê* are left out of it as nonpolitical forms of nature or as naked life. Agamben's argument about the politics of life—biopolitics as a fundamentally political process wherein life is an outcome of its inclusion in a particular social order—extends also from the core question ("what is life?") to the analysis of the more nuanced conditions of how the social can be understood to be produced by various relations of inclusions and exclusions.

Writing elsewhere about the anthropological machine in philosophy and the human sciences, Agamben (2004, 37) stated, following Foucault's similar argument found already in his 1966 archaeology of human sciences, *Les Mots et les Choses*, that "insofar as the production of man through the opposition man/animal, human/inhuman, is at stake here, the machine necessarily functions by means of an exclusion (which is also always already a capturing) and an inclusion (which is also always already an exclusion)."

Agamben's two interrelated arguments about "life as a politically secularized concept" and its relation to "communal life" serve as my second theoretical observation with regard to the theory of nation presented in chapter 1 of the present work. I claim that it is the very same anthropological machine that Agamben writes about that has long contributed to the exclusion of nonhumans in the study of the formation and constant renegotiation of modern nationhoods. Instead of being treated as the fleshly corporeal matter of nationhood, they have been dealt with as imagined projections of communal identity. In discussions of nation formation, rarely have nonhumans been regarded as anything more than symbolic figures or representations or metaphors of a national identity (e.g., Ritvo 1992; Michael 2001). The relationship between *Natura sacer* and sovereign properly describes the current direction of juridico-institutional biopower over bare life.

Nevertheless, nonhumans, despite the attempt to bring them under the rule of biopower, are more recalcitrant and hence not necessarily at odds with the Foucauldian way of understanding the control of populations. In novel technoscientific practices, the very line drawn between humans and nonhumans, already crossed both symbolically and materially in, for example, xenotransplantation and tissue engineering (e.g., M. Brown et al. 1998), has been challenged, and the utility of human/nonhuman dichotomies in the formation and/or description of current hybrid identities is urgently called into question. In other words, the anthropological machine, which lies at the very heart of our philosophical understanding of human and, hence, *bios* is becoming a problematic machine for production of useful identities in our current situation.

It is no wonder, then, that our understanding of the constitution of the collectives in which we live today, of which nation-states are arguably the most powerful, is also called into question (Latour 2003). In studies of nationhood and biopower, the nonhuman is routinely othered, its corporealities overlooked by an anthropocentric theoretical imagination. I have argued in this chapter, in contrast, that the paradoxical relations of nonhumans to the sovereign, at once captured and excluded, are constitutive to any modern state's governance. Nonhuman genetic resources provide a potential source of novel biowealth, but they also act as living genetic corporealities through which sovereign biopower is enacted. Nonhumans are indeed constitutive parts of any sovereign state, bodies through which nationhood is at once naturalized and vitalized.

Offering a startling diagnosis of today's problematic relationship between the human and the nonhuman, Agamben writes, "When the difference vanishes and the two terms collapse upon each other—as seems to be happening today—the difference between being and nothing, licit and illicit, divine and demonic also fades away, and in its place something appears for which we seem to lack even a name" (2004, 22). This is a complex interaction between the global political economy of genetic resources and national interests and stakeholders, with the latter seeking proprietary ownership of biowealth while at the same time redefining collective identity. It is this crisscrossing of the categories of the human and the nonhuman and its role in the biopolitics of state formation that nation-states are predicating and enacting their sovereignty via their claims of origins in and through nonhuman genetic resources.

CONCLUSION biogenetic paradoxes of the nation

Cattle, apples, sheep. These are just a few examples among the myriad life forms that are undergoing changes as motion in biodiversity conservation turns biological objects into valuable genetic resources. Other species and breeds in countries near and far are feeling changes in their ecological niches related to the changing political economies over life, new technologically enabled spaces and circuits of biovalue accumulation, and increasing global tensions over ownership claims. With these paths, the stakes in global biopolitics are rearticulated through these three key interests at the heart of current biodiversity-linked power struggles.

In these final pages, I reflect on some of the key arguments and reapproach the global politics of nature along with the role of nations in the actualization of all this as has been analyzed in the empirical chapters. This reflection casts into relief what is at stake in the national genetic-resource programs in Finland and, I claim, in all nations that are signatory to the CBD and the Nagoya Protocol, with others brought into the patterns, too, irrespective of not being signatories.

As argued in the introductory chapter and demonstrated in threads woven through all chapters of the book, the idea of the CBD and the subsequent Nagoya Protocol grew from three distinct roots leading to unresolved biopolitical entanglements—or into three mutually inextricable ethical plateaus—stretching from the global to the local. All of these are linked to the rise of modern agricultural technologies, dubbed the Green Revolution, and to the resulting new ways to categorize, objectify, and manipulate life across political and biological boundaries. These plateaus wait to be scaled, poised with the continuing biogenetic paradoxes that lie behind the historically unfolding paths toward the global agreements.

The first root is related directly to a series of agricultural innovations and their effects on the forms of life that are integral to the advancing of human civilizations along with the forms of life that are outside these relationships. New scientific rationalities, associated technologies, and innovated knowledge of the management of the living—especially knowledge from the Green Revolution—changed the economic and ecological landscape of the planet in the latter part of the twentieth century. Domesticated and nondomesticated natures, or agricultural and wild biodiversity, are arguably more homogenized and genetically uniform than ever before, and their ecological niches are becoming smaller, more standardized, and increasingly controlled. This narrative of the homogenization and depletion of genetic-resource pools is central to the birth of the internationally powerful discourses of conservation biology, a crisis discipline, as explained in the introductory chapter. The discourse is dominant in public articulations of biodiversity, but other powerful narratives are hidden beneath it.

One very influential yet largely unexplored strand in the current narratives of global biodiversity conservation involves how the effects of the Green Revolution have thrust the question of the nation into relief in the past few decades. Many, if not most, of the global tensions inherent in the global politics of the CBD stem from deep material-semiotic links forged in the convention text between the idea of nation and the nature asserted to belong to it. This link is central to the explicit biopolitical declaration found within the CBD. It drives a new convergence between nation and nature, and it forces into being new ethical plateaus in a complex terrain that is riven with new epistemological politics of the living and some vexing biogenetic paradoxes. These plateaus are occupied and brought to life by the figure of genetic resources assuming various material manifestations, which depend on the implementation of the CBD actions at a national level. Hence, in my fieldwork in Finland a few key phrases stood out from the very outset. For the scientists I followed, it was important to save genetic resources because they were seen as "our living past," "living national heritage," and a "corporeal form of national culture." For a social scientist who is primed to be keenly aware of the implicit dualism between nature and culture, these sorts of conceptualizations melding the two ostensibly separate realms of reality (and not arbitrary realms but the two basic ontological spheres of the West) sound problematic. But even if these kinds of hybrid concepts were readily used by the scientists at the level of their everyday speech, the practical articulation of national culture and the nonhuman corporealities that were suspected to be native was a challenge to them, too.

In her book on bioprospecting in Mexico, Hayden (2003b) described an analogous problematic situation facing biologists: they soon found that they were functioning as a nexus between the local communities and their international agreements with biotechnology companies and national governments. Thus, in addition to doing their research, they had to find balance among numerous political and economic requirements, mostly derived from access and benefit-sharing issues surrounding new active biochemical components. In other words, the scientists ended up doing political work through their scientific inquiry into new, promising futures of chemical derivatives of exotic plants. Her analysis shows well the interwoven nature of science and the politics of nationhood.

Throughout the chapters, I have been arguing that sovereignty over a nation's nature is produced by a bringing together of the scientists who are capable of aligning historical narratives, biological corporealities, and molecular readings of nonhuman life; the politicians and administrators at both global and local levels who are reacting to the changes in our understanding of biology at the molecular and genomic level and to what we can now do experimentally and materially to generate novel biovalue; and local farmers and other culturalists (e.g., horticulturalists) as keepers of national populations of nonhuman life so as to achieve a renewed technoscientific warrant for the nation (in this case, Finland). Unlike in the case of Mexican bioprospecting, the alignments found in my work are made not between multinational corporations and states but between a nation and new nonhuman genetics.

The inclusion of nonhuman forms of life as objects of ownership and as subjects of societal politics is most definitely not a novel phenomenon per se. Nonhuman species have always been part of our communal life and its day-to-day practices. This is a universally shared condition of *anthropos*, as the sheer volume of classical anthropological literature on the subject cited throughout the book attests. In Western countries, plants, animals, and nature have played a great role in the development of culture insofar as they have been considered central elements of national development. The era of the neoliberalization of natures and economic gains derived from the standardization and homogenization of nonhuman forms of life has, however, led to a crisis of genetic resources and reduced the diversity of the gene pools available for molding life, through biotechnologies, into particular forms pressed into service for increasing the production of biovalue (Kloppenburg 1988; Shiva 1991; Sunder Rajan 2006). Contemporary debates about access and benefit sharing linked to genetic resources and the related quarrels over intellectual property rights stand witness to a global competition between nations (and subnational local communities) and agropharma multinationals in the field of these matters that are so vital for future survival. The alleged breach of sovereignty over matters of national importance has prompted a strong resistance and a rebirth of the nation-state as the sovereign steward of bioresources worldwide, as witnessed with the CBD and the Nagoya Protocol.

The conservation of nature and cultural identities embodied in local life forms is inherently tied to the powerful interests of the nations that are now securing their populations by indexing, banking, and politically ordering the life found within the respective territories. What the global agreement promises to do at the international level—at least with regard to the signatory nations—is mobilize nationalism for the aims of naturalization, and thereby nativization, of genetic natures. In more precise terms, both the CBD and the Nagoya Protocol provide recognition of the signatory parties' sovereignty over their natural resources in their texts (specified in detail in both documents' annexes). Together these agreements create emerging forms of life that local practices of governmentality (where economic and other space is left to them for this) are left to decide on, and they legitimate the reinforcement of national boundaries that are inscribed at the genetic level of nonhuman life. Even if the mobilization of nationalism was introduced in the convention to fight the so-called biopiracy that has been framed as being practiced by the countries of the North against the biodiversity-rich countries of the South, one cannot but be impressed with how forceful and how alive the modern ideology of nation (and related subnational categories such as native breeds, indigenous communities, and traditional knowledge) is in our supposedly globalized world.

The global neoliberalization and related circuits that are generating capital out of vital materials face a tough ideological challenge through politically renaturalized national borders that are standing in the way of free movement of native bodies and embodied genetic information. Nations are increasingly regulating access and benefit sharing related to their native nonhuman populations called genetic resources. Herein lies a novel form of state-led biopolitics over their vital forces, biopolitics made possible by the pronounced articulation of national sovereignty through forms of life found in the respective national natures.

When looking at such a double bind of political forces (the contradiction resulting from marking off boundaries of a nation within its population and simultaneously taking care of its vital powers)[1] in more detail in the practices of implementation, one starts to see how the finest-granularity constituent practices of national sovereignty and biopower complement each other through the genetic identification, the gene banks, the national politics of nature, and the global political economy over genetic resources encapsulating and legitimating all this. It is interesting to compare this development to the ones made in the context of human genetics and to consider it in light of the discourse in recent debates about the role of nation-states in biopolitics. These have fallen into the trap of anthropocentrism in claiming that nations have lost much of their powers over life. I find a much closer connection between nations and their natures, between agriculture and culture, and between technologies of life targeting nonhuman and human species than is generally acknowledged.

Some years ago one of the main commentators on biopolitics today, Nikolas Rose, concluded that the role of the state in the control of genetic populations has been nothing less than abolished. In his book *The Politics of Life Itself*, he declared, "Life may, today more than ever, be subject to judgements of value, but those judgements are not made by a state managing the population en masse. Contemporary biopolitics in advanced liberal polities does not take the living body of the race and its vital components as resources whose fitness is to be maximized in a competitive struggle between states" (2007, 58).

My research on life beyond the human form leads to a paradoxical conclusion: I find that I must disagree with his diagnosis and conclude that the comment is presented in a form that does not take into account the inherent ties between human and nonhuman life as always-symmetrical targets of national interventions. It should be quite obvious from this research that his reading is an understanding wherein nation-states are composed of only human life. As I have attempted to show throughout this work, that understanding must give way to a much broader definition of what the nation consists of; how it, as a sovereign, orders and creates divisions of nonhuman life, too; and how biopower over them is practiced in a state-led manner today.

There is a nation-state-driven national and international identification of the most all-encompassing kind going on to save, secure, and maximize the value of patrimonial biowealth, the genetic resources of nations that are signatories to the CBD and the Nagoya Protocol. Sovereignty is still very much in operation and enacting powerful divisions over life, whether human or nonhuman in form, alongside biopolitics that target the maximization of its vital powers. The contemporary biogenetic paradoxes stem precisely from the efforts to salvage and reimagine the modern figures of the human, the nation, and the state in times when all these are intimately and inseparably bound up with new life forms in processes that reconfigure the symbolics and corporeal symbiosis, marking a time that Haraway (2015) calls the Chthulucene epoch.

BIOGENETIC PARADOXES OF THE NATION

To demonstrate how the troubling biogenetic paradoxes appearing in Finland emerged, I showed how early Finnish nation building in the late nineteenth century relied heavily on particular bovine companion species as external reference and justification for the cultural identity category of nation. Here, as I argued at length in chapter 1 on Finncattle, the creation of national biowealth, the scientific language of national breeds, the new technologies of life, and the creation of corporeal forms in parallel with the founding Finnish races have all been tightly interconnected in the making of the Finnish nation. Wealth and national territory, scientific language and national mythologies, and national life and biopolitics targeting animals came together in perfect symmetry between man and animal, and nation and nature, in the project of assembling the communal form of life called Finland. The history of Finncattle has served as one example of how the practical actualization of a nation's virtual presence—"imagination" as B. Anderson ([1983] 1991) calls it—takes place through nonhuman beings, nature.

As that chapter illustrates, the problem of defining the national population is not confined to the human sphere—natural populations are and have always been at the core of nationalist matters of concern. Foucault (2003), among others, has claimed that the concept of populations emerges in the human sciences with the aid of the natural sciences. The idea of humans as a natural species is derived from the reworking of natural history. Similarly, the idea of nonhuman life being a calculable resource, just as the human population is for a nation, proceeds from very early economic thinking (Mitchell 2002; Agrawal 2005).

In chapter 2, I showed how the transformation in the identification of national life forms that are today found living within the territory—in the so-called in situ conditions—is enabled by new biotechnologies that ultimately depend on the genetic identification of molecular differences between apple tree varieties in contrast to identification based only on morphological differences or production qualities. Here, the post-CBD world also explicitly mobilizes and legitimates national interests in novel forms of life, which do not really resemble apples, sheep, or cows. Apples are identified by the multiple relations enacted by various markers and genetic populations construed and individualized (identified) via genetic fingerprinting. The apples are increasingly known by genomic markers that were previously considered neutral but are now starting to code for nationality (in junk DNA), rerooted and naturalized in and through laboratory networks, made ingredients in national mandate lists that describe in detail what the nation consists of, and finally rewriting the natural history of the nation from the present.

Similarly, the analysis of how the transformation occurs between nonhuman genetic resources as found in situ and ex situ (as in most gene banks aimed most clearly at genetic conservation) reveals another side of the issues particular to genetic-resource programs: the question of reproduction through cryopreserved, frozen populations of national life and the new technological infrastructure within which these new forms of life find their ecological niche (chapter 3). What goes into the spinning whirlpool created by the strangely resonating fields of reasoning behind conservation discourse and related material practices comes out reshaped by the ecological, economic, and national interests. Here, technologies that were initially developed to reduce biodiversity and for agricultural production become technologies that promise the conservation of biodiversity. At the same time, the ecological niche of forms of life that are under peril is conditioned by the successful generation of novel goods in technological infrastructures, embedded within the political economy of international plant and animal production, and the virtualization of life via the cessation of animation actualizes the nation by creating an emergent form of life—stilled life. As I argued in chapters 2 and 3, other representational spaces and temporal fields that are emerging in our technoscientific contemporaneity can create new forms of life such as genetic resources stored in gene banks. Very special configurations of technoscientific space-times—new technologies and infrastructures—should be taken into account in the study of new types of nationhood (see also Haraway 1997) and the construction of a nation itself.

Finally, there is hence an implication to sovereignty that cuts deep with regard to the processes of nativization of national genetic resources. In this process, described in chapter 4, we see the breach of the outermost limits and the renaturalization of the body of a sovereign state: at the very moment when genetic resources are to be included in the body of the state, the state constitutes itself anew by forcing ministerial bodies into a state of exception in order to be able to include novel forms of life in both its institutional and its constitutional ordering of nature. If the sovereign is truly the one deciding on the state of exception (Schmitt 1985), we see here how novel biotechnological entities such as genetic resources are able to exert forces that are subversive enough to bring the sovereignty of a state into the light in order to enable new kinds of population-control programs and institutional infrastructures—a complementary reconfiguration of sovereignty and biopower. In other contexts, Sarah Franklin (2007a) has argued that nonhuman life has been, and remains, a matter of expanding frontiers (advancing colonial territorial spaces and simultaneously creating novel spaces for national technoscientific enterprises) and creating national wealth by circulating nonhuman animal bodies between and across spaces. Genetic resources, their connections to the Finnish territory, and their relations of difference show how new national relations of belonging for innovated natures are created through biotechnologies and related institutionalized spaces.

Much of my ethnographic work has been guided by a desire to follow empirically how the CBD translates into practical actions at national level in Finland and Finnish efforts to implement it. But as I have reiterated even in the earliest pages, my primary aim has not been to produce a commentary on contemporary debates about its (national or international) justification nor to look at what is really going on in the national genetic-resource conservation programs in Finland. Instead, the aim has been to question how the three biogenetic paradoxes—of changing political economies of animal and plant production meshed with growing concerns about biodiversity, the mission of conservation biology alongside the rearticulation of nature through the market idiom of genetic resources, and that surrounding the unresolved question about ownership rights over genetic resources—are interpreted, configured, and acted on with programs working on and through nonhuman genetic resources in Finland. This is a much more open-ended, and experimental, question about how the prevailing social form of organization of communal life is at once ideologically reinforced, institutionally redefined, and finally materially reconfigured both in practice and in theory.

THE TROUBLED ANATOMY OF NATIONAL POPULATIONS

Several studies bundled loosely under the headings of animal studies, cultural geography, and history of agriculture have shown that nonhuman biological entities have a long history in terms of nativization for the purposes of nations and territorial bio-geopolitics (e.g., Crosby 1986; Ritvo 1992; Pauly 1996; S. Franklin 1999; Taussig 2001; Mansfield 2003; Raber and Tucker 2005).

Considering the number of these studies, one may find it quite interesting that this thread has not received much attention among theorists of the nation or that these writers have not presented their findings in a more systematic way to respond to the central arguments of the theory of nationalism. In the previous chapters, I have described how various national nonhuman populations are created and managed through the local definition of nonhuman populations and related individualization practices. The kinds of nonhuman life that are important to a nation are always within its power interests and have direct effects on the corporeal character of these life forms and, perhaps equally, on the form of their life to reify as appropriate as they are brought under (however constrained) national management.

Such factors point to one of my core interests for the book: the questioning of an overly simple drawing of boundaries between humans and nonhumans, one inherited from the early philosophy of life and one that has persisted to this day. The usual question at issue in analytical quarrels involves the dualistic demarcation between human and animal (Kalof and Fitzgerald 2007; Calarco 2008) plus other forms of life. This strange fixation is rather problematic, especially when one wishes to map the complex terrain traced by these relationships, which encompasses reasons behind genetic conservation, the technoscientific practices of genetic resourcing, and the politics underlying them. All of these muddle the boundaries, together rendering it impossible to formulate an answer as to any one easy way of dividing life into human and nonhuman in the context of nation. Nation acts as an assembly of life that includes *both*. And instead of trying to draw lines of demarcation between these two forms of life, the nation enacts its sovereignty by drawing the boundaries of inclusion and exclusion *within* the category of the human (e.g., nonlegal immigrants, personae non gratae) and other living organisms (e.g., nonnative, nonendogenous species). Recently, the stream of anthropological inquiry that is called multispecies ethnography has been explicitly rearticulating the question of the boundaries between the human and other living beings by focusing on "how a multitude of organisms' livelihoods shape and are shaped by political, economic, and cultural forces" (Kirksey and Helmreich 2010, 545). The ethnographic work presented in this book is, in one respect, a contribution to this kind of intellectual program and its way of questioning these leaky boundaries and the political forces in which they are embedded.

Because of these historical trajectories of biotechnologies in the hands of the national politics of population management, we have not gotten rid of state-led biopolitics (state-led biopolitics does not, as is often assumed, equal eugenics). Instead, a change in its forms of operation was seen in the latter half of the past century into the turn of the millennium, rendering these techniques even more prevalent, subtle, and pervasive in our contemporary societies that are assembled everywhere in the name and form of the *nation-state*—a form of collective life (the form of a state) that naturalizes its form through the nation (life assembled together by natural similarities) and related technologies of population management (see also Metzler 2007). Of course, the neoliberalization of natures (Hayden 2003b, 48–52) has had a specific route of creating biovalue and managing biocapital, a path that has now been interrupted by the national questioning of rights over the new matter of life. The selection of nonhuman matter for the ends of biocapitalization has proceeded without the ethics problems posed by anthropocentric bioethics. Nonproductive plants are being woven out of the gardens and fields at an increasing pace in a parallel to the killing of animals that are unfit for the breeds deemed relevant—just as in the projects of centuries past, animals that possess horns, the wrong color of coat, or too low a milk yield. They have simply been slaughtered without any kind of ethical concern, even without statements of worry by activists for nonhuman (or at least animal) rights.

Beyond the examination of biopolitics and the extent to which it is applied to life forms beyond *Homo sapiens*, the analytical gaze should be extended toward the other boundary-making politics and practices that are made possible by new technologies, such as the ones involved in genetic identification for national inclusion and exclusion. It proves enlightening when any anthropological study of science and technology questions the ways in which new categories of life and the living are being constituted, and it is equally interesting to note how these do not really resemble the old biological categories of what many would call animalness or plantness. The very naturalness of these basic categories of nature is being stripped away by genetic knowledge practices that render very visible the fact that the category of life is not (and has never been) an uncontested biological category but rather a political project—for example, a nation-building exercise—as Agamben (2004) argued some years ago (see also Helmreich 2011). There is no clear category of life and then politics over it. Neither is there first a field of politics and then life produced. The two are in constant relation to each other, re-forming what the life looks like while also dictating what the power can get hold of via its knowledge practices, institutions, and material technologies. In these interactions among life and politics and the particular assembly of forces, a nation becomes. These interactions constitute a process that is steeped in biogenetic paradoxes.

I have been arguing throughout the book that the boundaries between the cultural and the natural are constantly negotiated and renegotiated at multiple sites and in many spheres of reasoning. This negotiation takes place in national narrations that make use of symbolic connections just as much as in the complex terrain of contemporary debate, through economic and ecological discourses and through both traditional territory and new natural locations for national rooting.

The inquiry into these three paradoxes also leads to a broader question about the idea of the nation and its populations, and while unfolding the main lines of the book, I have attempted also to open up new ways of questioning the composition of nations in general with the particular example of Finland. This is one way of doing empirical philosophy informed by the new anthropological approaches and their practices. One of the core concerns of any philosophical inquiry, as Deleuze and Guattari (1994) argue, is to advance our understanding via the creation of a new connection between things. Sometimes this connection also requires the construction of new concepts—a central task for any philosophy, empirical or analytical. While the questions and neologisms could be employed in an interventionist project, with this book I have tried to answer—though I have been able to do so only partially—the questions that Agamben has raised about the most important issue of our time. He has argued,

> We must learn . . . to investigate . . . the practical and political mystery of separation. What is man, if he is always the place—and, at the same time, the result—of ceaseless divisions and caesurae? It is more urgent to work on these divisions, to ask in what way . . . has man been separated from non-man, and the animal from the human, than it is to take positions on the great issues, on so-called human rights and values. (Agamben 2004, 16)

Nativization processes have made the question of nonhuman nationhood explicit. These are legitimated by the international and national politics over nature, they are performed by the technoscientific apparatus, and they reconfigure the signatory nations' visible nature politics. What once politically separated man and animal, human and nonhuman, is now being called into question in the context of sovereignty and the resulting separation between nations on account of the genetic difference between their natures. Nonhuman genetics has become woven in with the international question of national sovereignty, national questions about the politics of nativization, and a new way of articulating this connection. At the same time, genetics challenges old ways of thinking about life, both human and other. What seem to be at play here are the new ways of creating separations between the *human* and the *nonhuman*, purpose-appropriate forms of arranging the politics of the nation-state as well as the nation-state's configuration of its native nature, with a new way of making distinctions at the political, corporeal, and juridical levels.

I set out more generally to do just what I describe above: question the taken-for-granted separations between human and nonhuman, between national culture and its nature, between the process of *humanitas* making an *anthropos* and the process of *nativitization* making its *naturas* under the name of the nation. Nation requires our attention now if we are to consider properly the important politics at the junctures of current technoscience and the newly vital international nationalism being manifested in and through the Convention on Biological Diversity (and related global agreements such as the Nagoya Protocol), which together enact a separationalist politics of our current global situation that is practically enabled by the new genetic knowledge. This is because, through the current academic literature on nationalism, the national community appears to be homocentric (or *Homo sapiens*–centric), even with its acknowledgment of nature (with natural boundaries of territory) and natural metaphors (arborescent rootings) used in describing the link of humans-as-nations to a certain soil. But where does this acknowledgment lead? What kind of "third space of anthropology" does this allow?

Homi Bhabha has argued,

> The narrative and psychological force that nationness brings to bear on cultural production and political projection is the effect of the ambivalence of the "nation" as a narrative strategy. As an apparatus of symbolic power, it produces a continual slippage of categories, like sexuality, class affiliation, territorial paranoia, or "cultural difference" in the act of writing the nation. What is displayed in this displacement and repetition of terms is the nation as the measure of the liminality of cultural modernity. (Bhabha 2004, 207)

What I would add to Bhabha's claim is that one of the most certain aspects of the liminality of modernity that national theory can make visible is the naturalized limit of the representation of nation and its biopolitics. What I have attempted to show in tracing the empirical contours of this space are its limits: the space is bounded by theoretical fixation to the modern figure of Man and politics targeting the life of *Homo sapiens*, biopolitics of the state. The figure of Man in the social sciences has a very short history, as Foucault has argued, one that he once declared would eventually "be erased, like a face drawn in sand at the edge of the sea" (Foucault [1966] 2001, 422). Resisting his conclusion, however, this figure has shown its peculiar vitality in literature on nations and in broader academic theorization. The final sentence of Bhabha's contribution to the theory of "culture," *The Location of Culture* (2004, 367), makes a plea to think anew about the spatio-temporal idea of national culture, of nationhood, and to go beyond current understandings of it. He writes, "What is crucial to such vision of the future is the belief that we must not merely change the *narratives of* our histories, but transform our sense of what it means to live, to be, in other times and different spaces, both human and historical" (emphasis in original). I will add here that to transform our sense of living within the contemporary formations of life called nations, we must not only change the sense in which we claim to be humans, historical and contemporary cultural beings, but also look beyond the very figure of the human: to rethink our communal forms of living as a constant interaction with the life forms beyond *Homo sapiens*.

NOTES

INTRODUCTION

1 The legislative, administrative, and policy measures related to the Convention on Biological Diversity and the subsequent Nagoya Protocol are tracked by the Access and Benefit-Sharing Clearing-House, provided by the United Nations. Through the clearing-house mechanism, records are made available online at https://absch.cbd.int/search/nationalRecords.

2 The call for equity is often dichotomized into a struggle between the global South and the global North, stereotyped as the former being the domain of genetic resources while the latter possesses the technoscientific processing apparatus. This book does not delve into the details of the strides being made in this direction in the form of efforts to provide a scientific apparatus to the global South—especially Brazil, India, and China.

3 "Aporias" here refers to paradoxes, contradictions, opposed imperatives, or double binds, to use the terms popularized in the anthropology literature by Callison (2008), Fischer (2003; 2009), K. Fortun (2001), M. Fortun (2008), Haraway (1991; 1997), Masco (2006), Sunder Rajan (2006), and others who are concerned with the ethics and power of technoscientific rearrangements.

4 "Legal certainty" is what the official documents of the meeting laud as a key achievement, but I flag the expression since nothing is as uncertain as legal certainty decided at a global level. I will explore the issue in depth in chapter 4.

5 See the strategic goals at https://www.cbd.int/sp/elements/default.shtml.

6 This book focuses on productive tensions resulting from the main aporias set forth by the Convention on Biodiversity and its three goals of sustainability, sovereignty rights, and access and benefit sharing. Similar focus on the productivity of contradictions, double binds, and paradoxes as can be found in earlier works by Gregory Bateson (*Steps to an Ecology of Mind*, 1972) and Kim Fortun (*Advocacy after Bhopal*, 2001); see also Fischer 2003. More recently, Michael Fortun (2008) has analyzed the productive contradictions stemming from the deal between Roche and DeCode Genetics Inc. of Iceland, and used "×" to signal the different tensions contained in the deal and beyond in the subheadings of the book, for example, by starting his introduction with "Lava × Land." I follow the same kind of graphic signaling of the three key tensions inherent in the CBD in the introduction.

7 In simple terms, these are temporarily stable configurations that ultimately get upset as values, technologies, and local decision making change, requiring new balancing work, after which a new ethical plateau is created, which, in its turn, remains stable for a time.

8 The words of James Clifford (1988, 215–20) may be instructive here: "Description of culture is itself a form of collection. . . . Some sort of 'gathering' around the self and the group—the assemblage of a material 'world,' the marking-off of a subjective domain that is not 'other'—is probably universal. All such collections embody hierarchies of value, exclusions, rule-governed territories of the self. But the notion that this gathering involves the accumulation of possessions, the idea that identity is a kind of wealth (of objects, knowledge, memories, experience), is surely not universal. . . . In the West, however, collecting has long been a strategy for the deployment of a possessive self, culture, and authenticity."

9 For Latour, "macro" and "micro," "local" and "global" are just poorly chosen ways to speak about the extent of an "actor network," wherein translations and various mediations create and extend the spatio-temporal existence of an event. Various mediators do not just "localize" interactions and channel, divide, centralize, or reduce. They also "globalize" them: they increase them, translate them, complicate them, and carry them forward (Latour 1996). With regard to the process of globalization in this sense, Latour has stated that a better name for actor network in describing the assemblage of connections and relations would be "actant-rhizome" (Latour 1996, 19), a concept referring to Deleuze and Guattari's (1987) work on rhizomes. A rhizome has neither a beginning nor an end; instead, it connects any point of passage to any other. In contrast to that of the rhizome, the metaphor of the actor network is not primarily spatial. It also incorporates the idea of temporal and agential heterogeneity (see Latour 2002a, 248–49).

1. FINNCATTLE

Epigraphs: Foucault 1979, 228; Wilmot 2007, 412.

1 See DAD-IS, http://dad.fao.org/.

2 Several studies have established clear links between nations and the management of their natural animal populations, be they cattle (Ritvo 1992; Taussig 2004), sheep (S. Franklin 2007b), salmon (Lien 2005), or any of various plants and trees (Schiebinger 2004). I continue an exploration of these linkages and expand the analysis historically to the early moments of nation formation in Finland.

3 The precursor to the Senate, a governmental council, was established in 1809 when the Grand Duchy of Finland was declared a political entity. Tsar Alexander I of Russia named the institution the Senate to mark out independence from the Russian Senate. The economic and judicial functions evolved and were reinstitutionalized, respectively, to the Cabinet working under the

prime minister and to the Supreme Court in 1918, a year after Finland gained its full independence.

4 Letter from the Board of Agriculture to the Senate of the Grand Duchy of Finland dated December 10, 1892, cited by Simonen 1949, 111.

5 Horse-breeding programs were established, too, and this led to institutionalization of the national horse-breeding society in 1907 by order of the Senate, with the aim of breeding a pure Finnish horse, the Finnhorse, with explicitly agricultural purposes.

6 "Every attempt to absorb [Finland] into the Russian system, whether in administrative, military, juridical, or cultural aspects, collided with the fact that Finland had grown into a modern country with a high degree of self-awareness and a set of institutions and values that differed markedly from those of Russia," according to Lundin (1981, 357).

7 The movement that is centered on promotion of the Finnish language and associated cultural heritage gain, called Fennomania, is a nationalist force, one of whose forms was "Affairfennomania," which held that particular national forms of economy ought to be developed.

8 Bovine tuberculosis, anthrax, and cattle plague were common animal diseases in the eighteenth and nineteenth centuries and were a regular problem to anyone who kept cattle. To tackle these diseases, the majority of the animal regulations included in the old statutes of Finland dealt with the prevention of infectious diseases. The first published regulation ("The Regulation Concerning the Prevention of Animal Diseases and Cattle Plague") pertaining to prevention of infectious diseases in Finnish territory was issued in 1722. Accordingly, all interaction of people and animals (and fodder) between infected areas and healthy ones were prohibited, and some practical advice was offered on what to do if dead animals are found in healthy areas. With the penalty for breaking these rules set as high as forty silver talers (or more than the value of a whole shed full of cattle), the regulations were quite serious with their punitive enforcement, but they lacked any reasonable effectiveness in containing various outbreaks (Forsius 1979a). Large-scale actions against the infectious diseases were taken first in the autumn of 1734. In a royal letter the Collegium Medicum, which at that time was in charge of tackling both human and nonhuman diseases, was urged to study the cattle plagues in and around the provinces of Turku and Uusimaa and to think of measures to prevent them. But it was not until the late eighteenth century that the first books on animal diseases—especially cattle diseases—were published. Since infectious diseases, such as plagues, were economically taxing, it might not come as a surprise that it was the Finnish Society for Economics that both published and granted money for books on the prevention and curing of infections in cattle. For example, in 1802 it granted prize money in a writing competition aimed at producing a "clear and concise, but sufficiently inclusive, textbook on the diseases of cattle and their cures, applied to the Finnish climate and

economic system." The final book, however, never materialized (Forsius 1979a).

9 A large and essentially international cattle economy was already well developed in Continental Europe in the early modern period starting in the late fifteenth century (Blanchard 1986). The transatlantic trade grew especially with the late nineteenth century's craze for purebred cattle and sheep (e.g., Butzer 1988; Ritvo 1995; Walton 1999; Derry 2003; Franklin 2007b). Walton (1999, 444) wrote that "the customary reward of the late eighteenth-century livestock improver was nominal in the literal sense that animals descended from his stock were likely to be referred to as 'of Princept's breed' or 'of Mr Webster's breed.' This was a common though not exclusive usage of the word 'breed' in that period [until the first decades of the 1800s], and assumed an ancestral linkage to animals of a particular breeder."

10 The theory had many different articulations at agricultural conferences and elsewhere. For example, the agricultural expert C. J. Collins, in charge of national cattle imports and commissioned by the Senate for the search for perfect cattle for Finnish soil, was one among many who were convinced by the theory. In an 1847 speech to the nobility and a few fellow upper-class cattle farmers, he spoke for the import of foreign animals to Finland. He argued that "neither the climate nor the changes in feeding have any significant effect on the development of cattle breeds. Rather, the most important thing to be taken into account in the evaluation of this matter is the nervous system of different breeds, because it is in this character in which every breed has its power to overcome the effects of changes in both the climate and the feeding ratio" (Collins 1847, cited by Nylander 1906, 14). According to the theory, animal breeds would remain unchanged by the effects of the environment because their essential character—for example, the "nervous system" proposed above—was fixed at the heart of their very "being." The only thing a reasonable cattle farmer could do to enhance the milk production of his cattle was choose the "right" breed for his farm. In Finland this had led to importation of foreign breeds in large quantities by the Senate as well as by the farmers themselves (Nissinen 1923, 25; Myllylä 1991, 12).

11 For example, the grand duchy had acquired a new purebred cattle type, Algaun, in 1869 for one of its cattle-breeding stations to replace the old and plague-afflicted animals. However, from 1870 to 1879 Senate practice was to import only Ayrshire bulls for crossbreeding purposes all over the country. In addition, Holsteins and the Allgäu area's Brown Swiss were imported to the country in large quantities by private farmers and were also crossbred. Crossbreeding became the norm of cattle breeding in Finland in the second half of the century (see Liukko 1906; Nylander 1906; Nissinen 1923; Simonen 1964). It was only nonhistorical breeds and individual animals that were visible to the hereditary perception of the latter half of the nineteenth century in Finland.

12 In the original Danish, "Denne Betragtning savner ikke Berettigelse; thi I enver reen Race er der en umiskjendeling Overeensstemmelse mellem alle de enkelte Former og Livsyttringer, saaledes at de alle samvirke til et og samme Maal, nemlig der, at passe Dyret nøie ind I alle de ydre Forhold, I hvilke der er sat, hvad enten disse ere naturlige eller kunstige" (Prosch 1863, 141).

13 And this still holds true. No matter the wide dissemination of cattle catalogues and the recent communication revolution (including internet technologies) providing easy advertising of animals, these fairs act as important sites of value negotiation, with visual performance and related judgment procedures for finding the best animals for a particular breed (the elite individuals) in their trade and facilitating exchange between breeders (e.g., K. Anderson 2003).

14 For recent analyses of different functions and performances created through agricultural shows, the work of K. Anderson (2003) and Holloway (2005) is illuminating.

15 "Kyyttö" is a rarely used adjective. Today it is used as the nickname of eastern Finncattle. It denotes a zigzagged color pattern on the sides or on the back of the cattle. See figs. 1.2 and 1.3. "Ruunis" is a forgotten word for which I have not been able to recover the meaning, but it most likely refers to brown.

16 This origin story is found almost unaltered in the two editions of the national textbook on the breeding of domestic animals from 1943 and 1951 (Harmia 1943; 1951). Also, the national societies for the heritage landrace breeds use this story in their materials today (see http://www.maatiainen.fi/ and, in Finnish, http://www.kolumbus.fi/suomenalkuperaiskarja/).

17 Of course, to become myth, narratives need certain particular conditions of lingual and extralingual configurations (Barthes 1957, 181). In articulating the myth with the new science of breeding, the board and the local agricultural societies operating under it had all the extralingual pieces aligned—plagues, cattle-import bans, the Senate's official approval, and a new science—to make them heard as the official speakers for the landrace's history. From this new position, they began to narrate the origins of local bovine breeds in neatly packaged stories that would draw the nation and the cattle close to each other.

18 For example, Savolaiset were considered a mixed race of Karjalalaiset and Hämäläiset. A large amount of literature is available on this division in the human sciences of the day, extending into the first decades of the twentieth century. The literature cited is just an exemplary collection from the writings.

19 In the original Finnish, "Turha onpi erotella Länttä sekä Itää, yksi maa ja yks karja, niin se olla pitää."

20 Political organization in the countryside was quick and effective on a large scale, from the postwar period onward; see the work of Granberg 2004, 141–86.

21 In the original Finnish, "Olemme kokoontuneet juhlimaan suomalaisen karjanjalostuksen merkkipäivää. Tämä juhlahetki yhdistää sadattuhannet suomalaiset kautta maan, hiljaiset uurtajat, joiden työlle ei usein omisteta kiitollista, kunnioittavaa ajatusta. Tässä juhlassa he sen sitä suuremmalla syyllä ansaitsevat" (LSK 1958, 6).

22 The general stud book for thoroughbred horses was published relatively early on, in 1791.

23 An identical value process was seen for the English Shorthorn and other cattle types in the nineteenth and early twentieth centuries, especially in the transatlantic trade (Walton 1999; Derry 2003). Even if the milk yields were indicated in the herd books from 1905 onward, the desire for a pure national cattle breed remained the main principle of the breeding.

24 In a similar fashion, Sarah Franklin (2007b, 83) has described how in popular imagery Britishness is deeply entrenched in the form of various sorts of British sheep that "together offer images of nature, culture, and industry woven together in sheep's wool to suggest the fabric of a nation in which even the animals are man-made."

25 Reflecting on the changes in Finncattle breeding over the years, one breeder-historian complained about the mixture of too many guiding principles: "The first stupidity in this cattle-breeding was when all the attention was aimed at the color and the form. Finncattle had to be the smallest we could find for them to be the original landrace. . . . Furiously we searched for these until we found out that some of them were bad and only some good in milking. We found out that we should strive for good milking cows and not perfectly formed animals, and only after that we woke up to the fact that the animal can be big if the milk yield is good. . . . When we were looking for good milk yield, we made the mistake that we dismissed cows with a low milk fat ratio even if they would have had a good milk yield. Then into the picture came the cattle controls. . . . We controlled what the cattle ate and what they produced with that. It would have been good if we would have stayed on that path (relative production). But then started the production competition" (Pihkala 1968, 8).

26 Technologies such as sexing of the offspring and embryo transfer were used also, but they did not prove as effective in augmenting animal production as artificial insemination did (e.g., Clarke 2007).

27 Maijala was active in the EAAP for his whole career and was awarded the society's Distinguished Service Award in 1993.

28 Per author's unpublished 2005 interview with Maijala.

2. ALEXANDER AND THE (RE)BIRTH OF NATION

1 Frankel's article was one of the first to speak for the conservation of genetic matter outside the agricultural sciences, but he was not really the first to present the idea of protecting genetic diversity as a culturally valuable heritage and an economic potentiality. This argument was already highly relevant to

agricultural sciences on the heels of the Green Revolution in the 1950s, as I showed in the introductory chapter.

2 Metaphors of birth extend to DNA fingerprinting by the scientists' own choice of registers. This is a technique that was directly referred to as "a royal birth in the best British tradition" (Pena 1993, x) in an anthology on the "state of the science" of genetic fingerprinting in 1993.

3 These lists are particular objects of political-scientific-natural convergence, central mediation points between natures and nations, of a sort that can circulate over great distances and represent the sovereignty of nations over their genetic matter. They are a form of "immutable mobiles" (Latour 1987) endowed with the political cum scientific authorization to act as national representatives of genetic sovereignty at various levels (national, regional, and international politics of nature) while being at the very same time responsible for the discursive expression of the novel sphere of nature they represent. In technical terms, they make the literary inscription of genetic resources possible as a nationally centralized and structured inventory and extend the work across all nonhuman species within the nationally defined boundaries of the politics of nature (see chapter 4).

4 The Nordic Gene Bank has been a powerful actor in promoting research into genetic diversity and conservation practices in the Nordic region since its establishment in 1979.

5 According to Smirnoff (1894), the Alexander may have been imported from Turkey to be cultivated in Russia in unidentified "earlier periods," was cultivated at the Valamo monastery in the twelfth century, and was exported in the 1800s to other parts of the world.

6 In Whiteheadian terms, propositions must be located somewhere: "But according to the ontological principle, every proposition must be somewhere. The 'locus' of a proposition consists of those actual occasions whose actual worlds include the logical subjects of the proposition. When an actual entity belongs to the locus of a proposition, then conversely the proposition is an element in the lure for feeling of that actual entity" (Whitehead 1979, 186). The Alexander as a proposition is included in the actual world of mandate lists as much as tentative mandate lists are "lured" into/as propositions. Propositions also anticipate an actuality in the form of corporeality, of which paper lists are one form, living trees another.

7 Article 15, paragraph 3, states that genetic resources "are only those that are provided by Contracting Parties that are countries of origin of such resources," where "country of origin of genetic resources" means "the country which possesses those genetic resources in in-situ conditions." "In-situ conditions," in turn, refers to conditions where genetic resources exist within ecosystems and natural habitats, and in the case of domesticated or cultivated species, in the surroundings where they have developed their distinctive properties. The Alexander's distinctive properties, as we have seen above, are linked by Meeri with the cultivation tradition: the Alexander has distinctive

properties because it is part of the Finnish historical tradition of cultivation, a part of the Finnish natural heritage.

8 However, she has made minor adjustments to it to fit it better with her own laboratory configuration. This kind of tinkering is more of a rule than an exception, as is well known in the STS literature, and which the early texts attest (e.g., Knorr Cetina 1979), and is still a relevant question today (Jordan and Lynch 1998). This protocol tinkering itself is not the focus of my analysis, and I will not address it at greater length here.

9 Phylogenetic trees have for a long time been one of the central tools for biologists, from classical evolutionists to morphologists and practitioners of comparative physiology, for tracing the evolutionary genealogy of organisms. Molecular biologists, too, have adopted this representation technique. Reflecting on this history and aspirations pertaining to phylogenetic trees as a representational metaphor, two well-known researchers in the field of molecular evolutionary genetics have written that "from the time of Charles Darwin, it has been a dream for many biologists to reconstruct the evolutionary history of all organisms on Earth and express it in the form of a phylogenetic tree" (Nei and Kumar 2000, 3; see also Pálsson 2002). This dream shows again how the Western cultural representation of nature is centrally dependent on the arborescent metaphor (Deleuze and Guattari 1987), a metaphor that becomes increasingly problematic as my narrative nears its end.

10 Consequently, articles 15, 16, and 19, dealing with the ownership of genetic resources, do not govern access to the vast collections of these resources obtained before the convention entered into force (UNEP/CBD/COP/13).

11 In Finnish context, the plants seem predominantly relegated to female scientists, and they are brought together with the national animals carved out by selected male scientists to form the full Finnish family of resources, which is shepherded by predominantly male farmers.

3. STILLED LIFE

Epigraphs: Landecker 2007, 232; Waldby and Mitchell 2006, 33.

1 I think it is important to note here that Foucault deemed this new figure to be among "quasi-natural phenomena," in a contrast to the recent tendency in Anglo-American literature to reduce this concept to specific technologies that make "life itself" an object of knowledge practices (e.g., the work of Rose and Clarke). In the latter accounts, it is highly unclear what the ontological status of "life itself" is, an epistemological figure or really "life itself"?

2 Waldby and Mitchell (2006), for example, claim that human tissue economies are increasingly complex in their technicity, biotechnologies of global reach disentangling tissues from the local (national) context, and muddled ownership rights within the global politics over them.

3 Following the Marxist and Foucauldian tradition, many writers make this claim. Perhaps the most recent sustained analysis can be found in the work of Sunder Rajan (2006).

4 See the classical debate on interest explanations in STS (Barnes 1981; MacKenzie 1981; Woolgar 1981a; 1981b). I am more interested in both how particular "interests" become seen as legitimate justifications for particular actions and how they are mobilized to achieve these in practice through texts, technologies, and related practices.

5 Lynch (1988; see also Birke et al. 2006) discusses how animals in the laboratory are transformed step by step from what he calls "naturalistic" animals into "analytic" objects of scientific inquiry by a ritual of sacrifice. The transformation described in this chapter involves a comparable process of transformation, but instead of concentrating on the ritual aspects of the transformation, I will be discussing how the procedure is affected by the particular conditions—relations pointing at the same time to the inside and outside of the field lab in different phases of the process—of identification of the genetic material suitable for the ex situ bank. The question here is (to paraphrase Lynch) what an ex situ bank is if it is at the same time less than the sheep and always more than the breed.

6 "Lampaista," *Maanmiehen Ystäwä* 42, November 19, 1850.

7 This was an eighteen-page work prepared by H. Sawela (1919), "Lammashoito," in *Maatilahallituksen lentokirjasia lammashoidosta* no. 1, which was published by Helsinki's Valtioneuvoston kirjapaino. It was later published by SLSY (Suomen Lampaan- ja Vuohenhoitoyhdistys 1921) via Tyrvään Kirjapaino Osakeyhtio in Vammala.

8 Given that sheep were kept in small groups (two to three animals per family) and that Finland's human population was around three million in 1920, a quick calculation reveals that about one-third of all Finnish households kept these animals. Finnsheep were used mainly to produce wool and meat for the family in the early twentieth century (see also Soini 2007).

9 It should be kept in mind that the official reasons behind the conservation of "native breeds" have varied. Some conservation scientists make a division into (a) economic-biological, (b) scientific, and (c) cultural-historical reasons (this was, for example, Maijala's thesis between 1971 and 2004) while others have given genetic conservation of animal breeds five or more "value justifications," ranging from future market opportunities to ecological value (e.g., Oldenbroek 1999, 5). There are plenty of other justification frameworks for genetic conservation. However, all these concentrate on finding the inherent value of the genetic material to be conserved, not the reasons and rationalities behind what makes the entire global conservation effort so attractive that it is suddenly considered an imperative that it take as its object of the knowledge genetic diversity itself.

10 Recent genetic research suggests that the effective population (*Ne*) is not yet in immediate peril but will approach that state if no action is taken. Li, Strandén, and Kantanen (2009) write that "the current level of *Ne* suggests genetic diversity in the Finnsheep population is approaching critical levels both in conservation and in selection programmes. If the annual change in

mean inbreeding coefficient increases, for example, as a result of intensive use of a few rams, maintenance of genetic variability would become more difficult, and, then, strong actions would be needed."

11 B. G. Brackett, G.E. Seidel, and S. M. Seidel discussed the potentiality embodied in Finnsheep genes in a well-known book about technologies of animal breeding in the 1980s. They wrote, "There are valuable resources that individuals, agencies, and governments are willing to purchase. Valuable genetic traits include genes for milk production in North American Holsteins, high growth rates in Danish swine, prolificacy in Finnish sheep, agility in Arabian horses, disease resistance in African cattle, and fleece characteristics of Australian sheep. With frozen semen and/or embryos, it is possible to move these genetic resources around the globe easily and inexpensively, with the additional benefit that the possibility of disease transmission is markedly reduced, relative to moving animals. There is also an epigenetic and developmental advantage if an animal is born into the environment in which it is expected to perform and reproduce" (Brackett et al. 1981, 8).

12 Also, various national and regional health and quarantine regulations are normally in place for the reproductive material; that is, it must be collected at a nationally approved collection facility that meets standards set for the destination market (e.g., the EU, the United States, or South America). However, in the wake of outbreaks of bovine spongiform encephalopathy and foot-and-mouth disease, for example, countries such as Britain have banned the transport of farm animals over large distances for reasons of biosecurity (e.g., Seguin 2003).

13 For the last twenty years of the twentieth century, more than 200 million frozen semen doses, mostly for bovine animals, were produced worldwide every year. With these numbers, the theoretical size of the cattle-sperm economy reached a value one could conservatively estimate at up to $4–5 billion per year (of which about 5 percent comes from international trade; see, for example, Gollin and Blackburn 2007).

14 The hormone belongs to a group called prostaglandins, which have been a focus of intensive research. In the recent history of medicine, work on prostaglandins was awarded a Nobel Prize in Physiology or Medicine in 1982 (Bergström et al.).

15 For an interesting analysis of the social order of a slaughterhouse, see the work of LeDuff 2003; for a critical review of modern animal husbandry, see S. Franklin 1999, 126–44; and for a collection of analogous essays on the ordering of human-animal relationships, see Wolch and Emel 1998.

16 For discussion of other methods and analytical constructs used to evaluate and manage fertility indices in real (i.e., nonbarn) laboratory environments, see the work of Hulet and Ercanbrack 1962, Garner and Johnson 1995, and Piperelis et al. 2008.

17 At least in 2009, the technique still more closely resembled those which Fox Keller (1992) has analyzed—the bullroarer, Frankenstein's work, and the

A-bomb—which were aimed at producing life but ended up producing death: Dolly prematurely grew old and died for unknown reasons. There is also another interesting story line behind the technologies pointing to the partial connection of technologies of procreation and kinship, of the trajectories of technological fatherhood—Ian Walmut was a student of Christopher Polge, the scientist behind the cryopreservation technique, and so very much the scientific forefather for Walmut's nucleus-transfer technique. But where Polge's technique is aimed only at suspending life, Walmut's is intended for a complete redesign of the process of the reproduction of life.

4. EXPERIMENTAL ADMINISTRATION

1 But, for rare exceptions, see Cambrosio et al. 1990; N. Brown and Michael 2004.

2 Interestingly, the history of the CBD recounted on the official website (http://www.cbd.int/) starts only with the preliminary meetings in 1991 as if to hide the controversies leading up to its ratification among the nation-states involved in its making and in the final closure by its ratification. A great deal has been written about this process from various perspectives, and it is not my aim to recount these writings here (for analyses of the CBD's interesting genealogy, see the references cited).

3 This institutional identification amounts to Douglasian analysis centered on "purity and danger," especially as seen in Mary Douglas's example of the status of cattle in the book of Leviticus: "Cattle were literally domesticated as slaves. They had to be brought into the social order to enjoy the blessing. The difference between cattle and wild beasts is that the wild beasts have no covenant to protect them" (Douglas [1966] 2002, 68). Her early analysis resonates interestingly with Agamben's (1998; 2000) argument on the "hidden" birth of biopolitics through exclusion of life from society, and inclusion of it therein, via the distinction between pure or naked life (life form, or *zoê*) and the life brought into the society and its subjection to society's public decision-making processes (a form of life, or *bios*). One finds here, of course, a central link to the politics of the state in its body politics through his interpretations of ancient Greek and modern thinkers, of whom Hannah Arendt and Michel Foucault are especially important.

4 Mandate of the ABS Group, Dnro 580/041/2003.

5 These are: WTO/TRIPS: World Trade Organization—Agreement on Trade-Related Aspects of Intellectual Property Rights; WIPO: World Intellectual Property Organization; UPOV: International Convention for the Protection of New Varieties of Plants; FAO/IT: Food and Agriculture Organization of the United Nations—International Treaty on Plant Genetic Resources for Food and Agriculture.

6 As stated in Bonn Guidelines provisions IA3, IA4, and especially IA7a: "The present Guidelines are voluntary and were prepared with a view to ensuring their: (a) Voluntary nature: they are intended to guide both users and provid-

ers of genetic resources on a voluntary basis" (Bonn Guidelines 2030 (SCBD 2002)).

7 Bonn Guidelines IA10: "The guidelines should be applied in a manner that is coherent and mutually supportive of the work of relevant international agreements and institutions. The guidelines are without prejudice to the access and benefit-sharing provisions of the FAO International Treaty for Plant Genetic Resources for Food and Agriculture. Furthermore, the work of the World Intellectual Property Organization on issues of relevance to access and benefit-sharing should be taken into account. The application of the guidelines should also take into account existing regional legislation and agreements on access and benefit-sharing."

8 The mission of the Finnish Ministry of the Environment is publicly stated as "to promote sustainable development, and . . . to keep the environment safe and healthy, to preserve biodiversity, to prevent environmental degradation, and to improve housing conditions."

9 This is from an interview with the secretary of the ABS group on June 16, 2005.

10 The report was released under the name "Geenivarojen saatavuutta ja hyötyjen jakoa koskevien Bonnin ohjeiden kansallinen toimeenpano" (National implementation of the Bonn Guidelines related to the access and benefit-sharing issues of genetic resources) (MAF 2007). The report, accessible also via the web at www.mmm.fi/documents/1410837/1790809/trm2007_5.pdf, includes an English-language summary.

11 A separate international agreement on cultivated plant varieties and their wild relatives used in agriculture was made independently of the CBD under the auspices of the FAO in 2001. This agreement is called the International Treaty on Plant Genetic Resources (for more, see Whatmore 2002 and http://www.planttreaty.org/).

12 This is from an interview with the chair of the ABS group on March 7, 2006.

13 Only one national review on the issues of jurisdiction associated with genetic resources had been done before the work of the ABS group commenced (Wallius 2001). The problem with that review was that it was completed before the release of the Bonn Guidelines.

14 This is from an interview with an expert member of the ABS group on March 15, 2006.

15 This is from an interview with the secretary of the ABS group on June 16, 2005.

16 This does not involve ownership per se being automatically transferred to the state. Instead, it means that the primary authority to decide on the ownership of genetic resources in Finland would be given to the state. It is only after this initial rearrangement of the social contract between the state and its citizens that the state could legitimately fulfill its international obligations stemming from the CBD. Only after this kind of arrangement could it exercise its legitimate sovereignty implied in the international convention by being

legally competent to decide how these ownership relations should be configured in Finland (the state could, for example, give the ownership of genetic resources to the citizens).

17 Regulation (EU) no. 511/2014.

18 As explained on the main website for the CBD at https://www.cbd.int/abs/about/.

19 This is from an interview with a senior official in September 2015.

20 Interview with a senior official in September 2015.

21 This is from an interview with a senior official of the Ministry of Agriculture and Forestry in December 2015.

22 Interview with a senior official, December 2015.

23 See https://absch.cbd.int/.

24 See https://www.cbd.int/conferences/2016/cop-13/documents.

CONCLUSION

1 Since Foucault's early analysis presented in *The History of Sexuality* (1985) of the time of the rise of biopower, sovereign forms of power have been downplayed in analysis of biopolitics even if Foucault himself asserted the complementary nature of the two within modern societies. His lectures (2003; 2004; 2007) on the emergence of biopower and liberal societies contain a discussion of the relation of the two powers, which he sees as still being very much operational: "And I think that one of the greatest transformations [the] political right underwent in the nineteenth century was precisely that. I wouldn't say exactly that sovereignty's old right—to take life or let live—was replaced, but it came to be complemented by a new right, which does not erase the old right but which does penetrate it, permeate it. This, the right, or rather precisely the opposite right. It is the power to make live and 'let' die" (Foucault 2003, 240).

REFERENCES

ARCHIVAL SOURCES

ISK [Eastern Finnish Cattle Breeding Society]. (1899) 1901. *Letter to Breeders*, no. 1. FABA Archives

ISK [Eastern Finnish Cattle Breeding Society]. 1918. *Letter to Breeders*, no. 4. FABA Archives.

ISK [Eastern Finnish Cattle Breeding Society]. 1922. *Letter to Breeders*, no. 8. FABA Archives.

ISK [Eastern Finnish Cattle Breeding Society]. 1930. *Letter to Breeders*, no. 49. FABA Archives.

ISK [Eastern Finnish Cattle Breeding Society]. 1936. *Letter to Breeders*, no. 73. FABA Archives.

LSK [Western Finncattle Society]. 1904. *Kantakirja I*. Hämeenlinna, Finland: Länsi-Suomen Karjanjalostusyhdistys.

LSK [Western Finncattle Society]. 1958. *Letter to Breeders*, no. 34. Western Finnish Cattle Breeding Society. FABA Archives.

MTT [Agrifood Research Finland]. 2005. "Finnsheep. A Northern Specialty."

Preststånds Protocoll vid Laudtagen. 1809. National Archives of Finland.

PSK [Northern Finncattle Society]. 1906. *Kantakirja I*. FABA Archives

SK [Finncattle Society]. 1969. *Letter to Breeders*, no. 2. FABA Archives.

PUBLISHED SOURCES

Abu-Lughod, Lila. 1991. "Writing against Culture." In *Recapturing Anthropology: Working in the Present*, edited by R. Fox, 137–62. Santa Fe, NM: School of American Research.

Acquaah, George. 2002. *Horticulture: Principles and Practices*. 3rd ed. Upper Saddle River, NJ: Prentice Hall.

Agamben, Giorgio. 1998. *Homo Sacer*. Stanford, CA: Stanford University Press.

Agamben, Giorgio. 2000. *Means without Ends: Notes on Politics*. Minneapolis: University of Minnesota Press.

Agamben, Giorgio. 2004. *The Open: Man and Animal*. Stanford, CA: Stanford University Press.

Agrawal, Arun. 2005. *Environmentality: Technologies of Government and the Making of Subjects*. Durham, NC: Duke University Press.

Alapuro, Risto. 1988. *State and Revolution in Finland*. Berkeley, CA: University of California Press.

Alsaidi, Abdullah. 2010. "Statement on Behalf of the Group of 77 and China in the High-Level Meeting of the General Assembly as a Contribution to the International Year of Biodiversity." New York, September 22, 2010.

Anderson, Benedict. (1983) 1991. *Imagined Communities: Reflections on the Origin and Spread of Nationalism*. Rev. ed. London: Verso.

Anderson, K. 2003. "White Natures: Sydney's Royal Agricultural Show in Posthumanist Perspective." *Transactions of the Institute of British Geographers* 28: 422–41.

Antonius-Klemola, Kristiina. 1999. *DNA Fingerprinting in Rubus L. Breeding*. Helsinki: Yliopistopaino.

Appadurai, Arjun. 1981. "The Past as a Scarce Resource." *Man*, n.s., 2: 201–19.

Appadurai, Arjun. 1988. "Putting Hierarchy in Its Place." *Cultural Anthropology* 3: 36–44.

Bakhtin, Mikhail. M. 1981. *The Dialogic Imagination: Four Essays*. Edited by M. Holquist. Austin: University of Texas Press.

Barker, J. S. F. 1994. "Animal Breeding and Conservation Genetics." In *Conservation Genetics*, edited by V. Loeschcke, J. Tomiuk, and S. K. Jain, 381–98. Berlin: Birkhäuser.

Barnes, Barry. 1981. "On the 'Hows' and 'Whys' of Cultural Change (Response to Woolgar)." *Social Studies of Science* 11: 481–98.

Barron, Archibald F. 1884. *British Apples: Report of the Committee of the National Apple Congress, Held in the Royal Horticultural Gardens, Chiswick, October 5th to 25th, 1883*. London: Macmillan.

Barthes, Roland. 1957. *Mythologies*. Paris: Seuil.

Bateson, Gregory. [1972] 2000. *Steps to an Ecology of Mind*. Chicago: University of Chicago Press.

Benjamin, Walter. 1968. *Illuminations*. New York: Harcourt, Brace.

Berg, Marc, and Stefan Timmermans. 2000. "Orders and Their Others: On the Constitution of Universalities in Medical Work." *Configurations* 8: 31–61.

Bhabha, Homi K. 1990a. "DissemiNation: Time, Narrative, and the Margins of the Modern Nation." In *Nation and Narration*, edited by Homi K. Bhabha, 291–321. London: Routledge.

Bhabha, Homi K., ed. 1990b. *Nation and Narration*. London: Routledge.

Bhabha, Homi K. 1994. *The Location of Culture*. New York: Routledge.

Bhabha, Homi K. 1996. "Postmodernism/Postcolonialism." In *Critical Terms for Art History*, edited by Robert S. Nelson and Richard Shiff, 307–22. Chicago: University of Chicago Press.

Bhabha, Homi K. 2004. *The Location of Culture*. New York: Routledge.

Billig, Michael. 1995. *Banal Nationalism*. London: SAGE.

Birke, Lynda, Arnold Arluke, and Mike Michael. 2006. *The Sacrifice: How Scientific Experiments Transform Animals and People*. West Lafayette, IN: Purdue University Press.

Blanchard, Ian. 1986. "The Continental European Cattle Trades, 1400–1600." *Economic History Review* 39: 427–60.

Boa-Amponsem, K., and G. Minozzi. 2006. "The State of Development of Biotechnologies as They Relate to the Management of Animal Genetic Resources and Their Potential Application in Developing Countries." Rome: FAO, Commission on Genetic Resources for Food and Agriculture.

Bowker, Geoffrey C. 2000. "Biodiversity Datadiversity." *Social Studies of Science* 30: 643–83.

Bowker, Geoffrey C., and Susan Leigh Star. 2002. *Sorting Things Out: Classifying and Its Consequences*. Cambridge, MA: MIT Press.

Brackett, B. G. 1981. "Applications of In Vitro Fertilization." In *New Technologies in Animal Breeding*, edited by B. G. Brackett, G. E. Seidel Jr., and S. M. Seidel, 141–61. New York: Academic.

Brackett, B. G., G. E. Seidel, and S. M. Seidel, eds. 1981. *New Technologies in Animal Breeding*. New York: Academic.

Brennan, Timothy. 1990. "The National Longing for Form." In *Nation and Narration*, edited by Homi K. Bhabha, 44–70. London: Routledge.

Brown, Lester R. 2001. *Eco-Economy: Building an Economy for the Earth*. Washington, DC: Earth Policy Institute.

Brown, Michael F., J. A. Barnes, David A. Cleveland, Rosemary J. Coombe, Phiilippe Descola, L. R. Hiatt, Jean Jackson, B. G. Karlsson, Darrell Addison Posey, Willow Roberts Powers, Lawrence Rosen, Fernando Santos Granero, Carlo Severi, David J. Stephenson, Marilyn Strathern, and Donald Tuzin. 1998. "Can Culture Be Copyrighted? (and Comments and Reply)." *Current Anthropology* 39: 193–222.

Brown, Nik. 2007. "Shifting Tenses: From Regimes of Truth to Regimes of Hope?" *Configurations* 13: 331–55.

Brown, Nik, A. Kraft, and P. Martin. 2006. "Imagining Blood: The Promissory Pasts of Haematopoietic Stem Cells." *BioSocieties* 1: 329–48.

Brown, Nik, and M. Michael. 2004. "Risky Creatures: Institutional Species Boundary Change in Biotechnology Regulation." *Health, Risk, Society* 6: 207–22.

Brush, S. B. 1998. "Indigenous Knowledge of Biological Resources and Intellectual Property Rights: The Role of Anthropology." *American Anthropologist* 95: 653–86.

Brush, S. B. 1999. "Bioprospecting the Public Domain." *Cultural Anthropology* 14: 535–55.

Butzer, K. W. 1988. "Cattle and Sheep from Old to New Spain: Historical Antecedents." *Annals of the Association of American Geographers* 78: 29–56.

Calarco, Matthew. 2008. *Zoographies: The Question of the Animal from Heidegger to Derrida*. New York: Columbia University Press.

Callison, Candis. 2014. *How Climate Change Comes to Matter: The Communal Life of Facts*. Durham, NC: Duke University Press.

Callon, Michel. 1986. "Some Elements of a Sociology of Translation: Domestication of the Scallops and the Fishermen of St. Brieuc Bay." In *Power, Action, and Belief: A New Sociology of Knowledge?*, edited by John Law, 196–233. London: Routledge and Kegan Paul.

Cambrosio, A., and P. Keating. 1988. "Going Monoclonal: Art, Science and Magic in the Use of Hybridoma Technology." *Social Problems* 35: 244–60.

Cambrosio, A., C. Limoges, and D. Provonost. 1990. "Representing Biotechnology: An Ethnography of Quebec Science Policy." *Social Studies of Science* 20: 195–227.

Canguilhem, Georges. 2007. *The Normal and the Pathological*. New York: Zone.

CBD. The Convention on Biological Diversity of 5 June 1992 (1760 U.N.T.S. 69).

Chatterjee, Partha. 1998. *The Nation and Its Fragments: Colonial and Postcolonial Histories*. Princeton, NJ: Princeton University Press.

Chatterjee, Partha. 2005. "The Nation in Heterogeneous Time." *Futures* 37: 925–42.

Clarke, Adele. 1998. *Disciplining Reproduction: Modernity, American Life Sciences, and the Problems of Sex*. Berkeley: University of California Press.

Clarke, Adele. 2007. "Reflections on the Reproductive Sciences in Agriculture in the UK and US, c. 1900–2000." *History and Philosophy of the Biological and Biomedical Sciences* 38: 316–39.

Clifford, James. 1988. *The Predicament of Culture: Twentieth-Century Ethnography, Literature, and Art*. Cambridge, MA: Harvard University Press.

Clifford, James. 1996. *Routes: Travel and Translation in the Late Twentieth Century*. Cambridge, MA: Harvard University Press.

Clifford, James, and George E. Marcus, eds. 1986. *Writing Culture: The Poetics and Politics of Ethnography*. Berkeley: University of California Press.

Cole, H. H., and P. T. Cupps, eds. 1977. *Reproduction in Domestic Animals*. New York: Academic.

Collier, Stephen J. 2005. "Budgets and Biopolitics." In *Global Assemblages: Technology, Politics, and Ethics as Anthropological Problems*, edited by Aihwa Ong and Stephen J. Collier, 373–90. Malden, MA: Blackwell.

Cressey, Daniel. 2014. "Biopiracy Ban Stirs Red-Tape Fears: Critics Worry Nagoya Protocol Will Hamper Disease Monitoring." *Nature* 514: 14–15.

Crosby, Alfred W. 1986. *Ecological Imperialism: The Biological Expansion of Europe 900–1900*. Cambridge: Cambridge University Press.

Darwin, Charles. (1859) 1996. *On the Origin of Species*. Oxford: Oxford University Press.

Deleuze, Gilles, and Félix Guattari. 1987. *A Thousand Plateaus: Capitalism and Schizophrenia*. Minneapolis: University of Minnesota Press.

Deleuze, Gilles, and Félix Guattari. 1994. *What Is Philosophy?* New York: Columbia University Press.

Derry, Margaret E. 2003. *Bred for Perfection: Shorthorn Cattle, Collies, and Arabian Horses since 1800*. Baltimore, MD: Johns Hopkins University Press.

Douglas, Mary. (1966) 2002. *Purity and Danger: An Analysis of Concepts of Pollution and Taboo*. London: Routledge.

Eley, Geoff, and Ronald G. Suny, eds. 1996. *Becoming National: A Reader*. New York: Oxford University Press.

Eneroth, Olof. 1884. *Handbok i Svensk Pomologi* [Handbook of Swedish pomology]. Stockholm: Nordstedts.

Escobar, Arturo. 1998. "Whose Knowledge, Whose Nature? Biodiversity, Conservation, and the Political Ecology of Social Movements." *Journal of Political Ecology* 1: 53–82.

FAO [United Nations Food and Agriculture Organization]. 1967. "FAO Technical Conference on Exploration, Utilization and Conservation of Plant Gene Resources." Rome: Food and Agriculture Organization of the United Nations.

FAO [United Nations Food and Agriculture Organization]. 1983. "Animal Production and Health Paper 44, no. 1." Proceedings of the Joint FAO/UNEP Expert Panel Meeting, October 1983, Part 1. Rome: Food and Agriculture Organization of the United Nations.

FAO [United Nations Food and Agriculture Organization]. 1984. "Animal Genetic Resources Conservation by Management, Data Banks and Training." Rome: Food and Agriculture Organization of the United Nations.

FAO [United Nations Food and Agriculture Organization]. 1999. "Animal Genetic Resources: A Global Programme for Sustainable Development." Animal Production and Health Paper 80. Rome: Food and Agriculture Organization of the United Nations.

FAO [United Nations Food and Agriculture Organization]. 2007. "Global Plan of Action for Animal Genetic Resources and the Interlaken Declaration." Rome: Commission on Genetic Resources for Food and Agriculture, Food and Agriculture Organization of the United Nations.

Faulkner, Alex, Ingrid Geesink, Julie Kent, and David Fitzpatrick. 2003. "Human Tissue Engineered Products—Drugs or Devices?" *British Medical Journal* 326: 1159–60.

First, N. L., A. Sevinge, and H. A. Henneman. 1961. "Fertility of Frozen and Unfrozen Ram Semen." *Journal of Animal Science* 20: 79–84.

Fischer, Michael M. J. 1999. "Emergent Forms of Life: Anthropologies of Late or Postmodernities." *Annual Review of Anthropology* 28: 455–78.

Fischer, Michael M. J. 2003. *Emergent Forms of Life and the Anthropological Voice*. Durham, NC: Duke University Press.

Fischer, Michael M. J. 2009. *Anthropological Futures*. Durham, NC: Duke University Press.

Fischer, Michael J. 2013. "Biopolis: Asian Science in the Global Circuitry." *Science, Technology and Society* 18: 379–404

Fitzgerald, Heli, Marja Ruohonen-Lehto, and Katileena Lohtander-Buckbee. 2015. "Suomen arvokkaat geenivarat." Suomen ympäristökeskuksen raportteja 26. Helsinki: Suomen ympäristökeskus.

Fletcher, A. L. 2004. "Field of Genes: The Politics of Science and Identity in the Estonian Genome Project." *New Genetics and Society* 23: 3–14.

Foote, R. H. 1983. "The Artificial Insemination Industry." In *New Technologies in Animal Breeding*, edited by B. G. Brackett, G. E. Seidel Jr., and S. M. Seidel, 13–39. New York: Academic.

Foote, R. H. 2002. "The History of Artificial Insemination: Selected Notes and Notables." *Journal of Animal Science* 80: 1–10.

Forsius, Arno. 1979a. "Eläinten Lääkehuollon Kehitys Suomessa Ennen Vuotta 1865." *Suomen Eläinlääkärilehti* 85: 393–404.

Forsius, Arno. 1979b. "Eläinten lääkehuollon kehitys Suomessa vuoden 1865 jälkeen."*Suomen Eläinlääkärilehti* 85: 443–52.

Fortun, Kim. 2001. *Advocacy after Bhopal: Environmentalism, Disaster, New Global Orders*. Chicago: University of Chicago Press.

Fortun, Michael. 2008. Promising Genomics: Iceland and deCODE Genetics in a World of Speculation. Berkeley: University of California Press.

Foucault, Michel. 1966. *Les mots et les choses*. Paris: Gallimard, 1966.

Foucault, Michel. 1977. *Discipline and Punish*. New York: Vintage.

Foucault, Michel. 1985. *History of Sexuality*. New York: Vintage.

Foucault, Michel. 2001. *The Order of Things: Archaeology of the Human Sciences*. London: Routledge.

Foucault, Michel. 2003. *"Society Must Be Defended": Lectures at the Collège de France 1975–1976*. New York: Picador.

Foucault, Michel. 2007. *Security, Territory, Population: Lectures at the Collège de France 1977–1978*. New York: Palgrave Macmillan.

Fox Keller, Evelyn. 1992. *Secrets of Life, Secrets of Death: Essays on Language, Gender and Science*. London: Routledge.

Frankel, O. H. 1974. "Genetic Conservation: Our Evolutionary Responsibility." *Genetics* 78: 53–65.

Frankel, O. H., and Michael E. Soulé, eds. 1981. *Conservation and Evolution*. Cambridge: Cambridge University Press.

Frankham, Richard. 1995. "Conservation Genetics." *Annual Review of Genetics* 29: 305–27.

Frankham, Richard. 2005. "Genetics and Extinction." *Biological Conservation* 126: 131–40.

Franklin, Alex. 2001. *Animals and Modern Cultures: A Sociology of Human-Animal Relations in Modernity*. London: SAGE.

Franklin, Sarah. 1999. "What We Know and What We Don't about Cloning and Society." *New Genetics and Society* 18: 111–20.

Franklin, Sarah. 2001. "Sheepwatching." *Anthropology Today* 17: 3–9.

Franklin, Sarah. 2003. "Kinship, Genes and Cloning: Life after Dolly." In *Genetic Nature/Culture: Anthropology and Science beyond the Two-Culture Divide*, edited by Alan H. Goodman, Deborah Heath, and M. Susan Lindee, 95–110. Berkeley: University of California Press.

Franklin, Sarah. 2006. "Mapping Biocapital: New Frontiers of Bioprospecting." *Cultural Geographies* 13: 301–4.

Franklin, Sarah. 2007a. *Dolly Mixtures: The Remaking of Genealogy*. Durham, NC: Duke University Press.
Franklin, Sarah. 2007b. "Dolly's Body: Gender, Genetics, and the New Genetic Capital." In *The Animals Reader: The Essential Classic and Contemporary Writings*, edited by Linda Kalof and Amy Fitzgerald, 349–61. Oxford: Berg.
Franklin, Sarah, and Margaret Lock, eds. 2003. *Remaking Life and Death: Towards an Anthropology of the Biosciences*. Santa Fe, NM: School of American Research Press.
Franklin, Sarah, Celia Lury, and Jackie Stacey. 2000. *Global Nature, Global Culture*. London: SAGE.
Franklin, Sarah, and Susan McKinnon, eds. 2001. *Relative Values: Reconfiguring Kinship Studies*. Durham, NC: Duke University Press.
Franklin, Sarah, and Helena Ragoné, eds. 1998. *Reproducing Reproduction: Kinship, Power and Technological Innovation*. Philadelphia: University of Pennsylvania Press.
Friedman, Jonathan. 1992. "Myth, History, and Political Identity." *Cultural Anthropology* 7: 194–210.
Friedman, Jonathan. 1994. *Cultural Identity and Global Process*. London: SAGE.
Garner, D., and L. Johnson. 1995. "Viability Assessment of Mammalian Sperm Using SYBR-14 and Propidium Iodide." *Biology of Reproduction* 153: 276–84.
Gaudillière, Jean-Paul. 2007. "The Farm and the Clinic: An Inquiry into the Making of Our Biotechnological Modernity." *Studies in History and Philosophy of Biological and Biomedical Sciences* 38: 521–29.

Gayon, Jean. 2000. "From Measurement to Organization: A Philosophical Scheme for the History of the Concept of Heredity." In *The Concept of the Gene in Development and Evolution: Historical and Epistemological Perspectives*, edited by Peter Beurton, Raphael Falk, and Hans-Jörg Rheinberger, 69–90. Cambridge: Cambridge University Press.
Gellner, Ernest. 1983. *Nations and Nationalism*. Ithaca, NY: Cornell University Press.
Gianfranceschi, L., N. Seglias, R. Tarchini, M. Komjanc, and C. Gessler. 1998. "Simple Sequence Repeats for the Genetic Analysis of Apple." *Theoretical and Applied Genetics* 96: 1069–76.
Gibbons, Ann. 1992. "Conservation Biology in the Fast Lane." *Science* 255: 20–22.
Glowka, Lyle, Françoise Burhenne-Guilmin, and Hugh Synge. 1994. "A Guide to the Convention on Biological Diversity." Environmental Policy and Law Paper 30. Gland, Switzerland: IUCN—the World Conservation Union.
Gollin, D., and H. Blackburn. 2007. "International Flows of Animal Genetic Resources: An Economic and Biological Analysis." http://www.fao.org/Ag/againfo/programmes/en/genetics/documents/Interlaken/sidevent/5_1/Gollin.pdf.
Gottweis, Herbert. 1998. *Governing Molecules: The Discursive Politics of Genetic Engineering in Europe and the United States*. Cambridge, MA: MIT Press.

Gottweis, Herbert, and Alan Petersen. 2008. *Biobanks: Governance in Comparative Perspective*. London: Routledge.

Granberg, Leo. 2004. "Tuotannon Kasvun Vuosikymmenet." In *Kasvun ja kriisien aika 1870-luvulta 1950-luvulle Suomen Maatalouden historia*, edited by M. Peltonen, 141–85. Helsinki: Suomen Kirjallisuuden Seura.

Greiber, Thomas, Sonia Peña Moreno, Mattias Åhrén, Jimena Nieto Carrasco, Evanson Chege Kamau, Jorge Cabrera Medaglia, Maria Julia Oliva, and Frederic Perron-Welch, in cooperation with Natasha Ali and China Williams. 2012. "An Explanatory Guide to the Nagoya Protocol on Access and Benefit-Sharing." IUCN Environmental Policy and Law Paper 83.

Grotenfelt, K. 1926. "Suomen Suomalaisten Heimojen Vanhin Historia." In *Suomen Suku*, edited by I. A. Kannisto, E. N. Setälä, U. T. Sirelius, and Y. Wichhmann, 264–71. Helsinki: Otava.

Grove, Richard H. 1996. *Green Imperialism: Colonial Expansion, Tropical Island Edens and the Origins of Environmentalism, 1600–1860*. Cambridge: Cambridge University Press.

Gupta, Akhil, and James Ferguson, eds. 1997a. *Anthropological Locations: Boundaries and Grounds of a Field Science*. Berkeley: University of California Press.

Gupta, Akhil, and James Ferguson, eds. 1997b. *Culture, Power, Place: Explorations in Critical Anthropology*. Durham, NC: Duke University Press.

Hacking, Ian. 1992. "The Self-Vindication of the Laboratory Sciences." In *Science as Practice and Culture*, edited by Andrew Pickering, 29–64. Chicago: University of Chicago Press.

Hajer, Maarten, and Hendrik Wagenaar. 2003. "Introduction." In *Deliberative Policy Analysis: Understanding Governance in the Network Society*, edited by Maarten Hajer and Hendrik Wagenaar, 1–32. Cambridge: Cambridge University Press.

Hall, Stuart. 2007 (with Fredric Jameson). "Interview with Stuart Hall," in *Jameson on Jameson: Conversations on Cultural Marxism*, edited by Ian Buchanan, 113–22. Durham, NC: Duke University Press.

Haraway, Donna. 1991. *Simians, Cyborgs and Women: The Reinvention of Nature*. New York: Routledge.

Haraway, Donna. 1997. *Modest_Witness@Second_Millennium.FemaleMan_Meets_Oncomouse*. New York: Routledge.

Haraway, Donna. 2003. *The Companion Species Manifesto: Dogs, People, and Significant Otherness*. Chicago: Prickly Paradigm.

Haraway, Donna. 2015. "Anthropocene, Capitalocene, Plantationocene, Chthulucene: Making Kin." *Environmental Humanities* 6: 159–65.

Harmia, Aarne. 1943. *Kotieläinjalostuksen Oppikirja*. Helsinki: Werner Söderström Osakeyhtiö.

Harmia, Aarne. 1951. *Kotieläinjalostuksen Oppikirja*. 2nd rev. ed. Helsinki: Werner Söderström Osakeyhtiö.

Hastrup, Kirsten. 1992. *Other Histories*. London: Routledge.

Hayden, Corinne. 2003a. "Suspended Animation: A Brine Shrimp Essay." In *Remaking Life and Death*, edited by Sarah Franklin and Margaret Lock, 193–226. Santa Fe, NM: School of American Research Press.
Hayden, Corinne. 2003b. *When Nature Goes Public: The Making and Unmaking of Bioprospecting in Mexico*. Princeton, NJ: Princeton University Press.
Hedrick, Philip. W. 2001. "Conservation Genetics: Where Are We Now?" *Trends in Ecology and Evolution* 16: 629–36.
Heikkinen, I., and Interministerial Group of Editors. 2007. *Saving Nature for People: National Strategy and Action Plan for Conservation and Sustainable Use of Biodiversity in Finland 2006–2016*. Helsinki: Ministry of the Environment.
Heller, Chaia, and Arturo Escobar. 2003. "From Pure Genes to GMOs: Transnationalized Gene Landscapes in the Biodiversity and Transgenic Food Networks." In *Genetic Nature/Culture: Anthropology and Science beyond the Two-Culture Divide*, edited by Alan H. Goodman, Deborah Heath, and M. Susan Lindee, 155–75. Berkeley: University of California Press.
Helmreich, Stefan. 2003. "Trees and Seas of Information: Alien Kinship and the Biopolitics of Gene Transfer in Marine Biology and Biotechnology." *American Ethnologist* 30: 341–59.
Helmreich, Stefan. 2005. "How Scientists Think, about 'Natives,' for Example: A Problem of Taxonomy among Biologists of Alien Species in Hawaii." *Journal of the Royal Anthropological Institute* 11: 107–27.
Helmreich, Stefan. 2007. "Blue-Green Capital, Biotechnological Circulation and an Oceanic Imaginary: A Critique of Biopolitical Economy." *BioSocieties* 2: 287–302.
Helmreich, Stefan. 2010. *Alien Ocean: Anthropological Voyages in Microbial Seas*. Berkeley: University of California Press.
Helmreich, Stefan. 2011. "What Was Life? Answers from Three Limit Biologies." *Critical Inquiry* 37: 671–96.
Hiemstra, S. J., T. van der Lende, and H. Woelders. 2006. "The Potential of Cryopreservation and Reproductive Technologies for Animal Genetic Resources Conservation Strategies in the Role of Biotechnology in Exploring and Protecting Agricultural Genetic Resources." Rome: Food and Agriculture Organization.
Hjerppe, Ritta. 1988. *The Finnish Economy 1860–1985: Growth and Structural Change*. Helsinki: Bank of Finland, Government Printing Centre.
Hobsbawm, Eric J. 1990. *Nations and Nationalism since 1780: Programme, Myth, Reality*. Cambridge: Cambridge University Press.
Hobsbawm, Eric, and Terence Ranger. 1983. *The Invention of Tradition*. Cambridge: Cambridge University Press.
Hodges, John. 1999. "Jubilee History of the European Association for Animal Production." *Livestock Production Science* 60: 105–68.
Holling, C. S., and W. C. Clark. 1975. "Notes toward a Science of Ecological Management." In *Unifying Concepts in Ecology*, edited by W. H. Dobben and R. H. McConnell, 247–51. The Hague: W. Junk.

Hollo, Erkki. 2012. *Nagoyan pöytäkirjan geenivarojen saatavuutta ja hyödyn ja- kamista koskevat sääntelytarpeet luonnonvaraisten sekä maa- ja metsätalouden geenivarojen hyödyntämisessä*. Helsinki: Suomen Ympäristöinstituutti.

Holloway, Lewis. 2005. "Aesthetics, Genetics, and Evaluating Animal Bodies: Locating and Displacing Cattle on Show and in Figures." *Environment and Planning D: Society and Space* 23: 883–902.

Holloway, Lewis, and Carol Morris. 2008. "Boosted Bodies: Genetic Techniques, Domestic Livestock Bodies and Complex Representations of Life." *Geoforum* 39: 1709–20.

Hulet, C. V., and S. K. Ercanbrack. 1962. "A Fertility Index for Rams." *Journal of Animal Science* 21: 489.

Inskeep, E. K., and J. B. Peters. 1981. "Economic Benefits of Reproductive Management, Synchronization of Estrus, and Artificial Insemination in Beef Cattle and Sheep." In *New Technologies in Animal Breeding*, edited by B. G. Brackett, G. E. Seidel Jr., and S. M. Seidel, 243–54. New York: Academic.

Itkonen, T. I., and K. Donner. 1926. "Lappalaiset." In *Suomen Suku II*, edited by A. Kannisto, E. N. Setälä, U. T. Sirelius, and Y. Wichhmann, 205–68. Helsinki: Otava.

Jasanoff, Sheila. 2004. *Designs on Nature: Science and Democracy in Europe and the U.S.* Princeton, NJ: Princeton University Press.

Jeffreys, A. J., and S. D. J. Pena. 1993. "Brief Introduction to Human DNA Fingerprinting." In DNA *Fingerprinting: State of the Science*, edited by S. D. J. Pena, R. Chakraborty, J. T. Epplen, and A. J. Jeffreys, 1–20. Berlin: Birkhäuser.

Jeffreys, A. J., V. Wilson, and S. L. Thein. 1985a. "Hypervariable 'Minisatellite' Regions in Human DNA." *Nature* 314: 67–73.

Jeffreys, A. J., V. Wilson, and S. L. Thein. 1985b. "Individual-Specific 'Finger-prints' of Human DNA." *Nature* 316: 76–79.

Jordan, K., and M. Lynch. 1998. "The Dissemination, Standardization and Routinization of a Molecular Biological Technique." *Social Studies of Science* 28: 773–800.

Juniper, Barrie E., and David J. Mabberley. 2006. *The Story of the Apple*. Portland, OR: Timber.

Jussila, Osmo. 2004. *Suomen Suuriruhtinaskunta 1809–1917*. Helsinki: WSOY.

Kajava, Yrjö. 1926. "Suomalaisten Rotuominaisuuksia." In *Suomen Suku*, edited by I. A. Kannisto, E. N. Setälä, U. T. Sirelius, and Y. Wichhmann, 215–50. Helsinki: Otava.

Kalof, Linda, and Amy Fitzgerald, eds. 2007. *The Animals Reader*. Oxford: Berg.

Kaltio, M. J. 1958. *60 Vuotta Suomenkarjan Jalostusta*. Vammala, Finland: Suomen Karjanjalostusyhdistys R. Y.

Kamau, Evanson Chenge, Bevis Fedder, and Gerd Winter. 2011. "The Nagoya Protocol on Access to Genetic Resources and Benefit Sharing: What Is New and What Are the Implications for Provider and User Countries and the Scientific Community?" *Law, Environment and Development Journal* 246: 254–55.

Kangas, Pekka, Jukka-Pekka Jäppinen, Marina von Weissenberg, and Hannu Karjalainen, eds. 1997/8. *National Biodiversity Action Plan in Finland, 1997–2005*. Vantaa, Finland: Ministry of the Environment. https://helda.helsinki.fi/handle/10138/185077.

Kay, Lily E. 1993. *The Molecular Vision of Life: Caltech, the Rockefeller Foundation, and the Rise of the New Biology*. New York: Oxford University Press.

Kay, Lily E. 2000. *Who Wrote the Book of Life?* Stanford, CA: Stanford University Press.

Kelty, Chris. 2001. "Final Report: Linux and Dot.com in Bangalore." Washington, DC: National Science Foundation.

Kiianlinna, Akseli. 1907. *Länsi-Suomen Karjanjalostusyhdistys I*. Hämeenlinna, Finland: Länsisuomen Karjanjalostusyhdistyksen Julkaisuja.

King, G. J., ed. 1993. *Reproduction in Domestic Animals: World Animal Science Series, B9*. Amsterdam: Elsevier Science.

Kirby, D. G., ed. 1975. *Finland and Russia, 1808–1920: From Autonomy to Independence—A Selection of Documents*. London: Macmillan.

Kirksey, S. Eben, and Stefan Helmreich. 2010. "The Emergence of Multispecies Ethnography." *Cultural Anthropology* 25: 545–76.

Klinge, Matti. 1990. *A Brief History of Finland*. Keuruu, Finland: Otava.

Kloppenburg, Jack Ralph. 1988. *First the Seed: The Political Economy of Plant Biotechnology, 1492–2000*. Cambridge: Cambridge University Press.

Knoppers, Bartha Maria, ed. 2003. *Population and Genetics: Legal and Socio-Ethical Perspectives*. Leiden, Netherlands: Brill.

Knorr Cetina, Karin D. 1979. "Tinkering toward Success: Prelude to a Theory of Scientific Practice." *Theory and Society* 8: 347–76.

Knorr Cetina, Karin D. 1982. "Scientific Communities or Transepistemic Arenas of Research." *Social Studies of Science* 12: 101–30.

Knorr Cetina, Karin D. 1999. *Epistemic Cultures: How the Sciences Make Knowledge*. Cambridge, MA: Harvard University Press.

Kohler, Robert E. 1994. *Lords of the Fly: Drosophila Genetics and the Experimental Life*. Chicago: University of Chicago Press.

Kohler, Robert E. 2002. *Landscapes and Labscapes: Exploring the Lab-Field Border in Biology*. Chicago: University of Chicago.

Kohler, Robert E. 2006. *All Creatures: Naturalists, Collectors, and Biodiversity, 1850–1950*. Princeton, NJ: Princeton University Press.

Krohn, J. 1887. *Maantieteellisiä kuvaelmia XIV. Suomen Suku*. Jyväskylä, Finland: Jyväskylän yliopiston kirjasto.

Lähdeoja, V. 1969. *Maataloushallituksen 75-Vuotistaival*. Helsinki: Valtion painatuskeskus.

Landecker, Hannah. 2003. "On Beginning and Ending with Apoptosis: Cell Death and Biomedicine." In *Remaking Life and Death: Towards an*

Anthropology of the Life Sciences, edited by Sarah Franklin and Margaret Lock, 23–60. Santa Fe, NM: School of American Research Press.

Landecker, Hannah. 2007. *Culturing Life: How Cells Became Technologies*. Cambridge, MA: Harvard University Press.

Latour, Bruno. 1987. *Science in Action: How to Follow Scientists and Engineers through Society*. Cambridge, MA: Harvard University Press.

Latour, Bruno. 1988. *The Pasteurization of France*. Cambridge, MA: Harvard University Press.

Latour, Bruno. 1990. "Drawing Things Together." In *Knowledge and Society: Studies in the Sociology of Culture Past and Present*, edited by Elizabeth Long and Henrika Kuklick, 1–40. Greenwich, CT: Jai Press.

Latour, Bruno. 1993. *We Have Never Been Modern*. Cambridge, MA: Harvard University Press.

Latour, Bruno. 1996. "On Interobjectivity." *Mind, Culture, and Activity* 3: 228–45.

Latour, Bruno. 1999. *Pandora's Hope: Essays on the Reality of Science Studies*. Cambridge, MA: Harvard University Press.

Latour, Bruno. 2002a. *La Fabrique du Droit: Une Ethnographie du Conseil d'État*. Paris: La Découverte.

Latour, Bruno. 2002b. "Morality and Technology: The End of the Means." *Theory, Culture and Society* 19: 247–60.

Latour, Bruno. 2003. "Is Re-modernization Occurring—And If So, How to Prove It? A Commentary on Ulrich Beck." *Theory, Culture and Society* 20: 35–48.

Latour, Bruno. 2004a. *Politics of Nature: How to Bring the Sciences into Democracy*. Cambridge, MA: Harvard University Press.

Latour, Bruno. 2004b. "Why Has Critique Run Out of Steam? From Matters of Fact to Matters of Concern." *Critical Inquiry* 30: 225–48.

Latour, Bruno, and Steve Woolgar. 1986. *Laboratory Life: The Construction of Scientific Facts*. 2nd ed. Princeton, NJ: Princeton University Press.

Law, John. 2008. "Culling, Catastrophe and Collectivity." *Distinktion* 16: 61–76.

Law, John, and Michael Lynch. 1988. "Lists, Field Guides, and the Descriptive Organization of Seeing: Birdwatching as an Exemplary Observational Activity." *Human Studies* 11: 271–303.

LeDuff, Charlie. 2003. "At a Slaughterhouse, Some Things Never Die." In *Zoontologies*, edited by Cary Wolfe, 183–98. Minneapolis: University of Minnesota Press.

Le Prestre, Philippe G. 2002. "The CBD at Ten: The Long Road to Effectiveness." *Journal of International Wildlife Law and Policy* 5: 269–85.

Leskinen, Aapo. 1977. *Käytännön Hedelmänviljely*. Helsinki: Puutarhaliitto.

Li, M.-H., I. Strandén, and J. Kantanen. 2009. "Genetic Diversity and Pedigree Analysis of the Finnsheep Breed." *Journal of Animal Science* 87: 1598–605.

Li, Y. C., A. B. Korol, T. Fahima, A. Beiles, and E. Nevo. 2002. "Microsatellites: Genomic Distribution, Putative Functions and Mutational Mechanisms: A Review." *Molecular Ecology* 11: 2453–65.

Lien, M. E. 2005. "'King of Fish' or 'Feral Peril': Tasmanian Atlantic Salmon and the Politics of Belonging." *Environment and Planning D: Society and Space* 23: 659–71.

Liukko, E. 1906. "Karjanhoidon kehityksestä Keski-Suomen Maanviljelysseuran alueella." In *Itä-Suomen Maatiaiskarja. Kokoelma*, edited by H. Nylander, 25–97. Helsinki: Itä-Suomen Karjanjalostusyhdistys.

Lock, Margaret. 2003. "On Making Up the Good-as-Dead in a Utilitarian World." In *Remaking Life and Death: Towards an Anthropology of the Biosciences*, edited by Sarah Franklin and Margaret Lock, 165–92. Santa Fe, NM: School of American Research Press.

Lundin, C. L. 1981. "Finland." In *Russification in the Baltic Provinces and Finland, 1855–1914*, edited by Edward C. Thaden, 357–408. Princeton, NJ: Princeton University Press.

Lynch, Michael E. 1988. "Sacrifice and the Transformation of the Animal Body into a Scientific Object: Laboratory Culture and Ritual Practice in the Neurosciences." *Social Studies of Science* 18: 265–89.

Lynch, Michael E. 2002. "Protocols, Practices, and the Reproduction of Technique in Molecular Biology." *British Journal of Sociology* 53: 203–20.

MacKenzie, D. 1981. "Interests, Positivism and History." *Social Studies of Science* 11: 498–504.

MAF [Finnish Ministry of Agriculture and Forestry]. 1983. *Kotieläinten Geeniainestoimikunnan Mietintö* [Report of the National Committee for the Genetic Material of Domestic Animals] 1983: 76. Helsinki: Maa- ja metsätalousministeriö.

MAF [Finnish Ministry of Agriculture and Forestry]. 2002. *Suomen Kansallinen Kasvigeenivaraohjelma* [National plant genetic resources programme]. Helsinki: Maa- ja metsätalousministeriö.

MAF [Finnish Ministry of Agriculture and Forestry]. 2003. *Country Report on Farm Animal Genetic Resources*. Helsinki: Maa- ja metsätalousministeriö.

MAF [Finnish Ministry of Agriculture and Forestry]. 2004. *Suomen Kansallinen Eläingeenivaraohjelma* [National animal genetic resources programme]. Helsinki: Maa- ja metsätalousministeriö.

MAF [Finnish Ministry of Agriculture and Forestry]. 2007. "Geenivarojen Saatavuutta ja Hyötyjen Jakoa Koskevien Bonnin Ohjeiden Kansallinen Toimeenpano. Taustaselvitys" [The national implementation of the Bonn guidelines with regard to ABS issues: A background review]. Työryhmämuistio, MMM, report, 2007: 5.

MAF [Finnish Ministry of Agriculture and Forestry]. 2012. Public description of institutional responsibilities. mmm.fi/en/task-and-objectives.

MAF [Finnish Ministry of Agriculture and Forestry]. 2015. Maa- ja metsatalousministerion lausunto luonnoksesta hallituksen esitykseksi Nagoyan poytakirjan hyvaksymisesta seka laiksi sen lainsaadannon alaan kuuluvien maaraysten voimaansaattamisesta ja laiksi geenivarojen ja niihin liittyvan perinteisen tiedon saatavuudesta. Lausunto 9.4.2015. Maa-ja metsätalousministeriö. Lausunto 192651. [Statement concerning the proposal for genetic resource law]

Maijala, Kalle. 1971. “Need and Methods of Gene Conservation in Animal Breeding.” *Annales de Génétique et de Sélection Animale* 2: 403–15.

Malkki, Liisa. 1992. “National Geographic: The Rooting of Peoples and the Territorialization of National Identity among Scholars and Refugees.” *Cultural Anthropology* 7: 24–44.

Mansfield, B. 2003. “From Catfish to Organic Fish: Making Distinctions about Nature as Cultural Economic Practice.” *Geoforum* 34: 329–42.

Marcus, George E. 1995. “Ethnography in/of the World System: The Emergence of Multi-sited Ethnography.” *Annual Review of Anthropology* 24: 95–117.

Markkola, Pirjo. 2004. “Johdanto: Maatalous jälleenrakennuksesta EU-aikaan.” In *Suomen maatalouden historia III: Suurten Muutosten Aika. Jälleenrakennuskaudesta EU-Suomeen*, edited by Pirjo Markkola, 14–23. Helsinki: SKS.

Martin, Emily. 1997. “Citadels, Rhizomes, and String Figures.” In *Technoscience and Cyberculture*, edited by Stanley Aronowitz, Barbara Martinsons, and Michael Menser, with Jennifer Rich, 97–109. New York: Routledge.

Martin, P., C. Coveny, A. Kraft, N. Brown, and P. Bath. 2006. “The Commercial Development of Stem Cell Technology: Lessons from the Past, Strategies for the Future.” *Regenerative Medicine* 1: 901–7.

Masco, Joseph. 2006. *The Nuclear Borderlands. The Manhattan Project in Post-Cold War New Mexico*. Princeton, NJ: Princeton University Press.

M’Charek, Amade. 2005. *The Human Genome Diversity Project: An Ethnography of Scientific Practice*. Cambridge: Cambridge University Press.

Medaglia, Jorge Cabrera, Frederic Perron-Welch, and Freedom Kai Phillips. 2014. *Overview of National and Regional Measures on Access and Benefit Sharing: Challenges and Opportunities in Implementing the Nagoya Protocol*. 3rd ed. Montreal: Centre for International Sustainable Development Law. https://www.absfocalpoint.nl/upload_mm/5/f/4/008c9cc8-19f3-4926-b380-5f13fd1eb705_Overview%20of%20national%20and%20regional%20measures%20on%20access%20and%20benefit%20sharing.pdf.

Meine, Curt. 2010. “Conservation Biology: Past and Present.” In *Conservation Biology for All*, edited by Navjot S. Sodhi and Paul R. Ehrlich, 7–26. Oxford: Oxford University Press.

Metzler, Ingrid. 2007. “Nationalizing Embryos: The Politics of Human Embryonic Stem Cell Research in Italy.” *BioSocieties* 2: 413–27.

Meurman, Olavi, and Olavi Collan. 1943. *Suomen Hedelmäpuut ja Viljellyt Marjat. Ensimmäinen Osa, Omenat*. Helsinki: Oy Suomen Kirja.

Michael, M. 2001. “Technoscientific Bespoking: Animals, Publics and the New Genetics.” *New Genetics and Society* 20: 205–24.

Mitchell, Timothy. 2002. *Rule of Experts: Egypt, Techno-Politics, Modernity*. Berkeley: University of California Press.

Moran, Katy, Steven R. King, and Thomas J. Carlson. 2001. “Biodiversity Prospecting: Lessons and Prospects.” *Annual Review of Anthropology* 30: 505–26.

Müller-Wille, Staffan, and Hans-Jörg Rheinberger. 2007. "Heredity: The Production of an Epistemic Space." In *Heredity Produced: At the Crossroads of Biology, Politics and Culture, 1500–1870*, edited by Staffan Müller-Wille and Hans-Jörg Rheinberger, 3–34. Cambridge, MA: MIT Press.

Myllylä, L. 1991. *Suomenkarja. Maan Alkuperäinen Karjarotu*. Vantaa, Finland: Suomenkarjan Jalostussäätiö.

Nash, Richard 2005. "'Honest English Breed': The Thoroughbred as Cultural Metaphor." In *The Culture of the Horse: Status, Discipline, and Identity in the Early Modern World*, edited by Karen Raber and Treva Tucker, 245–72. New York: Palgrave.

Nei, Masatoshi, and Sudhir Kumar. 2000. *Molecular Evolution and Phylogenetics*. New York: Oxford University Press.

Nimmo, Richie. 2008. "Governing Nonhumans: Knowledge, Sanitation and Discipline in the Late 19th- and Early 20th-Century British Milk Trade." *Distinktion* 16: 77–97.

Nissinen, Tatu. 1923. *Itä-Suomen Karjan Jalotustyö*. Helsinki: WSOY.

Nybom, Hilde. 1991. "Applications of DNA Fingerprinting in Plant Breeding." In *DNA Fingerprinting: Approaches and Applications*, edited by T. Burke, G. Dolf, A. J. Jeffreys, and R. Wolff, 294–311. Berlin: Birkhäuser.

Nylander, Hannes. 1906. "Piirteitä Karjanjalostusperiaatteiden vaihteluista Suomessa ja Niitten Vaikutus maatiaiskarjan jalostukseen." In *Itä-Suomen Maatiaiskarja. Kokoelma Kirjoituksia*, edited by H. Nylander. Helsinki: Itä-Suomen Karjanjalostusyhdistys.

Odum, Eugene P. (1953) 1975. *Fundamentals of Ecology*. Philadelphia: W. B. Saunders.

Ohnuki-Tierney, Emiko. 1987. *The Monkey as Mirror: Symbolic Transformations in Japanese History and Ritual*. Princeton, NJ: Princeton University Press.

Ohnuki-Tierney, Emiko. 1993. *Rice as Self: Japanese Identities through Time*. Princeton, NJ: Princeton University Press.

Oldenbroek, J. K., ed. 1999. *Genebanks and the Conservation of Farm Animal Genetic Resources*. Lelystad, Netherlands: ID–DLO.

Östman, A. C. 2004. "Mekanisoinnin Ensimmäinen Aalto" [The first wave of mechanization]. In *Kasvun ja kriisien aika 1870-luvulta 1950-luvulle Suomen Maatalouden historia II*, edited by M. Peltonen, 19–76. Helsinki: Suomen Kirjallisuuden Seura.

Owen, John B. 1976. *Sheep Production*. London: Baillière Tindall.

Ozden-Schilling, Canay. 2016. "The Infrastructure of Markets: From Electric Power to Electronic Data." *Economic Anthropology* 3: 68–80.

Ozden-Schilling, Thomas. 2016. "Salvage Cartographies: Mapping, Futures, and Landscapes in Northwest British Columbia." PhD thesis, Massachusetts Institute of Technology. http://hdl.handle.net/1721.1/104558.

Pálsson, G. 2002. "The Life of Family Trees and the Book of Icelanders." *Medical Anthropology* 21: 337–67.

Parry, Bronwyn. 2001. *Trading the Genome: Investigating the Commodification of Bio-Information*. New York: Columbia University Press.

Pauly, P. J. 1996. “The Beauty and Menace of the Japanese Cherry Trees.” *Isis* 87: 51–73.

Peltonen, M. 2004. “Uudet kaupallistumisen muodot” [New forms of commercialization of agriculture]. In *Kasvun ja kriisien aika 1870-luvulta 1950-luvulle Suomen Maatalouden historia II*, edited by M. Peltonen, 77–135. Helsinki: Suomen Kirjallisuuden Seura.

Pena, Sergio D. J. 1993. “Overview—DNA Fingerprinting: State of the Science.” In *DNA Fingerprinting: State of the Science*, edited by S. D. J. Pena, R. Chakraborty, J. T. Epplen, and A. J. Jeffreys, x. Basel: Birkhäuser.

Pertoldi, Cino, R. Bijlsma, and Volker Loeschcke. 2007. “Conservation Genetics in a Globally Changing Environment: Present Problems, Paradoxes and Future Challenges.” *Biodiversity and Conservation* 16: 4147–63.

Pihkala, Rurik 1968/9. SK [Finncattle Society]. 1969. *Letter to Breeders*, no. 2. FABA Archives, 8.

Pilling, D., R. Cardellino, M. Zjalic, B. Rischkowsky, K. A. Tempelman, and I. Hoffmann. 2007. “The Use of Reproductive and Molecular Biotechnology in Animal Genetic Resources Management—A Global Overview.” *Animal Genetic Resources Information* 40: 1–14.

Piperelis, S. G., D. Vafiadis, C. M. Boscos, C. Brozos, E. Kiossis, E., and C. Alexopoulos. 2008. “Efficiency Assessment of a Swift Method to Enhance Substandard Viability Ram Ejaculates.” *Reproduction in Domestic Animals* 43: 111–16.

Pistorius, Robin J. 1997. *Scientists, Plants and Politics: A History of the Plant Genetic Resources Movement*. Rome: International Plant Genetic Resources Institute.

Polanyi, Karl. (1944) 2001. *The Great Transformation: The Political and Economic Origins of Our Time*. Boston: Beacon.

Polge, C., A. U. Smith, and A. S. Parkes. 1949. “Revival of Spermatozoa after Vitrification and Dehydration at Low Temperatures.” *Nature* 164: 666.

Prosch, V. (1863) 1872. *Haandbog i det Almindelige Huusdyrbrug. Udarbeidet Naermest til Brug for Veterinairer og Landmaend. 2den Udgrave*. Copenhagen: Reitzels Forglag.

Pugh, D. G. 2002. *Sheep and Goat Medicine*. Maryland Heights, MO: Saunders.

Pyyhtinen, Olli, and Sakari Tamminen. 2011. “We Have Never Been Only Human: Foucault and Latour on the Question of the Anthropos.” *Anthropological Theory* 11: 135–52.

Quinn, Michael. 1993. “Corpulent Cattle and Milk Machines: Nature, Art and the Ideal Type.” *Society and Animals* 1: 145–57.

Raber, Karen, and Treva J. Tucker, eds. 2005. *The Culture of the Horse: Status, Discipline, and Identity in the Early Modern World*. New York: Palgrave Macmillan.

Rabinow, Paul. 1992. “Artificiality and Enlightenment: From Sociobiology to Biosociality.” In *The Science Studies Reader*, edited by Mario Biagioli, 407–16. New York: Routledge.

Rabinow, Paul. 1997. *Essays on the Anthropology of Reason*. Princeton, NJ: Princeton University Press.

Rasbech, N. O. 1993. "Artificial Insemination." In *Reproduction in Domesticated Animals*, edited by Gordon J. King, 365–86. Amsterdam: Elsevier.

Rasila, V., E. Jutikkala, and A. Mäkelä-Alitalo, eds. 2003–4. *Suomen Maatalouden Historia 1* [The history of Finnish agriculture I]. Helsinki: Suomalaisen Kirjallisuuden Seura.

Raustiala, K., and D. G. Victor. 1996. "Biodiversity since Rio: The Future of the Convention on Biological Diversity." *Environment* 38: 17–43.

Raustiala, K., and D. G. Victor. 2004. "The Regime Complex for Plant Genetic Resources." *International Organization* 34: 277–309.

Renan, Ernest. (1882) 1996. "What Is a Nation?" In *Becoming National: A Reader*, edited by Geoff Eley and Ronald G. Suny, 42–56. New York: Oxford University Press.

Rheinberger, Hans-Jörg. 1997. *Toward a History of Epistemic Things: Synthesizing Proteins in the Test Tube*. Stanford, CA: Stanford University Press.

Rheinberger, Hans-Jörg. 2000. "Beyond Nature and Culture: Modes of Reasoning in the Age of Molecular Biology and Medicine." In *Living and Working with the New Medical Technologies*, edited by Margaret Lock, Alan Young, and Alberto Cambrosio, 19–30. Cambridge: Cambridge University Press.

Riles, Annelise. 2006. "[Deadlines]: Removing the Brackets on Politics in Bureaucratic and Anthropological Analysis." In *Documents: Artifacts of Modern Knowledge*, edited by Annelise Riles, 71–92. Ann Arbor: University of Michigan Press.

Ritvo, Harriet. 1987. *The Animal Estate: The English and Other Creatures in the Victorian Age*. Cambridge, MA: Harvard University Press.

Ritvo, Harriet. 1992. "Race, Breed, and Myths of Origin: Chillingham Cattle as Ancient Britons." *Representations* 39: 1–22.

Ritvo, Harriet. 1995. "Possessing Mother Nature: Genetic Capital in Eighteenth-Century Britain." In *Early Modern Conceptions of Property*, edited by John Brewer and Susan Staves, 413–26. London: Routledge.

Roiko-Jokela, Hekki. 2004. "Asutustoiminnalla Sodasta Arkeen." In *Suomen Maatalouden Historia III*, edited by Pirjo Markkola, 27–90. Helsinki: Suomalaisen Kirjallisuuden Seura.

Rosaldo, Renato. 1986. "From the Door of His Tent: The Fieldworker and the Inquisitor." In *Writing Culture*, edited by James Clifford and George E. Marcus, 77–97. Berkeley: University of California Press.

Rose, Nikolas. 2007. *The Politics of Life Itself: Biomedicine, Power, and Subjectivity in the Twenty-First Century*. Princeton, NJ: Princeton University Press.

Roth, W.-M., and G. M. Bowen. 1999. "Digitizing Lizards or the Topology of Vision in Ecological Fieldwork." *Social Studies of Science* 29: 719–64.

Ruane, John, and Andrea Sonnino. 2006. *The Role of Biotechnology in Exploring and Protecting Agricultural Genetic Resources*. Rome: Food and Agriculture Organization.

Salamon, S. 1967. "Observations on Fertility of Ram Semen Frozen by Different Methods." *Australian Journal of Experimental Agriculture and Animal Husbandry* 7: 559–61.

Salamon, S., and W. M. C. Maxwell. 1995a. "Frozen Storage of Ram Semen I: Processing, Freezing, Thawing and Fertility after Cervical Insemination." *Animal Reproduction Science* 37: 185–249.

Salamon, S., and W. M. C. Maxwell. 1995b. "Frozen Storage of Ram Semen II: Causes of Low Fertility after Cervical Insemination Improvement." *Animal Reproduction Science* 38: 1–36.

Santoro, Pablo. 2009. "From (Public?) Waste to (Private?) Value: The Regulation of Private Cord Blood Banking in Spain." *Science Studies* 22: 3–23.

Sawela, Herman. 1919. "Lammashoito." In *Maatilahallituksen lentokirjasia lammashoidosta*. Helsinki: Valtioneuvoston kirjapaino.

SCBD [Secretariat of the Convention on Biological Diversity]. 2002. "Bonn Guidelines on Access to Genetic Resources and Fair and Equitable Sharing of the Benefits Arising out of Their Utilization." Montreal: Secretariat of the Convention on Biological Diversity.

SCBD [Secretariat of the Convention on Biological Diversity]. 2011. "Nagoya Protocol on Access to Genetic Resources and the Fair and Equitable Sharing of Benefits Arising from Their Utilization to the Convention on Biological Diversity." Montreal: Secretariat of the Convention on Biological Diversity.

SCBD [Secretariat of the Convention on Biological Diversity]. 2014. "Global Biodiversity Outlook 4." Montreal: Secretariat of the Convention on Biological Diversity.

Schiebinger, Londa. 2004. *Plants and Empire: Colonial Bioprospecting in the Atlantic World*. Cambridge, MA: Harvard University Press.

Schiebinger, Londa, and Claudia Swan, eds. 2005. *Colonial Botany: Science, Commerce, and Politics*. Philadelphia: University of Pennsylvania Press.

Schmitt, Carl. 1985. *Political Theology: Four Chapters on the Concept of Sovereignty*. Cambridge, MA: MIT Press.

Seguin, E. 2003. "The BSE Saga: A Cannibalistic Tale." *Science as Culture* 12: 3–22.

Serres, Michael, and Bruno Latour. 1998. *Conversations on Science, Culture, and Time*. Ann Arbor: University of Michigan Press.

Shapin, Steven. 1996. *The Scientific Revolution*. Chicago: University of Chicago Press.

Sharp, L. 2002. "Bodies, Boundaries and Territorial Disputes: Investigating the Murky Realms of Scientific Authority." *Medical Anthropology* 21: 369–79.

Shiva, Vandana. 1991. *The Violence of the Green Revolution: Third World Agriculture, Ecology and Politics*. New Delhi: Zed.

Shiva, Vandana. 1993. *Monocultures of the Mind: Perspectives on Biodiversity and Biotechnology*. London: Zed.

Simonen, Seppo. 1949. *Lypsykarjatalousvaltainen Maataloudellinen Tuotantojärjestelmä Suomessa*. Helsinki: Helsingin Yliopisto.

Simonen, Seppo. 1950. *Suomen Ayrshire-Yhdistyksen Historia 1901*. Helsinki: Suomen Ayershireyhdistys.

Simonen, Seppo. 1964. *Raivaajia ja Rakentajia. Suomen Maatalouden*. Helsinki: Kirjayhtymä.

Sirelius, U. T. 1924. "Heimot, Antropologia ja Kansan Luonne." In *Suomi: Maa. Kansa. Valtakunta II*, edited by A. Donner, A. Grotenfelt, L. Hendell, E. Hjelt, K. S. Laurila, A. Renqvist, K. S. Setälä, and R. Tigerstedt, 150–203. Helsinki: Otava.

Skarstad, Guro Ådnbgard. 2008. "Balancing Fish: A Meeting between Food Safety and Nutrition in an Assessment of Benefits and Risks." *Distinktion* 16: 99–114.

SLSY [Suomen Lampaan- ja Vuohenhoitoyhdistys]. 1921. "Lammashoito" in *Maatilahallituksen lentokirjasia lammashoidosta*. Vammala, Finland: Tyrvään Kirjapaino Osakeyhtio, No. 1.

Smirnoff, Alexandra. 1894. *Suomen Pomologiian Käsikirja*. Porvoo, Finland: WSOY.

Smith, Anthony D. 1986. *The Ethnic Origins of Nations*. Oxford: Blackwell.

Smith, Anthony D. 2000. *The Nation in History: Historiographical Debates about Ethnicity and Nationalism*. Hanover, NH: University Press of New England.

Soini, Katriina. 1937. *Länsi-Suomen Karja 1906–1936*. Tampere, Finland: Länsi-Suomen Karjanjalostusyhdistys.

Soini, Katriina. 2007. "Maatiaiseläinten monet arvot." In *Alkuperäisrotujen säilyttämisen taloudelliset, sosiaaliset ja kulttuuriset lähtökohdat*, edited by Miia Karja and Taina Lilja, MTT: Jokioinen, 17–40.

Soulé, Michael E. 1985. "What Is Conservation Biology?" "The Biological Diversity Crisis." Special issue, *BioScience* 35 (11): 727–34.

Steiner, Achim. 2010. "Message from the Executive Director of UNEP." In *Global Biodiversity Outlook 3. Secretariat of the Convention on Biological Diversity* 6. SCBD: Montréal

Stone, Jeffrey C. 1988. "Imperialism, Colonialism and Cartography." *Transactions of the Institute of British Geographers* 13: 57–64.

Stone, Glenn. 2010. "The Anthropology of Genetically Modified Crops." *Annual Review of Anthropology* 39: 381–400

Strathern, Marilyn. 1991. *Partial Connections*. Savage, MD: Rowman and Littlefield.

Strathern, Marilyn. 1993. *Reproducing the Future: Anthropology, Kinship and the New Reproductive Technologies*. Manchester: Manchester University Press.

Strathern, Marilyn. 1996. "Potential Property: Intellectual Rights and Property in Persons." *Social Anthropology* 4: 17–32.

Strathern, Marilyn. 2005. *Kinship, Law and the Unexpected: Relatives Are Always a Surprise*. Cambridge: Cambridge University Press.

Sunder Rajan, Kaushik. 2006. *Biocapital: The Constitution of Postgenomic Life*. Durham, NC: Duke University Press.

Takacs, David. 1992. *The Idea of Biodiversity: Philosophies of Paradise*. Baltimore, MD: Johns Hopkins University Press.

Tamminen, Sakari. 2015. "The Changing Value of Animal Genetic Resources: From Global Commons to National Genetic Landscapes." *Frontiers in Genetics* 6. https://doi.org/10.3389/fgene.2015.00279.

Tapio, M., M. Nurbiy, M. Ozerov, M. Inkulov, G. Gonzarenko, T. Kiselyova|, M. Murawski, H. Viinalass, and J. Kantanen. 2006a. "Sheep Mitochondrial

DNA Variation in European, Caucasian, and Central Asian Areas." *Biology and Evolution* 23: 1776–83.

Tapio, I., S. Värv, J. Bennewitz, J. Maleviciute, E. Fimland, Z. Grislis, T. H. Meuwissen, I. Miceikiene, I. Olsaker, H. Viinalass, J. Vilkki, and J. Kantanen. 2006b. "Prioritization for Conservation of Northern European Cattle Breeds Based on Analysis of Microsatellite Data." *Conservation Biology* 20: 1768–79.

Taussig, K. S. 2004. "Bovine Abominations: Genetic Culture and Politics in the Netherlands." *Cultural Anthropology* 19: 305–336.

Thaden, Edward C., with Marianna Foster Thaden. 1984. *The Western Borderlands of Russia, 1710–1870*. Princeton, NJ: Princeton University Press.

Thibier, M., and H.-M Wagner. 2002. "World Statistics for Artificial Insemination in Cattle." *Livestock Production Science* 74: 203–12.

Timmermans, Stefan and Marc Berg. "Standardization in Action: Achieving Local Universality through Medical Protocols." *Social Studies of Science* 27, 273–305.

Tsing, Anna Lowenhaupt. 2005. *Friction: An Ethnography of Global Connection*. Princeton, NJ: Princeton University Press.

Vida, G. 1994. "Global Issues of Genetic Diversity." In *Conservation Genetics*, edited by V. Loeschcke, J. Tomiuk, and S. K. Jain, 9–22. Berlin: Birkhäuser.

Vihola, Teppo. 1991. *Leipäviljasta Lypsykarjaan: Maatalouden Tuotantosuunnan Muutos Suomessa 1870-Luvulta Ensimmäisen Maailmansodan Vuosiin*. Historiallisia tutkimuksia 159. Jyväskylä, Finland: Suomen Historiallinen Seura.

Vogel, J. F. 1994. *Genes for Sale: Privatisation as a Conservation Policy*. Oxford: Oxford University Press.

Vogel, Joseph Henry, Nora Álvarez-Berríos, Norberto Quiñones-Vilche, Jeiger L. Medina-Muñiz, Dionisio Pérez-Montes, Arelis I. Arocho-Montes, Nicole Vale-Merniz, Ricardo Fuentes-Ramirez, Gabriel Marrero-Girona, Emmanuel Valcárcel Mercado, and Julio Santiago-Rios. 2011. "The Economics of Information, Studiously Ignored in the Nagoya Protocol on Access and Benefit Sharing." *Law, Environment and Development* 7: 47–74.

von Herder, Johann Gottfried. (1789) 1968. *Reflections on the Philosophy of the History of Mankind*. Chicago: University of Chicago Press.

Waldby, Catherine, and Robert Mitchell. 2006. *Tissue Economies: Blood, Organs, and Cell Lines in Late Capitalism*. Durham, NC: Duke University Press.

Wallius, Johanna. 2001. *Oikeus Geenivaroihin* [The right to genetic resources]. Helsinki: Talentum Media Oy.

Walsh, V., and J. Goodman. 2002. "From taxol to Taxol®: The Changing Identities and Ownership of an Anti-Cancer Drug." *Medical Anthropology* 21: 307–36.

Walton, John. 1986. "Pedigree and the National Cattle Herd Circa 1750–1950." *Agricultural History Review* 34: 149–70.

Walton, John. 1999. "Pedigree and Productivity in the British and North American Cattle Kingdoms." *Journal of Historical Geography* 25: 441–62.

Waterton, Claire. 2002. "From Field to Fantasy: Classifying Nature, Constructing Europe." *Social Studies of Science* 32: 177–204.

Webster, A. D. 2003. "Breeding, Selection of Apple and Pear Rootstocks." *Acta Horticulturae* 622: 499–505.
Westwood, Melvin N. 1993. *Temperate Zone Pomology*. Portland, OR: Timber.
Whatmore, Sarah. 2002. *Hybrid Geographies: Natures, Cultures, Spaces*. London: SAGE.
Whitehead, Alfred North. 1979. *Process and Reality: An Essay in Cosmology*. New York: Free Press.
Williams, Raymond. 1980. *Problems in Materialism and Culture*. London: Verso.
Wilmot, Sarah. 2007. "From 'Public Service' to Artificial Insemination: Animal Breeding Science and Reproductive Research in Early Twentieth-Century Britain." *Studies in History and Philosophy of Science Part C: Studies in History and Philosophy of Biological and Biomedical Sciences* 38: 411–41.
Wilson, E. O. 1988. *Biodiversity*. Washington, DC: National Academy of Sciences Press.
Wolch, Jennifer, R, and Jody Emel. 1998. *Animal Geographies: Place, Politics, and Identity in the Nature-Culture Borderlands*. London: Verso.
Woolgar, Steve. 1981a. "Critique and Criticism: Two Readings of Ethnomethodology." *Social Studies of Science* 11: 504–14.
Woolgar, Steve. 1981b. "Interests and Explanation in the Social Study of Science." *Social Studies of Science* 11: 365–94.
Woolgar, Steve. 1988. *Science: The Very Idea*. London: Routledge.
World Resources Institute, World Conservation Union, United Nations Environment Programme, Food and Agriculture Organization of the United Nations, and United Nations Educational Scientific and Cultural Organization. 1992. "Global Biodiversity Strategy: Guidelines for Action to Save, Study, and Use Earth's Biotic Wealth Sustainably and Equitably." Washington, DC: World Resources Institute.

INDEX